Education Policy & Social Inequality

Volume 4

Series Editor

Trevor Gale, University of Glasgow, Glasgow, UK

This series publishes monographs and edited collections that investigate relations between education policy and social inequality. Submissions that provoke new and generative ways of thinking about and acting on relations between education policy and social inequality are particularly invited from early career, emerging and established scholars.

While education policy has often been understood as having a normative function and is proposed as the solution to social inequality, the series is interested in how education policy frames, creates and at times exacerbates social inequality. It adopts a critical orientation, encompassing (1) innovative and interdisciplinary theoretical and conceptual studies – including but not exclusively drawing on sociology, cultural studies, social and cultural geography, history – and (2) original empirical work that examines a range of educational contexts, including early years education, vocational and further education, informal education, K-12 schooling and higher education.

The series sees critique and policy studies as having a transformative function. It publishes books that seek to re-articulate policy discourses, the realm of research, or which posit (1) new dimensions to understanding the role of education policy in connection with enduring social problems and (2) the amelioration of social inequality in ways that challenge the possibility of equity in the liberal democratic state, as well as in other forms of governance and government.

Education Policy and Social Inequality is edited by Professor Trevor Gale.

Please contact the publishing editor, Nick Melchior (email: nick.melchior@springer.com) if you are interested in submitting a proposal to this series.

Members of the series editorial board include:
Professor Nafsika Alexiadou (Umeå universitet, Sweden)
Dr. Annette Braun (Institute of Education, University of London, UK)
Professor Aslam Fataar (University of Stellenbosch, South Africa)
Professor Jane Kenway (Monash University, Australia)
A/Professor Zeus Leonardo (University of California – Berkeley, USA)
Professor Bob Lingard (University of Queensland, Australia)
Professor Chris Lubienski (University of Illinois - Urbana Champaign, USA)
Professor Ka Ho Mok (Hong Kong Institute of Education, China)
Professor Mark Olssen (Surrey University, UK)
A/Professor Wanda S. Pillow (University of Utah, USA)
A/Professor Taylor Webb (University of British Columbia, Canada)
Professor Agnes Van Zanten (Science Po/CNRS, France)

More information about this series at http://www.springer.com/series/13427

Louis Volante · Sylke V. Schnepf ·
John Jerrim · Don A. Klinger
Editors

Socioeconomic Inequality and Student Outcomes

Cross-National Trends, Policies, and Practices

Editors
Louis Volante
Faculty of Education
Brock University
Hamilton, ON, Canada

Sylke V. Schnepf
European Commission's
Joint Research Centre
Ispra, Italy

John Jerrim
UCL Institute of Education
London, UK

Don A. Klinger
University of Waikato
Hamilton, New Zealand

ISSN 2520-1476   ISSN 2520-1484   (electronic)
Education Policy & Social Inequality
ISBN 978-981-13-9862-9   ISBN 978-981-13-9863-6   (eBook)
https://doi.org/10.1007/978-981-13-9863-6

© Springer Nature Singapore Pte Ltd. 2019, corrected publication 2019
This work is subject to copyright. All rights are reserved by the Publisher, whether the whole or part of the material is concerned, specifically the rights of translation, reprinting, reuse of illustrations, recitation, broadcasting, reproduction on microfilms or in any other physical way, and transmission or information storage and retrieval, electronic adaptation, computer software, or by similar or dissimilar methodology now known or hereafter developed.
The use of general descriptive names, registered names, trademarks, service marks, etc. in this publication does not imply, even in the absence of a specific statement, that such names are exempt from the relevant protective laws and regulations and therefore free for general use.
The publisher, the authors and the editors are safe to assume that the advice and information in this book are believed to be true and accurate at the date of publication. Neither the publisher nor the authors or the editors give a warranty, expressed or implied, with respect to the material contained herein or for any errors or omissions that may have been made. The publisher remains neutral with regard to jurisdictional claims in published maps and institutional affiliations.

This Springer imprint is published by the registered company Springer Nature Singapore Pte Ltd.
The registered company address is: 152 Beach Road, #21-01/04 Gateway East, Singapore 189721, Singapore

This volume is dedicated to the millions of teachers and educators worldwide who devote tireless energy to improve the educational outcomes and life chances of disadvantaged students.

Foreword

For over 50 years, international comparisons of educational achievement have been part of the world research and evaluation enterprise. Starting with comparisons led by academics and funded haphazardly and periodically, the comparative enterprise has transformed into more regularly occurring, government-sanctioned, and methodologically sophisticated studies. This book, *Socioeconomic Inequality and Student Outcomes—Cross-National Trends, Policies, and Practices,* focuses attention on comparisons within and among countries relative to differences in student status and implicitly raises the question of the utility of international comparisons focused only on achievement at the margin. Countries obviously differ dramatically in their culture, economy, stability, diversity of population as well as educational systems. Simple bottom-line comparisons seem to relegate have and have-not nations to a pre-ordained rank order. Should the policy lesson from such data simply be to try harder?

Data from other fields, for instance, healthcare, show that wealthy countries do not predictably attain the optimal outcomes assumed by their "advanced" status and level of expenditures. In education, the situation is similar. Although the credibility of educational achievement measures is somewhat more suspect than hard data like mortality rates, contrasts of achievement among countries of different sub-groups, identified by socioeconomic and ethnic membership have much to recommend them from a policy and improvement viewpoint. Comparisons of achievement moderated by classification variables demonstrate whether and how much rhetorical claims about equity and opportunity can be trusted as well as the efficacy of policy interventions. Studies over time of the range and disparity of performance by gender, region, group, and individual differences can highlight the areas where policies have been effective. They can identify principal outcomes and unanticipated side effects of compensatory investments. But, at the heart of the matter is whether there is a sustainable commitment by authorities and by practitioners to raise the quality and level of performance of all of the nation's students.

The extent and depth of commitment to improved learning by all is often justified within countries in competitive, economic terms rather than from a moral stance. Even so, the rise of "nationalism" has new implications for this line of inquiry. Nationalism may explicitly or tacitly imply the deserved right of differential success. Nevertheless, an inhibitor to success may be the structural nature of opportunity in communities as well as schools. The latter is likely exacerbated by the increased and hardened political divisions emerging within countries across the world. On a larger scale, the emergence of nationalism as a reaction to refugee migration or to other perceived or manufactured threats to sovereignty could presage a wider rejection of globalism. Such dismissals must be short-lived and self-defeating, given connected nature of economies, of international corporations, of systems of higher education, and of the ecology of the planet itself.

This book then anticipates a continued future of international studies that provide lenses on how various nations attempt to achieve quality and equity in their educational systems. Noteworthy is the approach taken by the editor and authors to demonstrate their own commitment to quality and equity. They do so by preparing provocative chapters using state of the art methods and analyses and teams of authors. The writers of these chapters are illustrious scholars whose collaboration produces unusual value for the reader. Value, then, is the watchword of this volume, in its focus, methods, authors, and message.

Eva L. Baker
Distinguished Professor of Education
University of California
Los Angeles, CA, USA

The original version of this book was revised: Author provided affiliations are updated. The correction to the book is available at: https://doi.org/10.1007/978-981-13-9863-6_13

Acknowledgements

Understanding the relationships between socioeconomic inequality and student outcomes across a range of countries is particularly challenging. The editors of this volume would like to thank each of the contributors for their willingness to engage in this timely project and the resulting research and insights they have provided for the international community.

Portions of this edited volume were supported by the Social Sciences and Humanities Research Council of Canada (SSHRC).

Contents

Part I Socioeconomic Inequality in Education Systems

1 Socioeconomic Inequality and Student Outcomes Across Education Systems 3
John Jerrim, Louis Volante, Don A. Klinger and Sylke V. Schnepf

2 The Impact of Education Policies on Socioeconomic Inequality in Student Achievement: A Review of Comparative Studies 17
Rolf Strietholt, Jan-Eric Gustafsson, Nina Hogrebe, Victoria Rolfe, Monica Rosén, Isa Steinmann and Kajsa Yang Hansen

Part II National Profiles

3 Socioeconomic Inequality and Student Outcomes in English Schools 41
Jake Anders and Morag Henderson

4 Socioeconomic Inequality and Student Outcomes in German Schools 63
Horst Entorf and Maddalena Davoli

5 Socioeconomic Inequality and Student Outcomes in Italy 81
Nicola Pensiero, Orazio Giancola and Carlo Barone

6 Socioeconomic Inequality and Student Outcomes in Spanish Schools 95
Álvaro Choi and Jorge Calero

7 Socioeconomic Inequality and Student Outcomes in the Netherlands 111
Jaap Scheerens, Anneke Timmermans and Greetje van der Werf

8 Socioeconomic Inequality and Student Outcomes in Swedish Schools 133
Petra Löfstedt

xi

Contents

9 Socioeconomic Inequality and Student Outcomes in Finnish Schools 153
Katariina Salmela-Aro and Anna K. Chmielewski

10 Socioeconomic Inequality and Student Outcomes in Canadian Schools 169
Alana Butler

11 Socioeconomic Inequality and Student Outcomes in Australia 189
Philip Parker, Jiesi Guo and Taren Sanders

Part III Cross-Cultural Trends

12 Cross-National Trends in Addressing Socioeconomic Inequality in Education 207
Sylke V. Schnepf, Don A. Klinger, Louis Volante and John Jerrim

Correction to: Socioeconomic Inequality and Student Outcomes C1
Louis Volante, Sylke V. Schnepf, John Jerrim and Don A. Klinger

Editors and Contributors

About the Editors

Louis Volante (Ph.D.) is a Professor of Education at Brock University, Professorial Fellow at UNU-MERIT/Graduate School of Governance, and President of the Canadian Educational Researchers' Association (CERA). He is currently a Visiting Professor at the UCL Department of Social Science. His research, which has been widely disseminated and cited by scholars around the world, is focused on education and public policy analysis; international large-scale assessments and the politics of education reform; metrics, performance monitoring, and education governance; and migrant integration policies and social inequality in education. He serves on various advisory boards for academic journals and scholarly associations. He consults with governments, professional organizations, and universities around the world. With over 100 journal articles, technical reports, book chapters, and books that include diverse cultural contexts, Prof. Volante is an internationally recognized scholar in educational policy analysis.

Sylke V. Schnepf (Ph.D.) is a Senior Researcher in the Competence Centre on Microeconomic Evaluation of the European Commission's Joint Research Centre (Ispra, Italy) and a Research Fellow at the Institute for the Study of Labour IZA (Bonn, Germany). Previously, she was Associate Professor in Social Statistics at the University of Southampton. Her main research interests regard patterns of cross-national educational inequalities and counterfactual impact evaluation of policies aimed to mitigate these inequalities. She is also interested in survey design and has published a number of papers examining potential errors of achievement estimates deriving from cross-national educational achievement surveys.

John Jerrim (Ph.D.) is a Professor in Educational and Social Statistics at the Institute of Education, University College London. Professor Jerrim's research interests include the economics of education, access to higher education, inter-generational mobility, cross-national comparisons, and educational inequalities.

He has worked extensively with the OECD Programme for International Student Assessment (PISA) data, with this research reported widely in the British media. John was the recipient of an ESRC Research Scholarship 2006–2010 and awarded the prize as the "most promising Ph.D. student in the quantitative social sciences" at the University of Southampton. In October 2011, he was awarded a prestigious ESRC post-doctoral fellowship to continue his research into the educational and labor market expectations of adolescents and young adults. Since then he has won the inaugural ESRC Early Career Outstanding Impact award and has just received an ESRC grant to study cross-national comparisons of educational attainment and social mobility.

Don A. Klinger (Ph.D.) is the Dean of Education in the Te Kura Toi Tangata Faculty of Education at the University of Waikato in Hamilton, New Zealand. His research explores measurement theory, the evolving conceptions of formative and summative assessment, the uses of classroom assessment to inform teaching and learning, and the uses and misuses of large-scale assessments and databases to inform educational policy and practice. With over 130 research manuscripts and reports, and research projects that include both national and international contexts, Dr. Klinger is one of Canada's leading scholars regarding assessment practices, policies, and student achievement. He has served as the president for both the Canadian Society for the Study of Education (CSSE/SCEE) and the Consortium for Research on Educational Assessment and Teaching Effectiveness (CREATE).

Contributors

Jake Anders (Ph.D.) is Associate Professor of Educational and Social Statistics in the Department of Learning and Leadership at UCL Institute of Education, and Director of CREATE (Conducting Research, Evaluations, and Trials in Education) in UCL's Centre for Education Improvement Science. His research interests focus on understanding the causes and consequences of educational inequality and the evaluation of policies and programmes aiming to reduce it. His research, which has been funded by the Economic and Social Research Council, the Nuffield Foundation, the Education Endowment Foundation, the Sutton Trust, and the UK Department for Education among others, has been published in education, economics, sociology, and psychology journals. Recent projects include experimental and quasi-experimental evaluations of school-based interventions, investigations of the importance of curriculum in explaining inequality in university access, and explorations of continuing inequalities into the labor market.

Carlo Barone (Ph.D.) is Professor of Sociology at Sciences Po (Paris), where he is affiliated to the Observatoire Sociologique du Changement (OSC) and to the Laboratory for the Interdisciplinary Evaluation of Public Policies (LIEPP). His research focuses on the relationship between educational inequalities and social mobility in dynamic and comparative perspective. His recent work involves the recourse to randomized controlled trials for the design and evaluation of interventions to reduce inequalities in early skills accumulation, track choices, and access to Higher Education.

Alana Butler (Ph.D.) is an Assistant Professor in the Faculty of Education at Queen's University in Kingston, Ontario. In 2015, she graduated with a Ph.D. in Education from Cornell University in Ithaca, New York. Her specialization was Learning, Teaching, and Social Policy. She has worked on various research projects related to literacy, schooling, and race in education. She has taught in a range of settings that include preschool, ESL, adult literacy, and university undergraduate. Her research interests include race and gender studies, equity and inclusion, risk and resilience processes, student development, immigration and settlement studies, and multicultural education.

Jorge Calero (Ph.D.) is a tenured Professor of Applied Economics at the University of Barcelona, Department of Economics. He is also a researcher of the Barcelona Institute of Economics (Institut d'Economia de Barcelona). Professor Calero is currently the coordinator of the Interdisciplinary Research Group on Educational Policies GIPE-IGEP and previous Head of the Council of the Educational System Evaluation (Catalonia). His main research interests are the economics of education, educational policies evaluation, equity issues in education, and economics of the welfare state.

Anna K. Chmielewski (Ph.D.) is an Assistant Professor of Educational Leadership and Policy at the Ontario Institute for Studies in Education (OISE) of the University of Toronto. She holds a Ph.D. in Education and M.A. in Sociology from Stanford University. Chmielewski's research examines trends and patterns of educational inequality, both internationally and over time. She has studied socioeconomic disparities in academic achievement, school segregation, curricular differentiation/streaming/tracking, the consequences of childhood inequality for adult outcomes, and methods for the analysis of international large-scale assessments. Her research has been published in the *American Educational Research Journal* and the *American Journal of Education.*

Álvaro Choi (Ph.D.) is an Associate Professor at the University of Barcelona as well as Researcher at the Barcelona Institute of Education (IEB) and the Interdisciplinary Group on Educational Policies (GIPE-IGEP). His main research fields are related to the Economics of Education, Public Economics, and the Evaluation of Public Policies. He has participated in the evaluation of a number of educational policies and has led a project funded by the Ramón Areces Foundation which aimed to identify effective policies for enhancing educational achievement in Spain. He has worked intensively with international large-scale assessments and is an OECD's Thomas J. Alexander fellow.

Maddalena Davoli is a Ph.D. Candidate in Economics and Research Assistant at the Department of Applied Econometrics and International Economic Policy at Goethe University, Frankfurt. She holds a Master Degree in International Relations and Economics from the University of Bologna. Her research interests lie in the fields of applied microeconometrics, the economics of education and labor economics.

Horst Entorf (Dr. rer. pol.) is Professor of Econometrics at Goethe University. He has held previous research positions at the Université Catholique de Louvain-la-Neuve, CREST-INSEE, at Darmstadt University of Technology, CERGE-Prague, and at the University of Mannheim. He was SPES-fellow of the EU and a fellow of the Deutsche Forschungsgemeinschaft. Horst has contributed to various interdisciplinary fields, including labor economics, economics of education, migration, and the economics of crime. He has been affiliated with the Institute for Labor Economics (IZA) since 1997. He has published in international journals in the fields of economics and migration.

Orazio Giancola (Ph.D.) is a Researcher in the Department of Social and Economic Sciences of the Sapienza University of Rome. His main fields of study are the analysis of educational policies, the comparison of educational systems, the dynamics and processes that produce educational and social inequalities. His recent works concern the methodological analysis of the large-scale assessments in education, the effects of tracking and differentiation in educational systems, and the processes of educational choice at various levels of students' academic careers.

Jiesi Guo (Ph.D.) is a Research Fellow at the Institute for Positive Psychology and Education at the Australian Catholic University. His areas of interest include educational and developmental psychology with a particular focus on how multiple systems on the cultural, social, motivational, and behavioral development of youth shape individual and gender difference in achievement choice. He completed his Ph.D. at the Australian Catholic University and had multiple international research stays with a fully funded scholarship to collaborate with prestigious researchers in Germany and Finland. He has published in international journals in the fields of psychology and education.

Jan-Eric Gustafsson (Ph.D.) is Professor Emeritus of education at the University of Gothenburg. His research has primarily focused on basic and applied topics within the field of educational psychology, and particularly on developing models for the structure of cognitive abilities, as well as assessment and development of abilities, knowledge, and skills. In parallel with the substantively oriented research, he has also been involved in the development of quantitative methodology, focusing on measurement and statistical analysis. To an increasing extent, he has become involved in national educational policy issues and he recently chaired a governmental School Commission, aiming for improvements of the quality and equity of the Swedish school system.

Kajsa Yang Hansen (Ph.D.) is Professor of education at the University of Gothenburg and at the West University, Sweden. The main focus of her research lies on educational quality and equity from a comparative perspective. To explain the variation in academic achievement between individuals, schools, across countries, and over time has always been her primary research interest. Her methodological interests focus on the analytical techniques for large-scale survey data. Currently, she is conducting projects investigating the impacts of the recent educational reforms in Sweden on the opportunity to learn, and consequently influence on educational quality and equity.

Morag Henderson (D.Phil.) is a quantitative sociologist and co-investigator of Next Steps, a longitudinal study of educational transitions in England. She currently works in the Department of Social Science at UCL Institute of Education as an Associate Professor. Henderson achieved her D.Phil. in Sociology from the University of Oxford. Her main research interest is educational inequalities and she has written extensively on the socioeconomic attainment gap; educational transitions; the influence of subject choice on subsequent educational and labor market outcomes; intergenerational educational mobility; the influence of parenting practices on attainment and academic self-concept.

Nina Hogrebe (Ph.D.) teaches and conducts research at the Department of Education, University of Münster. Her main fields of interest are early childhood education and care, educational inequalities, as well as educational governance and funding. As a response to observed social and ethnic segregation processes in early childhood, she has explored the effects of different demographic makeups in day-care centers on children's language skills in a project funded by the German Research Foundation. Beginning in 2019, she will be analyzing whether there is a connection between the provider of settings (e.g., parental initiatives, church-based) and segregation in a study which is funded by the German Ministry of Education and Research. Additionally, she is involved in analyses focusing on the effects of preschool participation on children's (cognitive) competencies based on international comparative data.

Petra Löfstedt (Ph.D.) has been an investigator at the Unit for Mental Health, Children and Youth at the Public Health Agency of Sweden since 2009. Petra's work mainly involves monitoring and analyzing health determinants, and is focused on children, young people, and mental health. Petra is the Principal Investigator of the Swedish team participating in the international study of Health Behavior in School-Aged Children since 2009. She is responsible for the collection, processing, and analysis of data. Recently, Petra has focused on the relation between young people's mental health and different factors in school. Petra has been affiliated with Department of Public Health and Community Medicine, Sahlgrenska Academy, University of Gothenburg since November 2018.

Philip Parker (Ph.D.) is a Professor and deputy director of the Institute for Positive Psychology and Education (IPPE) at the Australian Catholic University. His research uses large longitudinal databases from countries such as Australia, US, UK, Germany, and Finland where he focuses on career pathways, educational attainment, and individual differences related to youths' transition from school to work or further education. He completed his Ph.D. at the University of Sydney and undertook a post-doctoral research fellowship in the PATHWAYS to Adulthood program hosted at the University of Tübingen, Germany. He has published in international journals in the fields of psychology, education, and sociology.

Nicola Pensiero (Ph.D.) is a quantitative sociologist at UCL Institute of Education, University College London, where he joined in 2013 after completing his Ph.D. at the European University Institute. His research focuses on stratification and inequality, education systems, and income inequality. He has published extensively on those topics and has provided consultancy for Department for Education and Nuffield Foundation in the UK, as well as for the European Commission.

Victoria Rolfe is a Ph.D. Candidate in Education at the Department of Education and Special Education at the University of Gothenburg. She holds a Master Degree in Educational Research from the University of Gothenburg. Her research interests are in educational equity, opportunity to learn, and international assessment.

Monica Rosén (Ph.D.) is Professor of Education at the University of Gothenburg. Her main areas of research concern differences and change educational outcomes and their determinants at individual-, group- and system levels. She also has a strong interest in methodological issues related to educational measurement, educational evaluation and assessment, comparative educational research, and statistical modeling techniques.

Katariina Salmela-Aro (Ph.D.) is Professor of Educational Sciences at the University of Helsinki and at the moment Marie Curie Visiting Professor in the ETH Collegium for Advanced Studies in Zurich. She is also a Visiting Professor in the Institute of Education, University College London, and School of Education, Michigan State University and was a Visiting Scholar at the School of Education, University of California Irvine. She was previously a post-doctoral fellow at the Max-Planck Institute in Berlin, Germany. Currently, she is the President of the European Association for Developmental Psychology and was the previous Secretary General (first female) of the International Society for the Study of Behavioral Development (ISSBD). She is the director of several ongoing longitudinal studies among young people: FinEdu, PIRE, LEAD, and Mind-the-Gap. Her key research areas are school engagement, burnout, optimal learning moments, life-span model of motivation and related interventions. She is the founding member of Pathways International Interdisciplinary Post-doctoral fellowship program and a founding member of Academy of Finland Strategic Funding Council. She was Consulting Editor of *Developmental Psychology* (*APA*), and is an Associate Editor for the *European Psychologist* journal. She has published over 250 papers and chapters and received several national/international grants, including 10 large-scale grants from the Academy of Finland, National Science Foundation, EU Coordinator Marie Curie post-doctoral fellowship grant, and Horizon 2020.

Taren Sanders (Ph.D.) is a Research Fellow at the Institute for Positive Psychology and Education within the Australian Catholic University. His research focuses on social epidemiology, especially as it relates to youth health behaviors. His research covers topics such as predictors of physical activity and screen time, social and environmental influences on children's health, intervention development, and behavioral measurement techniques. He is especially interested in the intersection between research and policy.

Jaap Scheerens (Ph.D.) is Professor Emeritus at the University of Twente in the Netherlands. At the University of Twente, he coordinated a research program on school effectiveness. During his career, he was the scientific director of the national research school for postgraduate training in educational science ICO and director of the research institute OCTO of the Faculty of Education at the University of Twente. He was involved in many international research projects funded by international organizations. He has published 20 books and approximately 100 articles in scientific journals, mainly addressing educational effectiveness and educational evaluation.

Isa Steinmann (Ph.D.) is a researcher at the Technische Universität Dortmund. Her main research interests lie in the field of educational effectiveness research focusing on the outcomes of student achievement and educational inequality, as well as in the field of international comparative research. From a methodological perspective, she is interested in approaches that allow causal inference from observational data and in educational measurement. She is a former recipient of a scholarship of the German Academic Scholarship Foundation.

Rolf Strietholt (Ph.D.) is a researcher at Technische Universität Dortmund. He is also affiliated with the University of Gothenburg. His current interests lie in the field of international comparisons of educational systems, so-called comparative education, and include educational effective research studies with a special focus on measuring and explaining inequalities in student performance. He teaches courses on educational measurement and causal analysis. Recently, he was a guest researcher at the WZB Berlin Social Science Center and the Centre for Educational Measurement at the University of Oslo (CEMO). Rolf is a former recipient of the IEA Bruce H. Choppin Memorial Award.

Anneke Timmermans (Ph.D.) is an Assistant Professor at the Faculty of Behavioral and Social Sciences at the University of Groningen, The Netherlands. Her research interests include teacher expectations, factors related to the transition from primary to secondary schools in tracked educational systems, multilevel modeling, and the validity and reliability of school performance indicators. In 2016, Anneke received the Early Career Researcher Award from the *British Journal of Educational Psychology* for the paper "Accurate, inaccurate, or biased teacher expectations: Do Dutch teachers differ in their expectations at the end of primary education?".

Greetje van der Werf (Ph.D.) is Full Professor of learning and instruction and vice-Dean of the Faculty of Behavioral and Social Sciences at the University of Groningen, The Netherlands. Her main interests include educational effectiveness, civics and citizenship education, and the influence of psychological precursors of school success. Her expertise is in conducting large-scale multilevel longitudinal research in secondary education as well as evidence-based field experiments.

Part I
Socioeconomic Inequality in Education Systems

Chapter 1
Socioeconomic Inequality and Student Outcomes Across Education Systems

John Jerrim, Louis Volante, Don A. Klinger and Sylke V. Schnepf

Abstract This chapter provides an introduction to the topic of socioeconomic inequality and student outcomes, including methodological challenges associated with cross-cultural research on this topic. Particular attention is devoted to documenting socioeconomic differences noted in prominent international achievement surveys such as the Trends in International Mathematics and Science Study (TIMSS) and the Programme for International Student Assessment (PISA), including how these results have changed over time. We show how evidence regarding socioeconomic inequalities from such large-scale international assessments is limited due to challenges with missing parental education data and reliance upon student proxy reports. A key conclusion is therefore that a different approach to understanding socioeconomic inequalities across countries is needed if real progress is going to be made in raising the achievement of young people from disadvantaged socioeconomic backgrounds. A framework for the national profiles presented in the second part of this book is then discussed.

Keywords Student achievement · Socioeconomic status · Inequality · Comparative analysis

---

The original version of this chapter was revised: The author Sylke V. Schnepf's affiliation has been changed to "European Commission's Joint Research Centre, Ispra, Italy". The correction to this chapter is available at https://doi.org/10.1007/978-981-13-9863-6_13

J. Jerrim (✉)
Institute of Education, University College London, London, UK
e-mail: j.jerrim@ucl.ac.uk

L. Volante
Brock University, Hamilton, ON, Canada

D. A. Klinger
University of Waikato, Hamilton, New Zealand

S. V. Schnepf
European Commission's Joint Research Centre, Ispra, Italy

© Springer Nature Singapore Pte Ltd. 2019
L. Volante et al. (eds.), *Socioeconomic Inequality
and Student Outcomes*, Education Policy & Social Inequality 4,
https://doi.org/10.1007/978-981-13-9863-6_1

1.1 Introduction

Socioeconomic inequality in young people's academic achievement has become one of the key academic and political issues of the twenty-first century. Indeed, public policymakers across the globe are now seeking to raise the cognitive skills of young people from disadvantaged backgrounds, and to narrow the gap in achievement between this group and their more affluent peers. There are at least three reasons why this is now seen as such a pressing issue. The first is economic efficiency. In a competitive world, it is vital that each country is making the most of its human resources. Yet, if young people from poor backgrounds are failing to reach their academic potential, then this is unlikely to be the case. The second reason is social justice. Individuals do not pick the family and socioeconomic position they are born into. Rather, it is luck of the draw. Hence many would deem it to be "unfair" and inequitable if life chances are to a large extent determined by a factor, such as family background, that is largely outside of one's control. The final reason is the persistence of inequality. Many view education as a key driver of economic inequality and intergenerational mobility (Economic and Social Research Council, 2012; Goldthorpe, 2014). Consequently, persistence in educational inequalities will translate into continuing inequalities in later life. This is not only in terms of labor market outcomes (occupation and income), but also other wider factors that education is thought to influence, such as well-being and health (Chou, Liu, Grossman, & Joyce, 2010).

Figure 1.1, drawn from Jerrim and Macmillan's (2015) research, helps to formalize this argument by illustrating the link between parental education, their offspring's education, and their offspring's later lifetime outcomes. It also illustrates the three broad mechanisms that are thought to drive the parent–child relationship in educational achievement. The first is the biological channel of heredity transfers —genetic differences in individuals' academic potential that may be transmitted across generations. A growing body of research is highlighting the importance of genetics for our understanding of socioeconomic gaps in educational achievement (Ayorech, Krapohl, Plomin, & von Stumm, 2017), though the bio-molecular work in this area is still somewhat in its infancy (Jerrim, Vignoles, Lingam, & Friend, 2015). The second mechanism is non-financial resources. This encompasses a whole host of factors throughout childhood which, although not costing much money, differ (on average) between high and low socioeconomic parents. Examples include breastfeeding, reading and interactions with the child, helping regularly with homework, and parenting styles, each of which are plausibly linked to children's educational achievement (e.g., Sacker, Kelly, Iacovou, Cable, & Bartley, 2013). Finally, parents with lower levels of education will have fewer financial resources to invest in their children's education. They are consequently less likely to have access to the necessary educational materials that their children need to achieve high outcomes in school. Possible examples include access to books/computers, attending lower quality schools, and being unable to afford private tutors. Along with macro-economic forces (e.g., income inequality), public

1 Socioeconomic Inequality and Student Outcomes ...

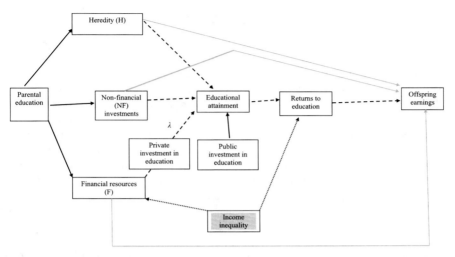

Fig. 1.1 Conceptual framework linking parental education to educational achievement and later lifetime outcomes. *Source* Jerrim and MacMillan (2015)

investment (e.g., government expenditure on education), and institutional structures (e.g., the design of the education system), these three forces combine to generate significant disparities in educational achievement by family background that can be observed across the developed world.

Figure 1.1 also serves as motivation as to why it is important to consider socioeconomic differences in educational achievement from an international comparative perspective. In order to judge whether inequality in achievement is large or small in any given country, it is necessary to have a yardstick to measure it against. For instance, is a correlation of 0.5 between parent and child years of schooling weak or strong? Drawing comparisons to other countries of a similar level of development provides an important and insightful context against which we can judge such results. Relatedly, Fig. 1.1 also has highlighted how heredity is thought to be one of the three key intergenerational mechanisms driving the intergenerational transmission of education. Yet, although this may help to explain parent–child links within a single country, it is difficult to see why this would cause differences *between* countries. In other words, the role of heredity transfers in generating intergenerational inequalities is likely to be approximately equal across nations. Hence, when considering why socioeconomic inequality in academic achievement is stronger in one country than another, we can largely rule this hereditary mechanism out. This then leaves factors that can be influenced by public policy—such as parental investments, macro-economic conditions, and institutional structures—as the remaining drivers of any cross-national differences. Indeed, as previous research has shown (e.g., Hanushek & Wossmann, 2006), cross-national comparisons also provide a natural way for one to consider how key institutional structures, such as the design of education systems, influences inequality in young people's outcomes.

1.2 Measurement Issues Regarding Socioeconomic Background

As the previous section has highlighted, there are important reasons to study inequality in educational achievement within an international comparative framework. There are, however, also important challenges, particularly with regards to the measurement of educational achievement across multiple countries and two generations. We provide an overview of these issues here, with a focus upon the measurement of family background. Although challenges also exist with respect to the robustness and international comparability of measures of children's academic achievement, we refer readers to chapters in previous edited volumes that have addressed this matter in detail (e.g., Goldstein, 2017).

The first decision one has to make when studying socioeconomic inequalities is which measure (or measures) of family background to use. Three main indicators are widely used in the literature: parental education, parental occupation, and (permanent) family income. Each has its advantages and disadvantages. For instance, while family income is easy to understand and interpret by a wide audience, and is arguably the most cross-nationally comparable, young people are unable to report it accurately, and it thus must be captured from parents directly. This means that it can be limited in terms of availability. On the other hand, young people generally can report parental occupation and parental education reasonably well (Jerrim & Micklewright, 2014), with these indicators therefore available within most datasets. Yet they suffer from a host of other measurement issues, as we shall discuss below.

An alternative to using just a single indicator is to combine several measures into a scale. This has been the preferred approach of the Organisation for Economic Co-operation and Development (OECD) in the Programme for International Student Assessment (PISA) study. This has the advantage of better capturing the multidimensional nature of any one indicator alone (Marks, 2011). However, such composite indicators are often difficult to interpret and communicate, while having also been criticized for their cross-national comparability (Rutkowski & Rutkowski, 2013). Additionally, composite indicators utilize cut scores to determine "low" versus "high" SES which varies largely across countries and reminds us of the important distinctions that exist between absolute versus relative poverty (Ravillion, 2016).

Throughout this volume, we have made a pragmatic choice of parental education (the highest level out of the child's mother and father) to be the preferred measure of socioeconomic position (wherever possible). Although we recognize that previous research has suggested that different family background indicators produce similar, but not identical, orderings of countries in terms of socioeconomic inequalities in student performance (Marks, 2011), we have decided to focus upon parental education for a number of reasons. First, this information is routinely collected in most social surveys across the world. Consequently, it is available in most national and international data sources within our countries of interest. Second, despite criticisms (Schneider, 2013), the International Standard Classification of Education (ISCED) framework provides (to some extent) a harmonized framework that allows for comparisons across surveys and international jurisdictions. This is not always true of the alternatives, such as with parental occupation or composite measures, which are sometimes recorded in datasets following national-specific categorizations. Third, as Fig. 1.1 has already demonstrated, there are clear mechanisms by which higher levels of parental education may cause their offspring to have higher levels of achievement at school. Fourth, the meaning of parental education is widely understood as a valid measure of family background among public policymakers and non-specialist audiences. Finally, it has also been the preferred measure in other cross-national research into socioeconomic inequalities (e.g., Bradbury, Corak, Waldfogel, & Washbrook, 2015) meaning that the work presented in this volume is consistent with much of the wider evidence base.

Yet it is also important that we highlight the potential challenges with parental education as a measure of socioeconomic position, and the care that readers of this volume will need to exercise when interpreting the results. As we shall illustrate in more detail below, the distribution of parental education varies markedly across countries. Consequently, a different proportion of the population will be classified as coming from a "disadvantaged" background depending upon the country. Whether this is a desirable property of a family background measure is open to debate. The reason for such large differences across countries is likely due, at least in part, to differences in the prestige of vocational qualifications across nations. For instance, while some countries have well-established vocational routes leading to highly regarded educational qualifications (e.g., Germany) other countries do not (e.g., England and the United States). Hence, despite the usefulness of the ISCED framework, there nevertheless remain some questions over whether one is truly comparing like-with-like.

Another important issue with respect to parental education is measurement error. Many surveys, including the large-scale international assessments, rely upon young people to provide proxy reports of their mother's and father's education level. However, as Jerrim and Micklewright (2014) illustrate, agreement between parent and child reports is far from complete. Moreover, cross-national patterns of socioeconomic inequality can vary in important ways, depending upon whose reports are used. In a similar manner, missing data can also be a problem, either because children are unwilling or unable to answer questions about their parents' education level, or because parents fail to complete the background questionnaire. Such issues may be particularly relevant for particular sub-groups. For instance, the educational qualifications of immigrants often do not easily fit into national reporting frameworks, and may, therefore, be particularly prone to non-response and miss-report. Each of the above, therefore, has the potential to impact upon the robustness of the conclusions that we can draw.

To conclude this section, we highlight these issues by illustrating the distribution of parental education across countries. Children have been grouped in low (ISCED 0–2), average (ISCED 3–5B), and high (ISCED 5A and above) parental education groups, along with those where this information is missing. Figures are presented data from the 2015 round of the Trends in International Mathematics and Science

Study (TIMSS) fourth grade (age 9/10), TIMSS eighth grade (age 13/14), and PISA (age 15/16) studies. Note that in TIMSS fourth grade, information on parental education is reported by parents in response to a background questionnaire, while in TIMSS eighth grade it is reported by participating children acting as proxy respondents.

A number of gaps appear in the TIMSS results due to countries either not participating in the study (Germany, Spain, Finland, and the Netherlands for the eighth-grade sample) or not participating in the home background questionnaire where information on parental education is reported (England and the United States in the case of the fourth-grade sample). Moreover, even where countries do participate, there continue to be serious problems with respect to missing parental education data. For instance, more than half of the fourth-grade sample is missing information on parental education in Australia and the Netherlands, mainly due to parents not returning the background questionnaire. Likewise, more than a third of the eighth-grade sample in Australia, Canada, England, and Sweden are missing parental education data, due to children either skipping this question or reporting that they "don't know" their mothers' and fathers' education level. Similar issues emerge with other socioeconomic background information in TIMSS, and in other international studies such as the Progress in International Reading Literacy Survey (PIRLS). There are, consequently, major limitations with using international resources such as TIMSS and PIRLS for studying the educational achievement of children from disadvantaged socioeconomic backgrounds, due to the serious risks posed by survey non-response.

In contrast, information on parental education is much more complete in PISA for most of the countries included in this volume (with the notable exception of Germany). Yet the distribution of parental education in the PISA study also helps to illustrate how the proportion falling into each of the different groups varies significantly across countries. For instance, whereas more than half of children report that at least one of their parents hold a degree in Finland, less than a quarter do in the Netherlands. Likewise, around a quarter of parents in Spain complete only basic education (ISCED level 0–2), compared to less than 5% of observations falling into this category in Finland, England, and Canada. Together, this helps to reiterate the point that, despite our use of comparable data and an internationally harmonized measure of educational qualifications, the size and composition of low parental-education groups across countries varies quite substantially.

1.3 Parent–Child Education Links in TIMSS and PISA

Despite the important caveats with the parental education measures in the large-scale international assessments documented above, it is nevertheless important to consider what they can tell us about the educational achievement of socioeconomically disadvantaged school children, and how this has changed over time. Table 1.2, therefore, illustrates the average mathematics scores of low education pupils according to the TIMSS/PISA 2015 studies (upper panel), and the size of the achievement gap relative to the high parental education group (lower panel). Lighter (darker) shading refers to "better" ("worse") performance relative to other countries at a given age. Note that, when reading this table, comparisons should only be made between countries at a single age, as it is not possible to directly compare scores between the various PISA and TIMSS studies. In other words, direct comparisons can be made when reading Table 1.2 vertically, but *not* when reading across horizontally.

Starting with the top panel, Germany stands out as a country where the low parental education group performs relatively well compared to the other countries. However, readers should interpret this finding in light of Table 1.1, and the fact that this group is larger (and hence likely to be somewhat less selective) than elsewhere. Sweden, on the other hand, is a country where children with low educated parents have comparatively poor mathematics skills. This is particularly true at age 15/16, based upon the PISA data, where both Sweden and the United States have lower levels of mathematics achievement than other countries. Otherwise, relatively few consistent patterns emerge, with the magnitude of most cross-national differences being relatively small. For instance, at age 9/10, Australia, Spain, Finland, and Italy are separated by just 10 TIMSS test points—roughly equivalent to an effect size of 0.1 standard deviations or less. The same holds true for Australia, Canada, Spain, Italy, and the Netherlands at age 15/16 with respect to the low parental education group's PISA scores. Our overall interpretation of the upper panel of Table 1.2 is that, on the whole, cross-national differences in the average mathematics skills of socioeconomically disadvantaged children are relatively small (at least with respect to the 10 countries included within this volume).

Table 1.1 The distribution of parental education across countries

TIMSS 2015								
	Age 9/10				Age 13/14			
	Low (%)	Medium (%)	High (%)	Missing (%)	Low (%)	Medium (%)	High (%)	Missing (%)
Australia	2	19	23	56	5	31	25	40
Canada	1	35	41	22	2	32	31	36
Germany	22	25	14	39	–	–	–	–
Spain	19	38	25	18	–	–	–	–
Finland	2	45	47	6	–	–	–	–
England	–	–	–	–	5	20	23	52
Italy	20	54	16	10	21	49	16	14
Netherlands	0	11	13	75	–	–	–	–
Sweden	4	36	40	21	4	26	31	40
USA	–	–	–	–	7	31	41	21

(continued)

Table 1.1 (continued)

PISA 2015	Age 15/16			
	Low (%)	Medium (%)	High (%)	Missing (%)
Australia	7	42	46	4
Canada	2	39	55	3
Germany	18	36	28	17
Spain	24	36	38	2
Finland	2	37	59	2
England	3	49	38	9
Italy	19	47	32	2
Netherlands	6	69	23	2
Sweden	5	39	52	4
USA	10	42	45	2

Notes Low refers to the highest parental education of ISCED level 0–2, medium ISCED level 3–5B and high to ISCED level 5A and above. Figures are row percentages

The lower panel of Table 1.2 turns to the gap in achievement between the "low" (ISCED level 0–2) and "high" (ISCED 5A/6) parental education groups. Similar findings emerge with respect to Germany and Sweden; the achievement gap tends to be comparatively small in the former and large in the latter (with the exception of the TIMSS results at age 13/14). There are also perhaps some surprising findings; achievement gaps in Finland do *not* stand out as particularly small, and are actually larger than in some of the other comparator countries. Likewise, across all three surveys, the magnitude of the mathematics achievement gap in Italy does not stand out as being particularly large (though, as Table 1.1 has already illustrated, Italy also has a greater proportion of children within the low parental education category than elsewhere). The other notable result is that socioeconomic inequality is quite pronounced in Australia relative to the other countries according to results from the two TIMSS studies, but this is not the case in PISA. Overall, the lower panel of Table 1.2 does provide some evidence that social inequality in educational achievement does to some extent vary across our 10 countries of interest.

To conclude this section, we consider how the mathematics skills of children from low parental education backgrounds have changed over time. As the survey with the most complete data in terms of both country coverage and available information on parental education, we have based this analysis upon PISA data alone. These results can be found in Table 1.3, with the top panel referring to average mathematics scores of the low parental education group, and the lower panel the gap in achievement between children from low and high parental education backgrounds. Note that the shading should now read across the table horizontally (i.e., it aids with comparisons made within each country over time), with darker cells indicating "worse" performance (lower average scores and larger achievement gaps).

1 Socioeconomic Inequality and Student Outcomes …

Table 1.2 The mathematics achievement of children from low parental education backgrounds

Mean scores

	Age 9/10	Age 13/14	Age 15/16
Australia	478	454	455
Canada	464	491	459
Germany	509	-	479
Spain	473	-	455
Finland	480	-	437
England	-	487	440
Italy	480	462	454
Netherlands	-	-	459
Sweden	460	470	420
USA	-	490	420

Gap between low and high parental education groups

	Age 9/10	Age 13/14	Age 15/16
Australia	86	88	68
Canada	72	68	72
Germany	52	-	58
Spain	64	-	57
Finland	74	-	89
England	-	81	76
Italy	59	63	55
Netherlands	-	-	79
Sweden	85	55	92
USA	-	55	74

Notes Estimates based upon children with available parental education data only. Age 9/10 based upon TIMSS 4th grade, age 13/14 TIMSS 8th grade, and age 15/16 PISA. The Netherlands has been excluded from age 9/10 estimates due to the small sample size of the low parental education group. Shading is within age-group (i.e., should be read vertically), with darker shading indicating "worse" outcomes (lower average scores and larger gaps) relative to the other countries

In terms of average scores, there has been some striking declines over the 12-year period considered. These have most notably occurred in the Netherlands, Finland, Canada, Sweden, and Australia, where there has been at least a 30 PISA test point drop between 2003 and 2015. (Note however that, for the Netherlands, response rates also tended to be lower in earlier waves of PISA, which could be having an impact upon the trends in this particular country.) In other nations, such as England, Spain, and the United States, the performance of this group has remained stagnant, with no obvious sign of progress having been made. Indeed, it is only really Germany where mathematics skills of the low parental education group has improved substantially over the last decade, with average scores in 2012/2015

Table 1.3 How is the relationship between parent and child education changing over time? Evidence from PISA mathematics

Mean scores of the low parental education group

	2003	2006	2009	2012	2015	Average
Netherlands	515	490	476	478	459	**484**
Finland	512	517	480	466	437	**482**
Canada	492	485	472	458	459	**473**
Australia	497	487	460	461	455	**472**
Germany	440	446	443	481	479	**458**
Spain	462	456	455	450	455	**456**
England	-	448	447	450	440	**446**
Italy	429	433	454	450	454	**444**
Sweden	461	462	426	429	420	**440**
USA	424	412	437	441	420	**427**

Gap between low and high parental education groups

	2003	2006	2009	2012	2015	Average
Italy	71	60	53	55	55	**59**
Spain	58	58	60	69	57	**60**
Finland	53	50	73	68	89	**67**
Netherlands	52	59	90	66	79	**69**
Canada	64	61	74	80	72	**70**
Australia	59	63	89	79	68	**72**
Sweden	63	51	88	65	92	**72**
England	-	79	71	79	76	**76**
USA	93	97	83	69	74	**83**
Germany	120	90	115	75	58	**92**

Notes Figures refer to PISA mathematics points. Average is the average between 2003 and 2015. Shading is within-country (i.e., should be read across horizontally), with darker shading indicating "worse" outcomes (lower average scores and larger gaps) relative to the other PISA rounds

around 40 points higher than in 2003/2006/2009 (this is roughly equivalent to a year of additional schooling; see Organisation for Economic Cooperation and Development, 2010, p. 167). Nevertheless, across the 10 countries considered, this seems to be the exception rather than the rule; rather than improving the mathematics skills of low socioeconomic status pupils over time, several of our 10 countries of interest are either showing no signs of progress or have gone into reverse.

Turning to the lower panel of Table 1.3, the gap in mathematics achievement between the high and low parental education groups seems to have increased in some countries, but fallen in others. Prominent examples where there has been a narrowing of achievement gaps include the United States, Germany, and (to some extent) Italy. Indeed, Germany has moved from having among the largest difference in children's mathematics achievement between the high and low parental education groups to among the smallest, at least out of the 10 countries considered. Sweden, the Netherlands, and Finland have, in contrast, moved in the other direction. Whereas the relationship between parental education and PISA mathematics scores was relatively weak in these nations in 2003, it has become much stronger by 2015. Again, the situation in some of the other countries has remained largely unchanged (e.g., England, Spain) or with no clear pattern to the results (e.g., Australia). Nevertheless, the recent experience of Germany and Italy does suggest it is possible to raise disadvantaged children's academic achievement and to narrow socioeconomic gaps in young people's skills. It is unfortunate, however, that several Western countries actually seem to be moving in the opposite direction.

1.4 The Structure and Contents of This Volume

The analysis presented in the previous section has highlighted that, although the major international large-scale assessments such as PISA, PIRLS, and TIMSS have some advantages, they also have important limitations with respect to improving our knowledge of educational achievement among low socioeconomic status pupils. Several key issues stand out. First, there are significant issues with either missing parental education data, or potential measurement error due to children acting as proxy respondents for their parents, as previously discussed. Second, even in countries where data are available, the youngest pupils within international surveys are age 9/10, and almost at the end of their primary school education. Yet a wide body of evidence documents how large socioeconomic gaps emerge very early in life (Cunha, Heckman, Lochner, & Masterov, 2006), and can be observed as young as age 3 (Jerrim & Vignoles, 2013). Therefore, in many ways, the international surveys only start collecting data after the point when much of the damage has already been done. Third, relatedly, none of the international studies follow the same group of children over time. Consequently, although they may be able to provide a single snapshot of young people's skills, they are unable to provide any information with regards to socioeconomic differences in developmental trajectories. Finally, as cross-sectional data, such studies can generally provide basic correlational evidence only. They are unable to reveal the wide set of factors likely to determine the poor educational outcomes of disadvantaged children, or provide much in the way of meaningful advice to education policymakers.

It is these limitations which have helped motivate the need for this volume. Rather than relying upon data from large-scale international assessments, this volume takes a somewhat different approach. Research teams from across 10 industrialized countries have been brought together to provide a series of case studies investigating socioeconomic inequalities in educational achievement from across a wide array of national contexts. This includes a diverse set of nations, ranging from those whose performance and equality according to PISA have been widely lauded (e.g., Canada, Finland) through to those whose international large-scale assessment scores are comparatively low, particularly among low parental education groups (e.g., Sweden, Italy). Although each chapter follows a similar structure, and utilizes parental education as the preferred measure of socioeconomic status (where possible), authors have also been free to exploit the full richness of the data and evidence available within their country, and have been encouraged to draw upon their detailed knowledge of their education system and subject expertise. This volume, therefore, seeks to provide readers with the latest empirical and policy evidence regarding how to improve educational achievement of young people from disadvantaged backgrounds, drawn from across the western world.

The volume is divided into three sections. Part I, including this introductory chapter, provides an overview of the topic of socioeconomic inequality and student outcomes, including methodological challenges associated with cross-cultural research on this issue. Particular attention has been devoted to explaining the strengths and limitations of PISA, TIMSS, and PIRLS for this purpose, including an investigation of what these resources tell us about the academic skills of young people from low socioeconomic backgrounds. The following chapter will consider some of the international trends related to the association between education policies and disadvantaged student populations.

Part II provides national profiles from scholars in nine countries (England, Germany, Italy, Spain, Netherlands, Sweden, Finland, Canada, and Australia). These countries have been selected because they represent Western industrialized nations that possess a range of datasets, many of which overcome some of the significant limitations with international achievement studies. These countries also vary widely in terms of their academic achievement results, education systems, and successes at addressing achievement gaps for socioeconomically disadvantaged student populations.

In order to promote a coherent approach and for the sake of comparability, each of the national profiles will be organized around four sections. An introductory section will provide a brief overview of the structure of compulsory school systems within a given country. The reader will gain an understanding of the general organizational and institutional features of the compulsory school system. This section also explains governance and administrative processes utilized to develop and refine education policies. The second section will describe the relative proportion of students who come from lower SES backgrounds within the national context. Although parental education will be the preferred measure (where possible), authors have been left to decide the most appropriate definition of the "low socioeconomic status" group using this variable within their own national context. Authors then outline the defining features associated with the disadvantaged student population, with particular attention given to explaining associated characteristics and mediating variables (i.e., gender, ethnicity, migrant status, single-parent households, and regional differences). Section 3 of the national profiles then describes the educational outcomes and choices of low SES children. These may include grades, grade repetition, graduation/dropout rates, aspirations, and standardized achievement scores, depending on the availability of data and relevance for the country context. Authors will also discuss the existing limitations of the available data and evidence within their particular national context. The final section of the national profiles then offers an analysis of the formulation, implementation, and effectiveness of education policies that are relevant for children with socioeconomic disadvantages.

Authors will also provide an explanation of the evolution of education policies as well as any refinements made to key institutional features (i.e., tracking provisions). Consequently, chapters will discuss the inherent linkages between children's background, educational outcomes, institutional features, and policy developments within an overarching cultural, social, and political context. On the basis of this discussion, the readers will have a clear indication of what kind of policies work the best, and what should be the way forward for the country with regards to improving educational outcomes and closing the achievement gaps of lower SES student populations.

Note that the aim of these profiles is *not* for results from individual countries to be directly compared. Rather, we hope that they help to facilitate thought, discussion, and debate among readers, and lead policymakers to consider whether what has "worked" in other education systems might usefully be applied in other national contexts.

The final part of this volume (Part III, the conclusion) then synthesizes findings from the national profiles about the role of institutional features, education policies, and societal-level forces that influence educational inequities. The conclusion also proposes future areas of inquiry stemming from the national profiles.

References

Ayorech, Z., Krapohl, E., Plomin, R., & von Stumm, S. (2017). Genetic influence on intergenerational educational attainment. *Psychological Science, 28*(9), 1302–1310. https://doi.org/10.1177/0956797617707270.

Bradbury, B., Corak, M., Waldfogel, J., & Washbrook, L. (2015). *Too many children left behind: The U.S. achievement gap in comparative perspective.* New York, NY: Russell Sage Foundation.

Chou, S. Y., Liu, J. T., Grossman, M., & Joyce, T. (2010). Parental education and child health: Evidence from a natural experiment in Taiwan. *American Economic Journal. Applied Economics, 2*(1), 63–91.

Cunha, F., Heckman, J., Lochner, L., & Masterov, D. (2006). Interpreting the evidence on life cycle skill formation. In E. Hanushek & F. Welch (Eds.), *Handbook of the economics of education* (pp. 698–812). Amsterdam, Netherlands: Holland North.

Economic and Social Research Council. (2012). *Education vital for social mobility* (ESRC social mobility evidence briefing). Retrieved from http://www.esrc.ac.uk/files/news-events-and-publications/evidence-briefings/education-vital-for-social-mobility/

Goldstein, H. (2017). Measurement and evaluation issues with PISA. In L. Volante (Ed.), *The PISA effect on global educational governance* (pp. 49–58). New York, NY: Routledge.

Goldthorpe, J. (2014). The role of education in intergenerational social mobility: Problems from empirical research in sociology and some theoretical pointers from economics. *Rationality and Society, 26*(3), 259–265. https://doi.org/10.1177/1043463113519068.

Hanushek, E., & Wossmann, L. (2006). Does educational tracking affect performance and inequality? Differences-in-differences evidence across countries. *The Economic Journal, 116*(510), C63–C76. https://doi.org/10.1111/j.1468-0297.2006.01076.x.

Jerrim, J., & Macmillan, L. (2015). Income inequality, intergenerational mobility and the Great Gatsby Curve: Is education the key? *Social Forces, 94*(2), 505–533. https://doi.org/10.1093/sf/sov075.

Jerrim, J., & Micklewright, J. (2014). Socioeconomic gradients in children's cognitive skills: Are cross-country comparisons robust to who reports family background? *European Sociological Review, 30*(6), 766–781. https://doi.org/10.1093/esr/jcu072.

Jerrim, J., & Vignoles, A. (2013). Social mobility, regression to the mean and the cognitive development of high ability children from disadvantaged homes. *Journal of the Royal Statistical Society Series A, 176*(4), 887–906. https://doi.org/10.1111/j.1467-985X.2012.01072.x.

Jerrim, J., Vignoles, A., Lingam, R., & Friend, A. (2015). The socio-economic gradient in children's reading skills and the role of genetics. *British Education Research Journal, 41*(1), 6–29. https://doi.org/10.1002/berj.3143.

Marks, G. (2011). Issues in the conceptualisation and measurement of socioeconomic background: Do different measures generate different conclusions? *Social Indicators Research, 104*(2), 225–251. https://doi.org/10.1007/s11205-010-9741-1.

Organisation for Economic Co-operation and Development. (2010). *PISA 2009 results: What students know and can do*. Paris, France: OECD Publishing. Retrieved from http://www.oecd.org/pisa/pisaproducts/48852548.pdf

Ravillion, M. (2016). *Poverty comparisons*. London: Routledge Press.

Rutkowski, D., & Rutkowski, L. (2013). Measuring socioeconomic background in PISA: One size might not fit all. *Research in Comparative and International Education, 8*(3), 259–278. https://doi.org/10.2304/rcie.2013.8.3.259.

Sacker, A., Kelly, Y., Iacovou, M., Cable, N., & Bartley, M. (2013). Breast feeding and intergenerational social mobility: What are the mechanisms? *Archives of Disease in Childhood, 98*(9), 666–671. https://doi.org/10.1136/archdischild-2012-303199.

Schneider, S. (2013). The international standard classification of education 2011. In G. E. Birkelund (Ed.), *Class and stratification analysis (Comparative social research* (Vol. 30, pp. 365–379). Bingley, UK: Emerald Group.

Chapter 2
The Impact of Education Policies on Socioeconomic Inequality in Student Achievement: A Review of Comparative Studies

Rolf Strietholt, Jan-Eric Gustafsson, Nina Hogrebe, Victoria Rolfe, Monica Rosén, Isa Steinmann and Kajsa Yang Hansen

Abstract This chapter reviews international comparative studies on the determinants of socioeconomic inequality in student performance. We were interested in studies of explanatory variables that are amenable to educational policy interventions. To identify such publications, we developed a comprehensive search strategy and conducted an electronic search based on six databases. We also manually searched two existing hand-picked reviews. After duplicates were removed, the search resulted in 814 references, of which a total of 35 studies met the eligibility criteria. The included studies investigated diverse topics such as learning environments inside and outside of school, educational expenditure, teacher education, autonomy, accountability, differentiation, and competition from private schools. Most studies are descriptive in nature and their findings are sometimes ambiguous. Despite these limitations, we tentatively conclude that the opportunity of choice reinforces inequality. Measures that target social selection can be effective.

Keywords Student achievement · Socioeconomic status · Inequality · Comparative analysis

---

R. Strietholt (✉) · J.-E. Gustafsson · V. Rolfe · M. Rosén · K. Y. Hansen
University of Gothenburg, Gothenburg, Sweden
e-mail: rolf.strietholt@tu-dortmund.de

R. Strietholt · I. Steinmann
TU Dortmund University, Dortmund, Germany

N. Hogrebe
University of Münster, Münster, Germany

K. Y. Hansen
University West, Trollhättan, Sweden

© Springer Nature Singapore Pte Ltd. 2019
L. Volante et al. (eds.), *Socioeconomic Inequality and Student Outcomes*, Education Policy & Social Inequality 4,
https://doi.org/10.1007/978-981-13-9863-6_2

2.1 Introduction

In virtually all countries, the socioeconomic status (SES) of students is correlated with their performance in standardized achievement tests. International large-scale assessments have become established as a unique resource to study such inequalities because they provide internationally comparable indicators to compare the degree of SES inequality in different countries. Even though it is inherently difficult to find internationally comparable measures of SES and achievement (see Chap. 1), there are at least three methodological advantages of such a comparative approach. First, many institutional features do not vary within a single country (e.g., the existence of national examinations) and as such, comparative studies are the only approach to observe variation in these features. Furthermore, even if determinants of inequality vary within a single country, the variations in the pooled international data from several countries are frequently much larger than those within a single county (Hanushek & Woessmann, 2011). Second, it is possible to replicate analyses to test the generalizability of research findings in different countries. Third, while within-country SES inequality may be in part due to genetics, cross-national inequalities are more likely to be due to differences in the learning environments. We restrict the present review to comparative studies that employ data from at least two countries. In addition to this cross-national perspective, the following chapters will complement the comparative perspective with in-depth descriptions of the situations in different countries.

Several studies have investigated determinants of academic success for all students, regardless of student SES, but few studies have focused on SES inequality as the issue of interest. Such studies on effect heterogeneity are precisely the research we are interested in. Common approaches to test for effect heterogeneity are (a) interaction effects between the main explanatory variable and SES, (b) two-step approaches where the computation of an SES inequality measure and modeling variation in this measure are two separate steps, and (c) replicating analyses for different SES groups. It seems also worth mentioning that studies focusing exclusively on the academic success of low SES students are outside the scope of this review because by design such studies permit no inferences about effect heterogeneity. Furthermore, we excluded studies that investigate whether the effect of SES on achievement changes after controlling for some other explanatory variables: changes in effects can be due to an association between the explanatory variable and SES (suggesting inequality in the access to educational opportunity), but they do not directly generate information about effect heterogeneity.

Our objective is to review the international comparative evidence on the determinants of SES inequality in achievement. We are interested in studies of explanatory variables that are amendable by educational policy interventions, but not in factors such as gender, geographical space (e.g., urban, rural), or economic development. Further, we do not consider motivational variables (e.g., interest, emotion) as determinants of SES achievement inequality because we think that they are essentially alternative educational outcomes. Therefore, SES inequality in motivational variables

2 The Impact of Education Policies on Socioeconomic … 19

is beyond the scope of this review. Studies that do not report the effect of single determinants of SES inequality but only the overall effect of several determinants will not be included (e.g., Heyneman & Loxley, 1983, and studies that replicated this study). To evaluate the quality of the existing body of evidence, we review the source studies and how SES inequality was measured in previous research.

2.2 Methods

2.2.1 Selection Criteria

We include studies that meet the following five criteria to synthesize the existing evidence determinants of socioeconomic inequality:

(1) Apply an indicator of SES inequality based on measures of SES and achievement.
(2) Apply a measure of a determinant of SES inequality.
(3) Report quantitative data on the relationship between (1) and (2) in sufficient detail.
(4) Include in its sample primary or secondary school students from two or more countries.
(5) Be published in a professional journal in English.

2.2.2 Keywords and Data Collection

The electronic search was conducted using *EconLit*, *ERIC*, *PsychINFO*, *Scopus*, *SocINDEX*, and *Web of Science*. We combined three sets of search terms for SES, achievement, and international study to search for references.[1] The search was limited

---

[1]The following search function for *Web of Science*: *TS = ("socioeconomic status" OR "socioeconomic status" OR "social class" OR "social status" OR "income or disadvantaged or poverty" OR "socioeconomic background" OR "socio-economic background" OR "social background" OR "social inequality" OR "socioeconomic inequality" OR "socio-economic inequality") AND TS = (achievement OR literacy OR performance) AND TS = ("international studies" OR "comparative analysis" OR "comparative education" OR "international assessment" OR cived OR fims OR firs OR fiss OR iccs OR icils OR pirls OR pisa OR sims OR sirs OR siss OR timss OR "civic education study" OR "first international mathematics study" OR "first international reading study" OR "first international science study" OR "international civic and citizenship education study" OR "international computer and information literacy study" OR "pilot twelve-country study" OR "programme for international student assessment" OR "progress in international reading literacy study" OR "reading literacy study" OR "second international mathematics study" OR "second international reading study" OR "second international science study" OR "six subject survey" OR "third international mathematics and science study"*

to journal articles published in English. After the removal of duplicates, the search resulted in 814 references. A second targeted search was conducted in two hand-picked reviews that are related to the topic of this paper resulting in six further publications (Hanushek & Woessmann, 2011; Van de Werfhorst & Mijs, 2010). In a final step, papers that were known by the authors were added. We conducted an initial screening of the title and abstract for all references and a full-text screening of the relevant references that passed the initial screening. A total of 35 studies met all eligibility criteria and their findings will be summarized in the next section. Most studies have focused on only one topic of investigation ($n = 24$) but a subset of studies has investigated two to five determinants ($n = 11$) of SES inequality. We used all available information on different topics of investigation in the present review.

2.3 Results

2.3.1 Source Studies

Several international large-scale assessments have been conducted since the late 1960s, but data from only a few of them have been used in the publications included in this review (for more information on this research see, e.g., Meyer, Strietholt, & Epstein, 2018; Strietholt, Gustafsson, Rosén, & Bos, 2014). Most studies in this review employed data from the Programme for International Student Assessment (PISA, $n = 19$), followed by the Trends in International Mathematics and Science Study (TIMSS, $n = 9$), the Progress in International Reading Literacy Study (PIRLS, $n = 6$), the Second International Mathematics Study (SIMS, $n = 2$), and the International Civic and Citizenship Education Study (ICCS, $n = 1$). Several references combined data from different cycles of the same study ($n = 5$) or different studies ($n = 3$). PIRLS tests primary school students, while PISA, SIMS, and ICCS focus on secondary school, and TIMSS includes both primary and secondary school samples. Most included references are concerned with SES inequality in secondary schools ($n = 29$), a few aimed to explain inequality at the end of primary school ($n = 5$), and only one study aimed to explain inequalities in primary as well as secondary school ($n = 1$). The observation that most studies are based on data from PISA, TIMSS, PIRLS, and SIMS implies that most comparative research is on SES inequality in mathematics, reading, and science performance.

The scope of the studies varies from three to 65 countries. In eight, data from less than 10 countries were used, in another eight, data from 10 to 25 countries, and 19 studies used data from more than 25 countries. Some of the studies limited their

---

OR "trends international mathematics and science study" OR "written composition study") along with the limiters *LANGUAGE: (English)* and *DOCUMENT TYPES: (Article)*. The search function and limiters were adapted to used for the other databases. *EBSCOhsost* were used to search *EconLit, ERIC, PsychINFO,* and *SocINDEX*. The electronic search was conducted on February 2, 2018.

analytical samples to a homogeneous set of countries like European, East Asian, or Organisation for Economic Co-operation and Development (OECD) members. One-quarter of the studies replicated analyses for different countries and three-quarters exploited variation in the pooled data. Two studies were published prior to 2001, eight studies between 2001 and 2010, and 29 studies from 2011 onwards.

2.3.2 Measures of Socioeconomic Inequality

In studies of children and adolescents, SES has long been conceptualized as a tripartite construct, incorporating measures of parental education, parental occupation, and parental income (Duncan, Featherman, & Duncan, 1972; Gottfried, 1985; Hauser, 1994; Mueller & Parcel, 1981; White, 1982). Further to these three traditional indicators, Sirin (2005) provides grounds for the inclusion of a fourth measure of socioeconomic status, home possessions.

The studies included in this review utilized a variety of items across three of the four domains of SES (parental income is frequently excluded due to the difficulty collecting data on this item) drawn from student, parental, and school questionnaires in their measures of SES, the creation of index variables approximating SES being a common data-handling technique. There are three broad trends in the measures of SES commonly seen in the analysis of international assessment data: the use of pre-calculated indices of SES, particularly the PISA index of economic, social, and cultural status (ESCS), which appears in 10 of the 35 studies included in this analysis; the use of one or more individual survey items, for example, the number of books in the home (23% of studies) or parental education (one-third of studies); or the computation of study-specific indices of SES (Bodovski, Byun, Chykina, & Chung, 2017; Caro and Lenkeit 2012; Chiu, 2015; Witschge & van de Werfhorst, 2015) or educational capital (Chudgar, Luschei, & Zhou, 2013; Luschei & Chudgar, 2011). SES measures are most commonly deployed in regression, however a notable subset of studies utilized SES as a grouping or stratification variable for replicating models across different groups (e.g., Akiba, LeTendre, & Scribner, 2007; Chiu, 2015; Falck, Mang, & Woessmann, 2018; Lavrijsen & Nicaise, 2015; Lavy, 2015).

2.4 Determinants of Socioeconomic Inequality in Student Achievement

2.4.1 Learning Environments Outside School

Children acquire skills and competences not only in school but also in their families and in preschool. A possible explanation for why the effect of parent–child communication may vary by socioeconomic background is that low SES parents arguably have more limited resources and skills to promote children's academic achievement. For this reason, parental involvement specifically may not have the same benefits for students from different SES families. With respect to preschool, children who grow up in less intellectually stimulating home environments may benefit more from spending time in preschool than privileged children who grow up in intellectually stimulating environments. The existing comparative research by and large supports the idea that learning environments before and outside compulsory schooling may reduce educational inequality if certain conditions are met.

2.4.2 Home Learning Environments

Park (2008) conducted separate regression analyses to investigate the interaction effect between SES and parent–child communication (discussing books, films, or school, and just talking) on achievement in 14 countries using PISA 2000 data. Some effects were positive, others negative, and most are nonsignificant. A striking result, however, is that the interaction effects were negative in all countries with a standardized school system (e.g., national curricula, textbooks, and exams) but positive in nonstandardized systems. Keeping the lack of statistical significance in mind, this finding suggests that efforts to increase parent–child communication could decrease the SES achievement gap because the payoff is greater for lower SES students in countries with standardized school systems. Park argues that low SES parents have greater access to the necessary knowledge about schooling in more standardized systems. In contrast, in countries with no such national standards, efforts to increase parent–child communication may actually widen the SES gap. Caro and Lenkeit (2012) replicated analyses of the interaction effect between parent–child communication and SES on achievement. They used PIRLS 2006 data, featuring a primary school sample, from five economically diverse countries and the main explanatory variable was the frequency with which parents talked to children about things they have done. Again, the interactions were small and nonsignificant.

To study the effect of shared book reading before the start of compulsory schooling on reading achievement end of primary school Araújo and Costa (2015) used PIRLS 2011 data from 22 European countries. Parents were asked how often someone in the household read to their children before the beginning of compulsory education on a three-point scale ("often", "sometimes", "never or almost never"). Separate comparisons were made for children from low and highly educated parents. They show that early book reading was positively associated with higher achievement in both groups, but the associations were stronger for disadvantaged children in most countries. This finding suggests that increasing book reading to young children may prevent later SES inequality. It is important to note, however, that today most parents read books to their children. The only exceptions were Bulgaria, Romania, and Wallonia (a region within Belgium) where 25–50% of the low-educated parents did *not* "often" read to their children.

Preschool children who grow up in less intellectually stimulating home environments may benefit more from spending time in preschool than privileged children who grow up in intellectually stimulating environments. To test this hypothesis, Cebolla-Boado, Radl, and Salazar (2016) employed the pooled PIRLS 2011 data from 28 developed countries. They regressed achievement on the time children spend in preschool, SES, and their interaction. The results reveal a positive main effect but a negative interaction effect. This finding suggests that preschool benefits are lower for children from more highly educated parents, and as such preschool reduces social inequality in educational achievement.

While participation in preschool is not compulsory in most countries, family background characteristics and preschool participation correlate (Hogrebe & Strietholt, 2016). For this reason, Schütz, Ursprung, and Woessmann (2008) hypothesized that the equalizing effect of preschool does not come into effect unless a large share of children are enrolled in preschool. To test this, they analyzed the pooled grade 8 TIMSS data from 57 countries. The results suggest an inverted U-shaped relationship between the preschool enrollment rate and the SES achievement gap. The authors argued that as long as few pupils attend preschools, these are probably students from privileged backgrounds; only when a substantial share of students are enrolled does the preschool system reach disadvantaged students and have an equalizing effect. Furthermore, preschool duration was negatively related to the achievement gap, which supports the idea that particularly disadvantaged children benefit from stimulating preschool environments. Schlicht, Stadelmann-Steffen, and Freitag (2010) provide further evidence for the idea that large preschool enrollment rates are associated with lower SES gaps. They find that the effect of parental education on student achievement is smaller in countries where more than 75% of the children in the relevant age group were enrolled in preschool, using PISA data from 25 European countries. In contrast, Burger (2016) did not find a significant association between the percentage of pupils who had attended pre-primary education (ISCED 0) and the SES gap within countries using a sample of 31 European countries that participated in PISA 2012. Burger, however, did not model a nonlinear relationship between preschool enrollment rates and SES inequality and his results analyses may simply be driven by selection effect in countries with low enrollment rates.

2.4.3 School Learning Environments

Several studies have searched for features of school learning environments that can reduce SES inequality. We grouped this research into different areas that concern quantity, quality, and emotional features of instruction and schooling as well as the social composition of the learning group.

2.4.4 Time for Learning

Some studies have related the amount of instructional time to student achievement following the sensible premise that learning something is a function of the time allocated to learn it. Again, disadvantaged children may benefit more from additional instructional time than privileged children who receive intellectually stimulating environments anyway (e.g., private tutoring). In a recent study, Lavy (2015) proposed an interesting approach to identify the effect of instructional time that can take possible selection bias into account when analyzing pooled cross-sectional PISA 2006 data from 58 countries. The study used information on instructional time and performance which was available for mathematics, reading, and science, and exploited the within-student between-subject variation in dependent and independent variables to minimize the endogeneity bias. The analyses were replicated for students from low and highly educated parents, and suggest that there is some heterogeneity in the effect of instructional time. The effects were higher for students from low-educated parents, implying that an increase in instructional time reduces SES inequality in achievement. Burger (2016) and Schlicht et al. (2010) confirmed this finding that additional time at school reduces the effect of parental education on student achievement. They studied the cross-sectional association between annual instruction time (across all subjects) and the SES achievement gaps using PISA 2012 data from 31 European countries and PISA 2006 data from 25 European countries, respectively. Both studies revealed a negative association between the amount of time that children spent at school during a school year and the SES gap in achievement.

Sandoval-Hernández and Białowolski (2016) studied whether time spent on homework predicts academic resilience—that is, high performance despite low SES. They conducted separate analyses for five high-performing Asian countries using TIMSS 2011 grade 8 data. The authors observed that the time spent on homework was positively associated with high-performing low SES students but not for high SES students in Singapore. Although this finding suggests that homework may be able to reduce SES inequality, it seems important to bear in mind that differential effects were observed in only one of the five countries.

2.4.5 Content Coverage

Another important dimension of opportunity is the exposure to learning contents. Two studies have investigated the interaction between content coverage and SES. Schmidt, Burroughs, Zoido, and Houang (2015) used the degree to which students were exposed to formal mathematics (e.g., cosine, exponential functions) as the main explanatory variable. Student achievement was regressed on student- and school-level measures of content coverage and SES. Individual-level measures of content coverage and SES were simply aggregated by school to arrive at the school-level measures. To test for differential effects, interactions between content coverage and SES were modeled on both levels. Using PISA data from 33 OECD countries, the study reveals positive interaction effects between content coverage and Opportunity to Learn (OTL) on student and school levels. Santibañez and Fagioli (2016) replicated the finding that the interaction between SES and content coverage predicts performance for a more diverse set of 50 countries using data from the same source study. The results from both studies suggest that content coverage is less effective for disadvantaged students, as well as for schools with a disadvantaged student body. Possible explanations for these unexpected findings are the cross-sectional design and methodological issues in the content coverage measures. In contrast to other studies, PISA does not use teacher but rather student data to measure content coverage and there are methodological issues in the wording of response scales (Scheerens, 2017; Yang Hansen & Strietholt 2018).

2.4.6 School Culture

Several scholars have emphasized that school culture is a determinant of student learning. Factors such as disciplinary climate, school emphasis on academic success, and a good relationship between students and teachers hinder or amplify student learning. It may be hypothesized that school culture is particularly important for disadvantaged students because they receive less parental support and grow up in a more unstable environment outside school. The existing comparative research, however, does not provide much—and sometimes counterintuitive—evidence for the assumption that a learning-oriented school culture can close the gap between low and high SES students. Sandoval-Hernández and Białowolski (2016) aimed to identify factors that support academic resilience. Using TIMSS 2011 grade 8 data from five high-performing Asian countries, four school climate variables were studied (emphasis on academic success, bullying, reinforcement by teachers, discipline). The main objective was to identify educational factors that are more effective for low SES students than for high SES students. The study provides no evidence for a heterogeneity in the effects of the four school climate variables in any of the four countries. Huang and Sebastian (2015) used PISA 2012 data to investigate a similar set of variables and, by and large, confirmed the previous neutral findings. They investigated variation in the within-school achievement gaps based on SES in 61 countries using PISA 2012 data. Since the SES gap varied statistically significantly in only 16 countries, all further analyses were replicated to this smaller subset of countries. Only two variables showed a somehow consistent relation with SES inequality: first, a positive student–teacher relationship—that is, students felt that their teachers got along with them, listened to them, and were fair, and could be approached if they needed help—was statistically significantly associated with lower within-school SES gaps in three countries and in most other countries the association was negative as well; and second, in five of the 16 countries, school discipline was significantly associated with higher SES inequality. It is, however, difficult to interpret that the achievement gaps were small in schools with problematic disciplinary climate (i.e., noise, disorder).

2.4.7 School Mix

Social segregation in the school system and measures of desegregation have been discussed for several decades. For example, transporting students by bus to schools in other districts to reduce prior racial segregation of schools (busing), ability tracking, and zoning-based school admission policies aim to influence school choice and social segregation. Several studies have used school-level SES as a predictor of performance levels but only few have related it to SES inequality in achievement. Specifically, we identified only two cross-national studies that have investigated the possibility that disadvantaged children gain more from their peers than do more advantaged children. These studies have proposed different measures of school mix. Research provides hardly any evidence that school mix is especially important for disadvantaged children.

Using PIRLS 2001 data from Germany, France, Iceland, the Netherlands, Norway, and Sweden, Ammermueller and Pischke (2009) studied the differential effects of the class mean SES on performance by SES groups. For this purpose, they regressed the achievement scores on the student-level measure number of books, the mean number of books in each classroom (social composition), and the interaction of the two variables. The data included data from more than one class per school and the authors added school fixed effects to control for unobserved confounding variables on school level. The analyses show that high SES classes perform better than low SES schools. The main finding, however, is that the interaction of student and class SES is nonsignificant in all six countries.

Chudgar et al. (2013) conceptualized school mix differently. First, they constructed a student-level SES indicator based on several possession variables (e.g., books, computer). Second, students in the bottom quartile of the national SES distribution were defined as low SES students. Third, the authors computed the absolute distance (i.e., ignoring the positive or negative sign) between the average classroom SES of all children in the classroom and the SES value of each student. The basic motivation behind this measure is that students who are closer to the average SES of their classmates may experience a less mixed environment compared to students who are further away from the average SES of their classmates. The final analytical model is regression of achievement on the dummy for low SES students, the distance measure, and their interaction. The model also contains school fixed effects. TIMSS 2007 grade 8 data were used to replicate the analyses in 15 countries. The main result is a positive main effect of the distance measure but a negative interaction in virtually all countries. This finding indicates that studying in diverse classrooms is beneficial for privileged students but not for low SES students.

2.4.8 Differentiation

Differentiation (or stratification) is one of the most contentious institutional features of educational systems. While some countries stream children into different ability schools after primary school, others keep their secondary school system comprehensive. A frequent argument against differentiation is that educational transitions depend mainly not on ability but on SES (parental assumptions and tastes). There is compelling evidence that early tracking increases SES achievement inequality. In contrast to the research on external (between-school) differentiation, only one study investigated the effect of internal (within-school course-by-course) differentiation, finding mostly no effect on SES inequality.

The most often used indicator of differentiation is the age of first selection in the education system. This indicator is also referred to as early tracking. The most reliable evidence comes from studies that compare SES achievement gaps in primary and secondary school in tracked and untracked educational systems; as such, a design has similar methodological advantages to other longitudinal designs. Dupriez and Dumay (2006) combined primary and secondary school data for 15 European countries that participated in both PIRLS 2001 and PISA 2000. To quantify the degree of differentiation, the age of first tracking was used. In the same vein, (Lavrijsen & Nicaise, 2015) combined PIRLS 2006 and PIRLS 2012 data from 33 countries. Both studies reveal a negative effect of the age of tracking SES gaps, which suggests that tracking increases SES gaps.

Some studies compare SES inequality in secondary school in tracked and untracked educational systems without controlling for initial levels of inequality. Even though studies with such a design arguably permit less strong claims, their results on the effects of early tracking are consistent with studies that exploit longitudinal variation in SES gaps. Higher SES gaps were found in early tracking countries using data from various cycles of TIMSS (Schütz et al., 2008) and PISA (Brunello & Checchi, 2007; Horn, 2009; Le Donné, 2014; Schlicht et al., 2010). The results are less conclusive for alternative indicators of differentiation, namely, the number of tracks (school types) for the 15-year-olds, the share of upper secondary students who are enrolled in vocational programs, and course-by-course tracking within schools (Horn, 2009; Huang & Sebastian, 2015; Le Donné, 2014). These findings may suggest that it is not differentiation per se but rather between-school tracking at a very early age that exacerbates SES inequalities.

2.4.9 Accountability

Accountability concerns measures to hold educational actors accountable for their performance. There are mixed assumptions about how accountability affects SES inequality. Central examinations, for example, may decrease achievement gaps because they establish transparent criteria for performance and such information may be particularly useful for low educated parents who have more limited information about the educational system and the performance of their children. Critics of accountability systems, on the other hand, are concerned that teachers and schools may try to remove poor-performing disadvantaged children to improve their results. The evidence from comparative studies is inconclusive for various accountability measures.

To investigate effects of the existence of curriculum-based external exit examination systems that are compulsory for all students, Woessmann (2005) used a large sample of 54 countries that participated in TIMSS 1995 or 1999 (grade 8) and a more homogeneous sample of 31 OECD countries. Central exams were associated with smaller gaps between children from educated and uneducated parents for TIMSS but with larger gaps for PISA data. For the number of books SES indicator, the effects were mostly neutral. Horn (2009) and Han (2018) replicated the analyses for OECD countries using data from the more recent PISA 2009 and 2012 cycles. They observed no association between the existence of national exams and SES (measured by the ESCS index) achievement gaps.

The mere existence of exams may not be effective unless there are actual consequences for educational actors. Horn (2009) used a broad index to measure whether achievement data is communicated to various actors (parents, local community, higher level) and used by parents to choose schools, or by authorities to reward or sanction schools. This index was measured on the country level. The analyses of PISA 2009 data from 29 countries suggest no relation between SES inequality and the usage of achievement data. Gándara and Randall (2015) used PISA 2006 data from Australia, Korea, Portugal, and the United States to investigate a similar issue on school level. Principals were asked if they inform parents about the performance of their children, if school achievement data is posted publicly, and if such data is used to evaluate teachers' or principals' performance; all this information was summarized into a single score of school accountability. The study suggests a positive association between the principals' perception of school accountability and SES inequality within their schools. This finding implies that accountability increases SES gaps. Woessmann (2011) argues the performance-related payment system motivates current teachers. He studied whether the existence of a payment system that rewards outstanding teacher performance affects SES gaps using PISA 2003 data from 27 OECD countries. The study finds positive effects for the main effect of teacher performance pay and the interaction with student SES on student achievement. These findings suggest that performance pay systems do indeed have an effect on student learning but the currently existing systems apparently do not motivate teachers to support specifically disadvantaged students. Current performance pay systems thus lead to larger SES performance gaps.

School inspection is another approach to evaluate schools and there is mixed evidence.

Horn (2009) used OECD data from PISA 2003 to compare 16 countries with and 10 countries without a national inspectorate. The analyses reveal no differences in the SES achievement gaps. Witschge and van de Werfhorst (2015) used data from the ICCS from 2009 to study SES inequality in civic knowledge; that is, students' knowledge and skills of reasoning and analysis of civic systems, principals, participation, and identities. The authors compared 23 countries with and without an external evaluation system where external evaluators report to a local, regional, or central education authority. The main finding are larger within-school SES gaps in countries with an external evaluation system.

2.4.10 Interaction Between Differentiation and Accountability

Central exams may hold schools accountable for their performance, which may encourage them to allocate students to tracks, not on the basis of SES. Bol, Witschge, Van de Werfhorst, and Dronkers (2014) discuss the relationship between differentiation and accountability and argue that educational tracking may be less problematic if countries implement measures to ensure that the selection into different tracks depends mainly on merit but not on SES. Specifically, they hypothesized that SES has a larger effect on student achievement in tracked systems without central examinations, whereas this relationship is attenuated in tracked systems with central examinations. Analyses based on PISA 2009 data from 36 developed countries confirmed a significant negative triple-interaction between SES, central exams, and tracking. This finding suggests that central examinations reduce the effect of early tracking on SES inequality.

In another contribution, Bodovski et al. (2017) conducted similar analyses on the interaction between institutional features using a sample of 8th-grade data from four TIMSS cycles (1999, 2003, 2007, 2011) and 37 countries. Like Bol and colleagues, they considered tracking as one institutional feature. However, in contrast to Bol et al., the second variable is no pure measure of accountability but a combined measure of the existence of central exams, national curriculum, and centrally prescribed textbooks. The study suggests a negative effect on the interaction of the two institutional features but the parameter does not reach statistical significance. The lack of significance may be due to the ambiguous second measure which is no pure measure of accountability.

2.4.11 Autonomy

Autonomy is a key feature of the new public management regime. Proponents of autonomy argue that giving local actors more freedom in how they manage the school and their staff increases efficiency. Critics of this system fear that the lack of standardization may result in a system of unequal schools that mainly serves children from privileged backgrounds.

Studies that use concrete measures of autonomy observe positive associations between school autonomy and SES inequality. Han (2018) used the pooled PISA 2012 data from 34 OECD countries to investigate autonomy in teacher hiring and achievement inequality. She classified the mode of decision-making in teacher hiring into three levels: fully school-based teacher hiring; shared hiring decisions by school and external authority; and fully external authority-based hiring. The smallest SES gaps were observed in countries where schools have no autonomy over teacher hiring. Horn (2009) computed the ratio of principals who report autonomy in staffing, budgeting, instructional content, and assessment practices for 28 countries using data from the PISA 2003 school questionnaire. This measure of school autonomy suggests higher SES inequality in countries with autonomous schools.

Centralization is the counterpart of autonomy. However, in contrast to the research on school autonomy, the research on centralization finds no associations between indicators of centralization and the level of SES inequality. Horn (2009) also computed the ratio of principals who report direct national or regional influence on staffing, budgeting, instructional content, and assessment practices as a measure of centralization. Witschge and van de Werfhorst (2015) used the existence of guidelines on how to assess students' active participation in school or in the community and the existence of national curricula and standards in civic education as indicators of centralization when analyzing ICCS data from 20 to 23 countries. A possible explanation for the neutral findings for centralization is that the measures used in previous research are poor indicators in comparative studies.

2.4.12 Private Schools and Competition Among Schools

Private schools may be more able to introduce new pedagogical concepts than public schools and they may be more effective because parents, teachers, principals, and the school board have shared values about education. Furthermore, private schools sometimes acquire additional resources from sponsors or by charging school fees. From a systemic perspective, private schools introduce competition among schools. With respect to social inequality in achievement, critics are particularly concerned that children from advantaged backgrounds are more likely to be schooled at private schools while disadvantaged children are schooled at public schools with less resources.

Analyses of country-level data have found no or even moderately negative associations between the share of private schools and SES inequality in achievement. This finding has been constantly replicated in studies that used data from a large set of countries and multiple cycles of TIMSS (grade 8; Bodovski et al., 2017; Schütz et al., 2008) and PISA (Burger, 2016; Schlicht et al., 2010). Two studies conducted additional analyses to test specifically the role of private funding. Schütz et al. (2008) found that a higher proportion of private sources of funds for educational institutions is associated with larger SES gaps. Another measure of private funding is the share of schools with fees in a country. PISA data suggests that SES achievement gaps are larger in countries with a high share of schools with fees (Le Donné, 2014). A tentative interpretation of the research findings is that private schools introduce new pedagogical concepts that narrow SES gaps *if* they are publicly funded. Private funding and school fees, on the other hand, introduce a barrier for poor families that increases social segregation and reinforces SES inequality in achievement.

Another research strand compared private and public schools within countries. A particularly interesting study has used longitudinal data of the Second International Mathematics Study (SIMS; 13–14-year-old students) which was conducted in 1980–1982. The 13–14-year-old students were tested in the beginning and at the end of the school year. Toma (1996) compared SES achievement gaps in public and private schools in Belgium, France, New Zealand, Canada, and the United States. Gain scores were regressed on indicators for private schools (vs. public), SES, and their interaction. The analyses suggest statistically significant interaction effects only in France and New Zealand where the main effects of private schools were positive, but their interaction was negative. This finding suggests that the superior achievement effects of private schooling are less for higher SES students than for lower ones. In further analyses, Zimmer and Toma (2000) used the same data to compare achievement gains in high and low SES schools in public and private schools. For this purpose, they computed the average parental education and occupation for each school. They estimated a model for the pooled data, not separate models for each country. The results for the school level, however, were similar to those for SES gaps on student level. The two main effects were positive but their interaction was negative. This finding implies that the achievement gaps between low and high SES schools were smaller among private schools compared to public schools. Jehangir, Glas, and van den Berg (2015) did not use longitudinal but cross-sectional PISA 2009 data to compare SES gaps at public and private schools in eight economically diverse countries from different world regions. In two countries, the gaps were larger in public schools, and in six there were no differences.

2.4.13 *Public Expenditure on Education*

Public educational expenditure and SES inequality in performance may be associated because low public investment is substituted by high private investment (e.g., private tutoring). Well-educated and rich parents may invest more in education because they value education more and have more resources than parents with low SES. High public investment may also send the symbolic policy message that education is important. While well-educated parents tend to value education anyway, such a message may be particularly important for less educated families.

International studies have consistently replicated the finding that high public expenditure is associated with low SES inequality in performance. The per capita educational expenditure, whether in purchasing power standards or as a percentage of total governmental expenditure, is negatively correlated with the SES achievement gap observed in TIMSS and PISA. Such a negative correlation has been observed for diverse samples of countries around the world (Akiba et al., 2007; Bodovski et al., 2017) and in more homogeneous samples of European (Schlicht et al., 2010) or Middle East and North African (Salehi-Isfahani, Hassine, & Assaad, 2013) countries. The negative association between public expenditure and SES inequality in achievement vanishes in studies that fail to take into account the countries' economic development by using the actual value of expenditures on public education (Salehi-Isfahani et al., 2013; Schütz et al., 2008).

2.4.14 Teacher Qualification

Educationalists frequently emphasize the role of teachers in learning. It seems natural to investigate if an unequal distribution of teaching quality is related to achievement gaps. Well-trained teachers may be particularly able to adapt to the needs of disadvantaged students who receive less parental support than advantaged children. Furthermore, teacher quality may mediate the effects of other institutional features on SES achievement inequality in performance (e.g., the most qualified teachers may cluster in the most prestigious track in a tracked system). The research findings from previous comparative studies are inconsistent.

Akiba et al. (2007) used TIMSS 2003 grade 8 data from 46 countries to compare educational systems with needs-based and unequal access to qualified teachers. Teaching certificates, mathematics as major, mathematics education as major, and teaching experience were used to measure teaching quality. In needs-based systems, disadvantaged children have greater access to qualified teachers, and in unequal systems vice versa. The analyses reveal that the SES achievement gaps are mostly unrelated to the distribution of teaching quality. The only exception was observed for access to teachers with a major in mathematics; the SES achievement gaps were higher in countries where advantaged children have greater access to teachers with a major in mathematics.

Effects of teacher qualifications have also been studied at both school and class level. Chiu (2015) used the pooled PISA 2009 data from 65 countries to investigate the effect of teacher education on social inequality in student performance. The study shows that SES gaps in achievement are larger in schools with a higher share of teachers with university degrees. This finding suggests that students with more cultural capital benefit more from teachers with university degrees, compared to other students. Luschei and Chudgar (2011) used TIMSS 2003 data from 25 economically diverse countries around the world to study teacher quality at classroom level. They estimated the interaction effect of various teacher characteristics (teacher gender, experience, degree, and competence) and SES on student performance at the end of primary school. The interaction effects were mostly neutral. Only a few parameters reached the level of statistical significance, but there were no consistent patterns across countries. This finding suggests that teacher characteristics are equally important for students of different SES.

2.4.15 Additional Results

Apart from the areas we have discussed so far, studies have been conducted on rather specific issues of education. Falck et al. (2018) used grade 4 (53 countries) and grade 8 (30 countries) data from TIMSS 2011 to investigate computer use in classrooms. The authors exploited the within-student between-subject variation in different computer usages in mathematics and science to circumvent bias from unobserved student and school characteristics. The results from the main analyses suggest that using computers to look up ideas and information has a positive effect on achievement, while using them to practice skills and procedures does not. Further analyses of different SES groups suggest that both positive and negative effects were more pronounced for high SES students. This finding suggests that using computers to look up information increases SES achievement inequality, while using them to practice skills narrows the SES gap. Põder, Lauri, and Veski (2016) use pooled PISA 2009 data from Estonia, Finland, and Sweden to compare whether different school admission policies translate into SES inequality in achievement. The main school-level explanatory variables were whether schools prioritize student admission by zoning (i.e., walking distance) or performance (i.e., past record). The main finding is that student admission by zoning is associated with lower SES gaps while student admission by performance is associated with higher SES gaps; however, these results are not very robust in robustness checks. Huang and Sebastian (2015) tested whether instructional leadership (e.g., developing professional development programs for instructionally weak teachers) and teacher leadership (e.g., teacher involvement in management decisions) predict SES inequality within schools. The analyses were replicated for 16 countries using PISA 2012 data. Both leadership variables were unrelated to the size of the school SES gaps in all 16 countries. Schlicht et al. (2010) investigated the relation between the average class size (pupil–teacher ratio) and SES achievement gap using the pooled PISA 2006 data from EU member states, of which 10 are Eastern countries with a communist legacy and 15 Western democracies. The study suggests that the association was positive in Eastern but negative in Western countries. This finding suggests that the SES gaps are smaller in Western countries with large average classes and vice versa in Eastern countries. The contradictory findings for the Western countries may, however, be due to an outlier in the small sample of countries.

2.5 Conclusions

International comparative research on the determinants of SES inequality in student achievement constitutes a relatively new approach to understand the emergence of performance gaps. There are still a manageable number of studies that applied this approach, and the selection of studies included in the present review may be overly optimistic as we did not apply strict inclusion criteria in terms of research designs. The studies we considered here sought to identify the effects of the various determinants of SES inequality. In fact, most of the existing research we synthesized is descriptive in nature, estimating simple correlations based on cross-sectional data. While we by no means want to criticize the authors for their pioneering work in an emerging field, we still should be cautious in the interpretation of the findings. At the same time, it seems worth mentioning some praiseworthy examples of studies where the authors developed quasi-experimental approaches to address selection bias, unobserved confounding variables, and other issues related to the identification of causal effects of determinants of SES inequality (for a more general discussion see Hanushek & Woessmann, 2011; Strietholt et al., 2014; Strietholt & Scherer, 2017). Such studies analyzed panel data (Toma, 1996; Zimmer & Toma, 2000), exploited within-student between-subject variation (Falck et al., 2018; Lavy, 2015), or combined different educational stages from various source studies (Dupriez & Dumay, 2006; Lavrijsen & Nicaise, 2015). At the same time, there is an ongoing debate on the limitations of combining certain test scores from international assessments (e.g., Jerrim, Lopez-Agudo, Marcenaro-Gutierrez, & Shure, 2017; Lockheed & Wagemaker, 2013).

Further methodological issues related to the reproducibility and generalizability of research findings. While these issues are certainly no distinctive feature of comparative studies (Open Science Collaboration, 2015) it seems pertinent to acknowledge some limitations of the international comparative research. The limited number of countries is a natural limitation of this approach. While the accumulated data from international assessment comprises data from about 100 countries, several studies we reviewed exploited data from only a few countries or were limited to certain regions (e.g. OECD, European, Northern countries). Another limitation relates to the representation of different educational stages in the research we reviewed. Only a handful of studies investigated SES achievement inequality at the end of primary school while most were about inequality in secondary school. From a policy perspective, it may be most efficient to prevent the emergence inequalities at an early stage. Thus, further research on primary school (or even earlier) is needed.

Despite the fact that it is inherently difficult to identify determinants of SES inequality, we would like to point to some tentative lessons learned. First, we repeatedly found that opportunity of choice reinforced inequality. SES inequality in achievement is higher in countries where preschool is not compulsory but voluntary, different tracks exist, the share of public funding is low, and private schools charge fees. Second, policies that narrow down choice reduce SES inequality. Preschool does not reinforce but rather reduces SES inequality if the preschool system serves not only a few but all children (i.e., also the disadvantaged). Tracking seems to be less problematic if countries implement measures to ensure that the selection into prestigious tracks depends mainly on merits but not on SES. A larger share of private funding and private schools with fees are associated with larger SES effects on achievement. In contrast to the country-level features that constitute an institutional framework for learning, there is little evidence regarding how to arrange school learning environments to reduce social inequality. The effects of school and classroom variables are mixed, and sometimes unexpected. However, the aforementioned methodological issue may explain at least some of the inconsistencies in the findings observed in previous research. Further research is needed, but we are confident that we are currently witnessing the emergence of a promising research approach that will help us to understand and influence the emergence of SES inequality in achievement.

Funding Note This project has received funding from the European Union's Horizon 2020 research and innovation programme under the Marie Skłodowska-Curie grant agreement No. 765400 and was supported by Swedish Research Council (Vetenskapsrådet) [grant number 2015-01080].

References

(* indicate that findings from the references were used in the present review)

* Akiba, M., LeTendre, G. K., & Scribner, J. P. (2007). Teacher quality, opportunity gap, and national achievement in 46 countries. *Educational Researcher, 36*(7), 369–387. https://doi.org/10.3102/0013189x07308739.
* Ammermueller, A., & Pischke, J. S. (2009). Peer effects in European primary schools: Evidence from the progress in international reading literacy study. *Journal of Labor Economics, 27*(3), 315–348. https://doi.org/10.1086/603650.
* Araújo, L., & Costa, P. (2015). Home book reading and reading achievement in EU countries: The progress in international reading literacy study 2011 (PIRLS). *Educational Research and Evaluation, 21*(5–6), 438.
* Bodovski, K., Byun, S. Y., Chykina, V., & Chung, H. J. (2017). Searching for the golden model of education: Cross-national analysis of math achievement. *Compare, 47*(5), 722–741. https://doi.org/10.1080/03057925.2016.1274881.
* Bol, T., Witschge, J., Van de Werfhorst, H. G., & Dronkers, J. (2014). Curricular tracking and central examinations: Counterbalancing the Impact of social background on student achievement in 36 countries. *Social Forces, 92*(4), 1545–1572. https://doi.org/10.1093/sf/sou003.
* Brunello, G., & Checchi, D. (2007). Does school tracking affect equality of opportunity? New international evidence. *Economic Policy, 22*(52), 781–861. doi: http://www.jstor.org/stable/4502215.
* Burger, K. (2016). Intergenerational transmission of education in Europe: Do more comprehensive education systems reduce social gradients in student achievement? *Research in Social Stratification and Mobility, 44*, 54–67. https://doi.org/10.1016/j.rssm.2016.02.002.
* Caro, D. H., & Lenkeit, J. (2012). An analytical approach to study educational inequalities: 10 hypothesis tests in PIRLS 2006. *International Journal of Research & Method in Education, 35*(1), 30.
* Cebolla-Boado, H., Radl, J., & Salazar, L. (2016). Preschool education as the great equalizer? A cross-country study into the sources of inequality in reading competence. *Acta Sociologica, 60*(1), 41–60. https://doi.org/10.1177/0001699316654529.
* Chiu, M. M. (2015). Family inequality, school inequalities, and mathematics achievement in 65 countries: Microeconomic mechanisms of rent seeking and diminishing marginal returns. *Teachers College Record, 117*(1), 1–32.
* Chudgar, A., Luschei, T. F., & Zhou, Y. (2013). Science and mathematics achievement and the importance of classroom composition: Multicountry analysis using TIMSS 2007. *American Journal of Education, 119*(2), 295–316. https://doi.org/10.1086/668764.
Duncan, O. D., Featherman, D. L., & Duncan, B. (1972). *Socio-economic background and achievement.* New York: Seminar Press.
* Dupriez, V., & Dumay, X. (2006). Inequalities in school systems: Effect of school structure or of society structure? *Comparative Education, 42*(2), 243–260. https://doi.org/10.1080/03050060600628074.
* Falck, O., Mang, C., & Woessmann, L. (2018). Virtually no effect? Different uses of classroom computers and their effect on student achievement. *Oxford Bulletin of Economics and Statistics, 80*(1), 1–38. https://doi.org/10.1111/obes.12192.

* Gándara, F., & Randall, J. (2015). Investigating the relationship between school-level accountability practices and science achievement. *Education Policy Analysis Archives, 23.* https://doi.org/10.14507/epaa.v23.2013.

Gottfried, A. (1985). Measures of socioeconomic status in child development research: Data and recommendations. *Merrill-Palmer Quarterly, 31*(1), 85–92.

* Han, S. W. (2018). School-based teacher hiring and achievement inequality: A comparative perspective. *International Journal of Educational Development, 61,* 82–91. https://doi.org/10.1016/j.ijedudev.2017.12.004.

Hanushek, E. A., & Woessmann, L. (2011). The economics of international differences in educational achievement. In E. A. Hanushek, S. Machin, & L. Woessmann (Eds.), *Handbook of the economics of education* (Vol. 3). Amsterdam: Elsevier.

Hauser, R. M. (1994). Measuring socioeconomic status in studies of child development. *Child Development, 65*(6), 1541–1545.

Heyneman, S. P., & Loxley, W. A. (1983). The effect of primary-school quality on academic achievement across twenty-nine high-and low-income countries. *Journal of Sociology, 88*(6), 1162–1194.

Hogrebe, N., & Strietholt, R. (2016). Does non-participation in preschool affect children's reading achievement? International evidence from propensity score analyses. *Large-scale Assessments in Education, 4*(1). https://doi.org/10.1186/s40536-016-0017-3.

* Horn, D. (2009). Age of selection counts: A cross-country analysis of educational institutions. *Educational Research and Evaluation, 15*(4), 343–366. https://doi.org/10.1080/13803610903087011.

* Huang, H. G., & Sebastian, J. (2015). The role of schools in bridging within-school achievement gaps based on socioeconomic status: A cross-national comparative study. *Compare—A Journal of Comparative and International Education, 45*(4), 501–525. https://doi.org/10.1080/03057925.2014.905103.

* Jehangir, K., Glas, C. A. W., & van den Berg, S. (2015). Exploring the relation between socio-economic status and reading achievement in PISA 2009 through an intercepts-and-slopes-as-outcomes paradigm. *International Journal of Educational Research, 71,* 1–15. https://doi.org/10.1016/j.ijer.2015.02.002.

Jerrim, J., Lopez-Agudo, L. A., Marcenaro-Gutierrez, O. D., & Shure, N. (2017). What happens when econometrics and psychometrics collide? An example using the PISA data. *Economics of Education Review, 61,* 51–58. https://doi.org/10.1016/j.econedurev.2017.09.007.

* Lavrijsen, J., & Nicaise, I. (2015). New empirical evidence on the effect of educational tracking on social inequalities in reading achievement. *European Educational Research Journal, 14*(3–4), 206-221. https://doi.org/10.1177/1474904115589039.

* Lavy, V. (2015). Do differences in schools' instruction time explain international achievement gaps? Evidence from developed and developing countries. *The Economic Journal, 125*(588), F397–F424. https://doi.org/10.1111/ecoj.12233.

* Le Donné, N. (2014). European variations in socioeconomic inequalities in students' cognitive achievement: The role of educational policies. *European Sociological Review, 30*(3), 329–343. https://doi.org/10.1093/esr/jcu040.

Lockheed, M. E., & Wagemaker, H. (2013). International large-scale assessments: Thermometers, whips or useful policy tools? *Research in Comparative and International Education, 8*(3), 296–306. https://doi.org/10.2304/rcie.2013.8.3.296.

* Luschei, T. F., & Chudgar, A. (2011). Teachers, student achievement and national income: A cross-national examination of relationships and interactions. *Prospects, 41*(4), 507–533. https://doi.org/10.1007/s11125-011-9213-7.

Meyer, H. D., Strietholt, R., & Epstein, D. Y. (2018). Three models of global education quality and the emerging democratic deficit in global education governance. In M. Akiba & G. K. LeTendre (Eds.), *Routledge international handbook of teacher quality and policy.* New York: Routledge.

Mueller, C. W., & Parcel, T. L. (1981). Measures of socioeconomic status: Alternatives and recommendations. *Child Development, 52*(1), 12–30.

2 The Impact of Education Policies on Socioeconomic … 37

Open Science Collaboration. (2015). Estimating the reproducibility of psychological science. *Science, 349*(6251), aac4716. https://doi.org/10.1126/science.aac4716.

* Park, H. (2008). The varied educational effects of parent-child communication: A comparative study of fourteen countries. *Comparative Education Review, 52*(2), 219–243. https://doi.org/10.1086/528763.

* Põder, K., Lauri, T., & Veski, A. (2016). Does school admission by Zoning affect educational inequality? A study of family background effect in Estonia, Finland, and Sweden. *Scandinavian Journal of Educational Research, 61*(6), 668–688. https://doi.org/10.1080/00313831.2016.1173094.

* Salehi-Isfahani, D., Hassine, N., & Assaad, R. (2013). Equality of opportunity in educational achievement in the Middle East and North Africa. *The Journal of Economic Inequality, 12*(4), 489–515. https://doi.org/10.1007/s10888-013-9263-6.

* Sandoval-Hernández, A., & Białowolski, P. (2016). Factors and conditions promoting academic resilience: A TIMSS-based analysis of five Asian education systems. *Asia Pacific Education Review, 17*(3), 511–520. https://doi.org/10.1007/s12564-016-9447-4.

* Santibañez, L., & Fagioli, L. (2016). Nothing succeeds like success? Equity, student outcomes, and opportunity to learn in high- and middle-income countries. *International Journal of Behavioral Development, 40*(6), 517–525. https://doi.org/10.1177/0165025416642050.

Scheerens, J. (2017). *Opportunity to learn, curriculum alignment and test preparation*. Berlin: Springer.

* Schlicht, R., Stadelmann-Steffen, I., & Freitag, M. (2010). Educational inequality in the EU the effectiveness of the national education policy. *European Union Politics, 11*(1), 29–60. https://doi.org/10.1177/1465116509346387.

* Schmidt, W. H., Burroughs, N. A., Zoido, P., & Houang, R. T. (2015). The role of schooling in perpetuating educational inequality: An international perspective. *Educational Researcher, 44*(7), 371–386. https://doi.org/10.3102/0013189x15603982.

* Schütz, G., Ursprung, H. W., & Woessmann, L. (2008). Education policy and equality of opportunity. *KyKlos, 61*(2), 279–308. https://doi.org/10.1111/j.1467-6435.2008.00402.x.

Sirin, S. R. (2005). Socioeconomic status and academic achievement: A meta-analytic review of research. *Review of Educational Research, 75*(3), 417–453. https://doi.org/10.3102/00346543075003417.

Strietholt, R., Gustafsson, J. E., Rosén, M., & Bos, W. (2014). Outcomes and causal inference in international comparative assessments. In E. Policy (Ed.), *Educational policy evaluation through international comparative assessments*. Münster/New York: Waxmann.

Strietholt, R., & Scherer, R. (2017). The contribution of international large-scale assessments to educational research: Combining individual and institutional data sources. *Scandinavian Journal of Educational Research,* 1–18. https://doi.org/10.1080/00313831.2016.1258729.

* Toma, E. (1996). Public funding and private schooling across countries. *Journal of Law and Economics, 9*(1), 121–148.

Van de Werfhorst, H. G., & Mijs, J. J. B. (2010). Achievement Inequality and the Institutional Structure of Educational Systems: A Comparative Perspective. *Annual Review of Sociology, 36*(1), 407–428. https://doi.org/10.1146/annurev.soc.012809.102538.

White, K. R. (1982). The relation between socioeconomic status and academic achievement. *Psychological Bulletin, 91*(3), 461–481. https://doi.org/10.1037/0033-2909.91.3.461.

* Witschge, J., & van de Werfhorst, H. G. (2015). Standardization of lower secondary civic education and inequality of the civic and political engagement of students. *School Effectiveness and School Improvement, 27*(3), 367–384. https://doi.org/10.1080/09243453.2015.1068817.

* Woessmann, L. (2005). The effect heterogeneity of central examinations: Evidence from TIMSS, TIMSS—Repeat and PISA. *Education Economics, 13*(2), 143–169. https://doi.org/10.1080/09645290500031165.

* Woessmann, L. (2011). Cross-country evidence on teacher performance pay. *Economics of Education Review, 30*(3), 404–418. https://doi.org/10.1016/j.econedurev.2010.12.008.

Yang Hansen, K., & Strietholt, R. (2018). Does schooling actually perpetuate educational inequality in mathematics performance? A validity question on the measures of opportunity to learn in PISA. *Zdm*, *50*(4), 643–658. https://doi.org/10.1007/s11858-018-0935-3.

* Zimmer, R., & Toma, E. (2000). Peer effects in private and public schools across countries. *Journal of Policy Analysis and Management, 19*(1), 75–92.

Part II
National Profiles

Chapter 3
Socioeconomic Inequality and Student Outcomes in English Schools

Jake Anders and Morag Henderson

Abstract This chapter explores socioeconomic inequality in educational outcomes in England. We begin by describing the key features of the English education system and highlight the characteristics of the student population. We explore the educational outcomes of socioeconomically disadvantaged young people through comparison of a number of different outcomes during educational careers. We analyze policies introduced or mooted in recent years to consider the extent to which they are likely to address these challenges successfully. These include the introduction of "academy" schools, reforms to the school curriculum, changes to education funding, the potential (re-)growth of academically selective schooling, increased investment in early years education, and an increased focused on gathering and disseminating robust evidence on "what works" in educational attainment. Many of these changes seem unlikely to hold many lessons for other countries wishing to reduce attainment gaps. However, there are notable exceptions, particularly regarding early years' education and improving the evidence base on what practical changes schools can make to promote attainment among those from disadvantaged backgrounds.

Keywords Student achievement · Socioeconomic status · Inequality · England

3.1 Introduction

This chapter explores socioeconomic inequality in educational outcomes in England. We focus on England rather than the whole of the UK because education policy in Wales, Scotland, and Northern Ireland is devolved to these countries' parliaments or assemblies. As such, the UK Government's Department for Education (DfE) only sets policy for England. We begin by describing the key features of the English education system and highlight the characteristics of the

---

J. Anders (✉) · M. Henderson
UCL Institute of Education, London, UK
e-mail: jake.anders@ucl.ac.uk

© Springer Nature Singapore Pte Ltd. 2019
L. Volante et al. (eds.), *Socioeconomic Inequality and Student Outcomes*, Education Policy & Social Inequality 4,
https://doi.org/10.1007/978-981-13-9863-6_3

student population; we explore the educational outcomes of socioeconomically disadvantaged young people and analyze the policies introduced or mooted in recent years to consider the extent to which they are likely to address these challenges successfully.

Children in England must participate in full-time education between the school terms after their 5th birthday until they turn 18.[1] State-funded schooling in England is free at the point of use at both primary (ages 5–11) and secondary (ages 12–18) phases. State and privately funded schools exist at both of these phases.

Private schools are funded by fees, bequests, and commercial activities. As such, they operate relatively independently; for example, they can set their own admission policies, which may include an admissions test, and school governance is a matter for the school itself (within some fairly light-touch regulations). Nevertheless, they are subject to an inspection regime, albeit one that is different to that which oversees state-funded schools. Approximately 7% of pupils in English education at any given time are in a privately funded school, while around 11% attend a privately funded school at some point in their educational career.

State-funded schools can be divided into two categories, generally known as "maintained" schools, which are funded and controlled by local authorities, and "academies" whose funding comes direct from the DfE and, thus, are outside local authority control but may instead be controlled by a sponsor or part of a multi-academy trust. The policy of academy schools as a turnaround model for schools deemed to be persistently failing had been introduced by the New Labour government in the mid-2000s with enforced academization being a package of measures including replacement of senior leadership and replacement of local authority oversight with external input from a sponsor. However, it was greatly extended post-2010 both for schools falling below floor standards (who would be sponsored by an external body), or outstanding schools keen for more autonomy and financial control: academies no longer had a portion of their funding diverted to their local authority but, in return, had to provide the back office, such as payroll, previously provided centrally. This position of "academization" as a way of increasing school autonomy so that they can respond to local demands was key to the rhetoric of the coalition government's academies program. Academies were also part of a shift to a "self-improving school-led system" (Greany & Higham, 2018) with academies (particularly those underperforming) encouraged to join multi-academy trusts which replaced many of the centralized functions of local authorities.

Formally, parents can exert a great deal of choice over the school to which they send their child. However, popular schools are often highly oversubscribed, resulting in schools picking pupils rather than vice versa. This school selection of pupils is largely based on geography (where the child lives) through a system of catchment areas, rather than on a child's attributes. Demand for high-performing

---

[1] In 2015 the DfE made an exception for deferring primary schooling in cases where the child was deemed not ready to start school, for example summer-born children (born between 1st April–31st August).

state schools is such that some parents may move to different neighborhoods to improve their child's chances of accessing a good state-funded school, resulting in what is sometimes referred to as selection by house prices. We describe school selection as being largely based on geography because there are some exceptions to this. No primary schools are allowed to select based on academic ability but some secondary schools are (see below), while some schools may select children based on other characteristics; for example, belonging to a particular faith.

English schools monitor the attainment of children throughout compulsory education by means of national examinations at age 7 (Key Stage 1), 11 (Key Stage 2) in primary school, and 16 (Key Stage 4/General Certificate of Secondary Education/GCSE) in secondary school. At age 18, students take A-Level examinations (Key Stage 5) or equivalent vocational qualifications, which are generally seen as a prerequisite for participation in higher education (although other routes are possible).

The remainder of the chapter proceeds as follows. We first describe the key characteristics of the student population in England; we then focus on differences in educational achievement by socioeconomic characteristics in order to present a contextualized picture of the academic performance of low SES pupils in England. We then turn to policy, reviewing work that has sought to evaluate the educational policies adopted or announced by the government which was designed to address (or are otherwise likely to have significant implications for) socioeconomic disadvantage in educational attainment. Lastly, we conclude by summarizing the current picture and future prospects.

3.2 Key Characteristics of the Student Population

According to figures from the UK's DfE in 2017, 91% of the 8.7 million school children in England attend state-funded schools (more specifically, 54% attend state-funded primary schools and 37% state-funded secondary schools), 7% attend privately funded schools, and 1% attend special schools (DfE, 2017d). This section of the chapter will explore the key characteristics of the student population in England, with a particular focus on disadvantage.

3.2.1 Gender

According to the school census from 2017 (DfE, 2017d), the population in state-funded primary schools is 51% boys and 49% girls, while in state-funded secondary schools the gender split is 50–50. In special schools and pupil referral units, we see a starker gender split, with the full-time student population comprising 72% boys and 28% girls. Lastly, in private schools 51% of pupils are boys and 49% are girls.

3.2.2 Household Income

Table 3.1 shows the proportion of children, by region, in absolute and relative poverty averaged across 2013–2016 (Department for Work and Pensions [DWP], 2017a, 2017b). Relative low income is measured by identifying those children who live in households with income below 60% of the median in that year, while absolute low income is measured by identifying households with inflation-adjusted income below 60% of the median income compared to 2010/11. The proportion of children in relative poverty before housing costs (BHC) was highest in West Midlands (23%) and lowest in the South East (13%). In London, the proportion of children living in poverty BHC was 17%, but we see a much higher proportion of living in poverty after housing costs (AHC, 27%) owing to the high costs of housing relative to other parts of the UK (McGuinness, 2018). In figures released by the DfE (2017d) about all school types, 14% of pupils claimed free school meals,[2] often used as a proxy for family income. This is the lowest proportion of all school students claiming free school meals since 2001.

3.2.3 Minority Ethnic Origins

According to the School Census (DfE, 2017d), the proportion of pupils from minority ethnic origins, that is, the pupils of compulsory school age and above who have been classified[3] to an ethnic group or origin other than White British, has been rising steadily since 2006. As of 2017, 32% of pupils in primary schools are of minority ethnic origins, and in secondary schools the proportion of minority ethnic origins is 29%. Asians make up the highest proportion of ethnic minority students in primary and secondary state schools (10.7% for both) with White non-British making up the second highest proportion of ethnic minorities in primary and secondary state schools (7.5 and 5.7%, respectively).

3.2.4 English as an Additional Language

The proportion of pupils whose family uses a language other than English at home has increased since 2006. This is not a measure of English proficiency (although it

---

[2]Children are eligible for free school meals if their parents are in receipt of income support, jobseekers allowance, child tax credit, or universal credit or if their annual gross income is no more than £16,190 and they are not entitled to Working Tax Credits.

[3]Ethnicity is collected for all pupils and records the ethnicity as stated by the parent/guardian or pupil.

3 Socioeconomic Inequality and Student … 45

Table 3.1 Proportion of children living in poverty 2013/14–2015/16, by region

	Percentage			
	Relative low income		Absolute low income	
	BHC	AHC	BHC	AHC
North East	20	28	19	28
North West	21	30	20	29
Yorkshire and the Humber	22	29	21	28
East Midlands	21	29	19	27
West Midlands	23	33	22	31
East of England	16	25	15	25
London	17	27	16	35
South East	13	25	13	24
South West	17	26	16	24
Total	**18**	**29**	**17**	**28**

Source DWP (2017b), *Households Below Average Income, 2016/17*, Tables 3.17ts, 3.18ts, 4.16ts, 4.17ts
BHC Before housing costs
AHC After housing costs

may be a proxy for this) nor a measure of recent immigration; instead, it should be seen as a measure of diversity. Twenty-one percent of pupils in primary schools are exposed to a language other than English at home, while in secondary schools the proportion is 16% (DfE, 2017d).

3.2.5 Regional Differences

In 2017, in England, there were 8,669,080 children in schools. In terms of the number of pupils by school type by region in England, there are some interesting statistics of note (DfE, 2017d). There are a greater number of school children of all ages in London (17%) and the South East (16%) than elsewhere, while the North East has the fewest school children of all ages (5%) followed by the East Midlands (8%). The breakdown of school population by schools are very similar by region, with the exception of private schools where the highest proportion of children attend private schools in South East (11%) and London (10%) and the least in the North East (3%), North West (4%), Yorkshire and the Humber (4%), and East Midlands (4%). There is also some variation in the number of children in state-funded nurseries with London, North East, North West, West Midlands, and East of England each accounting for 1%, and the South West accounting for 0.31%.

3.2.6 Family Structure

According to data from the UK's Office for National Statistics (2017), the most common type of family in the UK[4] with dependent children are opposite-sex married couples, comprising 62% of all families with children (based on survey data with $N = 7983$); 0.18% are accounted for by other types of legal partnership.[5] Lone parent families comprise 22% of all families with dependent children, 0.05% are same-sex cohabiting couples, and 16% opposite-sex cohabiting couples. The number of same-sex couples families in the UK has been increasing steadily since 1996; this is likely associated with larger proportions of the population identifying as lesbian, gay, or bisexual.

3.2.7 Parental Education

The PISA data from 2015 report the composition of parental education in England[6] using the International Standard Classification of Education (ISCED) scale ($N = 12,978$) based on students' report of their parents' qualifications. The conversion between ISCED and English qualifications is not straight forward, so our example qualifications are only illustrative. The results suggest that 43% of parents have achieved ISCED5A (equivalent to at least a first degree), that a fifth (20%) of parents have an ISCED5B qualification (higher education below degree level) and that slightly fewer than this (18%) have achieved ISCED 3A (A levels, taken 2 years after the end of compulsory education) as their highest qualification. A further 20% report their parents having qualifications equivalent to ISCED 3B (GCSEs, the UK's end of compulsory education examinations), while 3.3% of students report that their parents only having achieved ISCED1 or 2 (less than GCSEs) or have no qualifications.

3.3 Educational Outcomes of Low SES Children

In this section, we consider how the educational outcomes of low SES children compared to their more advantaged peers. We explore this through a number of different outcomes through their educational careers, including reporting the size of the difference in PISA scores in reading, math, and science by parental education and position in the distribution of PISA's SES index, the official measures of

---

[4]Data of family structure is based on the UK as a whole rather than England specifically.

[5]Civil partnerships were introduced in the UK in 2005; marriages to same sex couples were introduced in England and Wales in 2014.

[6]GCSEs are in category ISCED 3B & C, however GCSEs, the qualification taken at age 16 in England, do not easily fit into ISCED.

relative performance of disadvantaged pupils at ages 11 and 16, and post-16 and post-18 educational destinations. We also explore a number of factors that may be associated with the emergence of these gaps in an English context.

3.3.1 PISA

To explore relative performance in PISA scores by family background, we plot average test scores in reading[7] by parental education (using the measure described above) in Fig. 3.1. For these purposes, we dichotomize parental education in two different ways. First, ISCED0-2 (which averages 4% of the sample over the years considered) versus ISCED3B-6 (averaging 96% of the sample) for comparability with other chapters in this volume; second, ISCED0-3B (which averages 25% of the sample over the years considered) versus ISCED 3A-6 (averaging 75% of the sample) for approximate comparability with national measures of disadvantage. We emphasize that the small size for the ISCED0-2 group in the English context means these results are likely to be particularly volatile.

Whichever comparison we draw, there are substantial differences between children of parents with low parental education and the rest of the population in these outcomes. For the reasons given above, we focus on our national comparison definition (ISCED0-3B vs. ISCED 3A-6) where the gap between these two groups are approximately 25 PISA points (the same is true in math and science, which are not shown). There is little sign of significant or sustained narrowing over the time period we consider (PISA from 2006 to 2015).

3.3.2 Official Measure of Educational Inequality

For the purposes of English educational statistics, the government defines disadvantaged pupils as those who were registered as eligible for free school meals in the last 6 years; children who are "looked after" by a local authority; and children who left care in England and Wales through adoption or via a Special Guardianship or a Child Arrangements Order (DfE, 2018a). In 2017, 32% of pupils taking national tests at age 11 were classed as disadvantaged (DfE, 2017b), while 27% of pupils taking national tests at age 16 were classed as disadvantaged (DfE, 2018b).

The government's official measure relative to disadvantaged pupils' performance is known as the attainment gap index (DfE, 2014). It reports the difference in the average rank position on the relevant national test of pupils not classified as disadvantaged minus the average rank position of pupils classified as disadvantaged. Rank position is used to allow comparison over time despite changes in the assessments during this period.

---

[7]There are similar results if we use math or science scores, instead of reading.

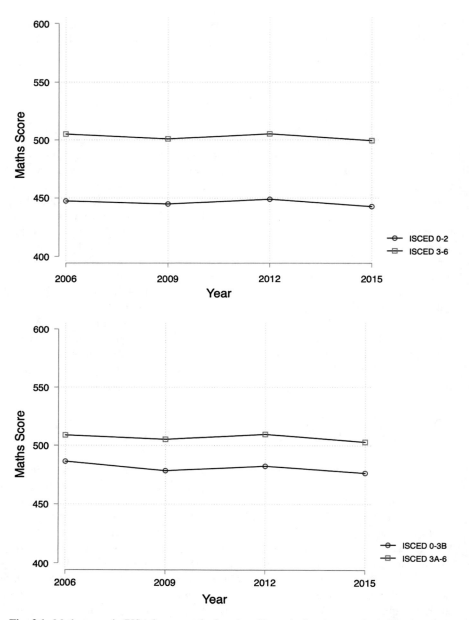

Fig. 3.1 Maths score in PISA by parental education. *Notes* Authors' own calculations based on data from PISA 2006/15. Uses first maths score plausible value

3 Socioeconomic Inequality and Student …

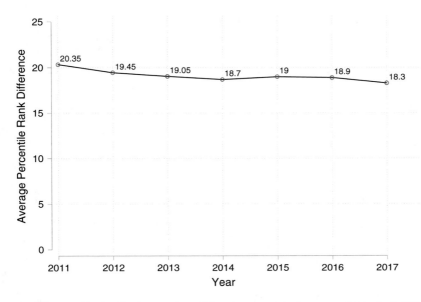

Fig. 3.2 Trend in the disadvantaged pupils' attainment gap index at age 16 England, 2011–2017 (state-funded schools). *Notes* Based on the Department for Education (2018b), with additional calculations by authors. Official DfE "gap index" is multiplied by 5 in order to aid interpretation, since this converts to average percentile rank difference between disadvantaged students and all other students

We adapt the official index slightly in order to improve interpretability. If we imagine that there are 100 children ranked by their test scores, our graphs report the difference in the average ranking (out of 100) in these pupils' test scores by whether they are deemed to be disadvantaged or not. We can also think of them as differences in mean percentile ranks between the two groups. Figure 3.2 reports this difference at age 16; the statistic is also produced at age 11, however, it tells a similar story to that at age 11.

Based on this official government definition of the attainment gap, there has been a narrowing of two percentile-rank places at age 16, from a difference of just over 20 (in 2011) to just below 18 (in 2017). The gap in average rankings is slightly narrower at age 11, but also narrows by two percentile ranks over the same period.

3.3.3   Post-16 Education

In terms of post-16 educational transitions in England, in 2015/16 the plurality of pupils continued into a school "sixth form" (39%), with a similar proportion going to a further education destination (38%). Thirteen percent of pupils went to a sixth form college, 6% went into an apprenticeship, and 3% went to an employment/

Table 3.2 Representation of children in post-16 educational tracks by parental education

Parental education	Sample overall (%)	In full-time education (%)	Taking A-levels (%)	Two or more facilitating subjects at A-level (%)
Degree or equivalent (ISCED5-6)	18.7	23.5	30.3	39.7
Other HE qualification (ISCED4)	13.5	14.5	16.1	16.0
A-levels (ISCED3A)	10.4	11.3	11.9	10.3
GCSE A-C (ISCED3C)	39.5	34.4	28.8	23.5
Level 1 equals and below (ISCED0-2)	17.9	16.2	12.9	10.4

Source Moulton et al. (2018) based on analysis of the Longitudinal Study of Young People in England. *Notes* Weighted to account for sample design and attrition. ISCED classifications are approximate and based on OECD classification described by Schneider (2008)

training destination (DfE, 2017a). Beyond this, almost 50% of pupils now go to Higher Education post-18 (DfE, 2017c).

We go on to consider a number of other important educational outcomes and how they differ by family background. Moulton, Sullivan, Henderson, and Anders (2018) find that children of parents with degrees are over-represented in full-time education post-16 among this cohort making educational transition decisions in 2006 (Table 3.2). Furthermore, they are more heavily over-represented among the increasingly more academic tracks of taking A-levels and taking two or more so-called "facilitating" subjects (identified by the Russell Group of highly competitive universities as particularly important for further studies at these institutions).

3.3.4 University Attendance Differences

A key educational outcome in an English context is attendance at university. According to an analysis by Anders (2012), there is a 43-percentage point gap in university attendance between the least and the most advantaged fifths of the population. Similar differentials in university entry have been documented by others using different data (Boliver, 2013; Chowdry, Crawford, Dearden, Goodman, & Vignoles, 2013). Furthermore, Wakeling and Laurison (2017) highlight a large socioeconomic differential in entry to postgraduate courses, with those from less privileged backgrounds "only about 28 per cent as likely to obtain a postgraduate degree when compared with their peers from privileged origins" (Wakeling & Laurison, 2017, p. 533). This gap is a relatively recent phenomenon occurring contemporaneously with the widening of access to undergraduate higher education.

3.3.5 When and Why Do These Differences Emerge?

Most evidence suggests that socioeconomic differences in educational attainment emerge early in life (Anders & Jerrim, 2017), although this is particularly difficult to quantify in children's early years. The evidence on how these gaps develop during schooling is difficult to interpret, with some finding little evidence that schools can be "prime movers" in reducing achievement gaps (Strand, 2016) and others finding that "there is less divergence in performance … [among] pupils who attend the same schools" (Crawford, Macmillan, & Vignoles, 2017, p. 88), suggesting schools can play a significant role in reducing divergence (at least among early high-achievers, who were the focus of this work).

There is a similar message from work by Anders (2017), considering the gap in university attendance in particular. This work tracks pupils' changes in expectations of university attendance through their adolescent years in order to understand differences by family background. It is notable that children from less advantaged backgrounds are considerably more likely to stop expecting to apply to university than those from more advantaged backgrounds during this period, suggesting that there is some widening of educational inequality through this period. This gap is not explained by differences in these individuals' academic attainment.

Having an advantaged social background (captured via a range of measures) is consistently linked to taking a more demanding and prestigious curriculum. As shown in Fig. 3.3, a lower proportion of young people who take applied subjects have highly educated parents and a higher proportion of young people who take more academically demanding subjects, such as STEM subjects, have highly educated parents. Henderson, Sullivan, Anders, and Moulton (2017) find that these socioeconomic differences in subjects studied (in particular applied, STEM and EBacc-eligible[8] subjects) are only partly explained by differences in prior attainment, while Anders, Henderson, Moulton, and Sullivan (2018b) highlight the important role that schools, and school composition, seem to play in shaping the subject choices that young people are able to make. Furthermore, Moulton et al. (2018) and Anders et al. (2018a) highlight how these differences are associated with subsequent educational transitions.

3.3.6 Limitations of Data Sources

It is important to acknowledge the limitations for assessing the differences in educational outcomes of low SES pupils of the datasets used as part of this chapter.

---

[8]The Ebacc subjects were identified by the government as important for future academic study. The "Ebacc" is a school performance measure introduced in 2010, comprising of five core subjects where students achieve a C grade or above in either: English, Mathematics, History or Geography, two sciences and a Modern or Ancient Language.

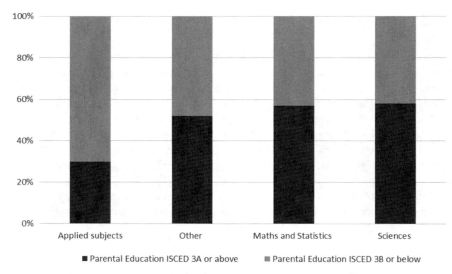

Fig. 3.3 GCSE subjects selected by parental education. *Notes* Authors' own additional analysis based on similar analysis by Henderson, Sullivan, Anders, Moulton (2017)

Several authors have highlighted the limitations of using the administrative National Pupil Database (e.g., Ilie, Sutherland, & Vignoles, 2017) and there are related limitations in using data from PISA, particularly in that information about SES is collected only from pupils and not from their parents (Jerrim & Micklewright, 2014). As a result, we also draw on studies using data from some of England's cohort studies, in particular, "Next Steps" (formerly known as the Longitudinal Study of Young People in England, LSYPE). These data include much richer measures of family SES, including direct parental reports, but the longitudinal data present possible limitations due to the reduction in representativeness of the sample (we make use of the appropriate survey and design weights to try to account for this). Taken together, these data sources paint a consistent picture of educational inequality and therefore we can have increased confidence in the general narrative that emerges.

3.4 Educational Policies Designed to Address Socioeconomic Disadvantage

In this section, we discuss policies aimed at addressing the socioeconomic attainment gap and evidence of their success or otherwise.

3.4.1 Free Early Education

England has increasingly invested in early education programs since the late 1990s. The "Sure Start" scheme was introduced in 1998 as an early intervention for children under age 4 to be delivered through local providers. These were designed to support families and parents; provide quality learning, play, and child care; and offer support regarding child health and special needs. Several policy changes since then have resulted in an entitlement to free early education effectively being universal across England since 2005 for 3- and 4-year olds. Since 2017, the government has offered 15 hours of early education for 38 weeks per year to all 3- and 4-year olds and the most disadvantaged 2-year olds. As a result of these policies, the number of 3- to 5-year olds accessing places grew: more specifically, between 2008 and 2010 the number of children taking up places increased by around 5% while between 2010 and 2015 it grew by 11% (DfE, 2010, 2015). However, the push to increase the number of disadvantaged children attending early years had limited success; evidence from the DfE show that 58% of eligible children took up their places by January 2015. Moreover, Stewart and Obolenskaya (2016) found that there was little evidence of the SES gap narrowing as a result of the increase in provision of early education from 1999 and 2004, but there was some evidence that the gap narrowed from 2007 to 2014. They speculate that this reflects the improvements in the quality of provision, including better-qualified staff, and the introduction of an early years foundation stage curriculum.

3.4.2 Curriculum Reform

The national curriculum,[9] which includes math, science, English, physical education, computing, and religious education at all key stages and sex and relationship education at secondary school, must be taught to pupils aged 5–16 in local authority-maintained state-funded schools in England. This includes the majority of primary schools but no longer the majority of secondary schools because of the rise of academies (including free schools, discussed further below) which do not have to follow the national curriculum (although many do and they are required by their funding agreements to offer a balanced range of subjects including English, math, sciences, and religious education). The national curriculum has been overhauled several times since it was first introduced in 1988 (see Roberts, 2018, for a summary). The policies of the Labour government up to 2007 focused on curriculum

---

[9]Key stage 1–3 national curriculum subjects from September 2014: Maths, English, science, history, geography, art and design, physical education, music, languages (key stage 2 and key stage 3), computing, design and technology, citizenship education (key stage 3). At key stage 4 the subjects include: Maths, English, science, physical education, computing and citizenship education (Roberts, 2018).

and assessment reform, including the introduction of vocational courses, deemed equivalent to GCSEs (Lupton, Thomson, & Obolenskaya, 2016). Beginning in 2010, under a Conservative–Liberal Democrat coalition government, there were some substantial changes to the curriculum including a reduction in the number of vocational qualifications included in the benchmarking of school results and changes to the way pupils are assessed at GCSE and A-level, reducing the use of coursework and increasing the emphasis on final exams. The curriculum itself was also reformed to put more emphasis on knowledge, seen as a more traditional manner of learning, in both primary and secondary schools. It was argued that this new "slimmed down" curriculum would give teachers the freedom to meet the needs of their students based on their professional judgment. The rationale for this change was to give all students the opportunity to gain access to "powerful knowledge" (Young, 2010, p. 5), however it has been argued that this was undermined by the lack of thought as to improvements in pedagogy to ensure all pupils can engage with these new curricula (Whitty, 2010).

In terms of the associated outcomes of these curriculum changes for narrowing the gap, there was an improvement in GCSE attainment between 2007 and 2010, with the proportion of young people achieving 5 A*-C grades increasing from 59.9 to 75.6%; however, this improvement was not found in the PISA tests over the same period, which gives rise to the possibility that the success was as a result of channeling students (especially those from less advantaged backgrounds; Henderson, Sullivan, Anders, Moulton, 2017) into vocational equivalent qualifications (Jerrim, 2012). There is also some evidence that the change to final-exam assessment has resulted in lower attainment for those at the bottom of the attainment distribution, but it may be too early to be certain of any long-term effects of these changes (Lupton et al., 2016).

3.4.3 Academies and Free Schools

The flagship education policy under the 2010–2015 Conservative–Liberal Democrat coalition government was perhaps the widespread role out of "academies" discussed above. However, evidence of systematic improvement as a result of widespread "academization" (Whitty & Anders, 2017), per se, or from being part of a multi-academy trust (Bernardinelli, Rutt, Greany, & Higham, 2018) is far from clear. There is some evidence of improvements in academic performance resulting from academization (e.g., Eyles & Machin, 2015; Machin & Vernoit, 2012). Eyles and Machin (2015) used a counterfactual design comparing academies' performance with maintained schools that went on to become academies after their data collection period and found that in academies an extra three percentage points of pupils achieved top grades (5 A*-C) at GCSE (or equivalents) compared to those yet to convert. However, further work suggested these academies improved their results by "further raising the attainments of students in the top half of the ability distribution, and in particular pupils in the top 20% tail" and not by improving the results of those in the bottom tail (Machin & Silva, 2013, p.ii).

Furthermore, as noted above there are significant differences between the academies program of the Labour government (as evaluated by most of the studies above) and that of the coalition government following 2010. Use of evidence of even modest improvements among such academies as evidence for their widespread roll-out has been criticized (Eyles, Machin, & Silva, 2015). Work evaluating the new cohort of academies, including previously high-performing "converter" academies, is only now starting to emerge (e.g., McDool, 2016) and it remains difficult to argue that there is strong and consistent evidence that academies will help to reduce the gap between low and high SES pupils.

3.4.4 Grammar Schools

State-funded academically selective schools in England are known as "grammar schools" and remain a controversial area of English education policy. Despite being phased out in most parts of England between the mid-1950s and the late-1980s, they have remained a fixture in a number of areas. Since these reforms, for the most part neither major political party has been in favor of altering this state of affairs. However, soon after Theresa May became Prime Minister in July 2016, she announced a number of significant changes to the education policies pursued by her predecessor, including plans to lift the formal restrictions on grammar school expansion introduced by the Labour government in 1998 (but de facto in place for some time before this). May's plan was to relax the restrictions on new and expanding selective schools and to allow alteration of admissions policies in non-selective schools to become more selective in some circumstances. There are 163 grammar schools in England and in the 2017 Conservative manifesto May pledged to open 140 new free schools, many of which were expected to be grammar schools, which would open from 2020. However, the performance of the Conservative party at the June 2017 election put some of these plans on hold, although some have been revisited more recently.

The PISA-based evidence on selective schooling internationally shows that academic selection in schools is negatively associated with equality and student motivation (Organisation for Economic Co-operation and Development, 2012). There is some evidence that selective schools across OECD countries achieve higher on average performance, even once taking account of family and demographic characteristics. However, on aggregate, an educational system's performance is not greater when a country has a higher proportion of academically selective schools. In England, the evidence is mixed; the Education Policy Institute found that in raw attainment terms 97% of grammar school pupils achieve the benchmark of five A*-C GCSEs compared to the state-funded national average of 57% (Andrews, Hutchinson, & Johnes, 2018). However, once pupil characteristics are adjusted for there is no difference on average pupil attainment between students who study in a selective-school area compared to those who do not study in a selective-school area (Andrews et al., 2018). This suggests that opening additional grammar schools will not raise attainment for all and joins others' evidence that expansion of selective schooling is likely to increase educational inequality (Burgess, Dickson, & Macmillan, 2014). Andrews et al. (2018) found an individual benefit in GCSE grades for students attending a grammar school, however it is known that access to grammar schools is highly socially graded with significant sums spent on private tuition for the grammar school entry tests by those who can afford it (e.g., Andrews et al., 2018; Jerrim & Sims, 2018).

3.4.5 Educational Funding

Work by Hanushek (1997) suggests that there is not a positive linear relationship between increasing school resources and student attainment. However, Hanushek acknowledges that depending on the way these resources are allocated and spent, funding can reduce the educational gap. Evidence from the UK has shown that there is a small but significant school resource effect (e.g., Dewey, Husted, & Kenny, 2000; Holmlund, McNally, & Viarengo, 2008). Holmlund et al. (2008) found that an increase of £1000 per pupil is associated with an increase in the number of pupils achieving the expected level of attainment at key stage 2 (taken at age 11). The increase is by 2.2 percentage points for English; 2 percentage points for math; and 0.7 percentage points in science. More recently the evidence suggests that an increase in school funding and resource has had a small positive influence on educational attainment (Gibbons, McNally, & Viarengo, 2017; Nicoletti & Rabe, 2014), but this has only been found to be statistically significant at the primary school level.

A recent review by Williams and Grayson (2018) summarizes the funding context in England since 2010. They note that in real-terms funding per pupil in state schools in England has increased from the 1990s to mid-2000s but this has subsequently declined in real terms. However, the targeting of the resources involves changes: in April 2011, the government introduced the "Pupil Premium", a form of per capita funding for schools favouring those with large numbers of students from disadvantaged backgrounds. Initially, each school received £488 per eligible pupil with this increasing to £1320 for primary school pupils and £935 for secondary school pupils in by 2016/17. In addition, schools receive an additional £1900 for students who were adopted, have a guardianship order, are in local authority care, or are a looked-after child (DfE, 2017d).

The aim of this targeted funding was to give schools the autonomy to use this funding to raise the attainment of the most disadvantaged. Schools were to be held to account through England's school inspection regime and performance tables that examined the Pupil Premium category specifically. However, it is not clear the extent to which targeted spending has happened as only a small proportion of the £1.25bn of Pupil Premium in 2012/13 was earmarked to be spent on activities that are known to improve attainment levels (The Sutton Trust, 2012). Furthermore, it was not until 2013/14 that the Pupil Premium exceeded the value of grants it replaced (Lupton & Thompson, 2015; Sibieta, Chowdry, & Muriel, 2008), although the policy did encourage redistribution of funds to the schools with the highest concentration of disadvantaged children.

One of the many challenges faced when trying to establish the impact of the Pupil Premium policy is that factors such as peer and school composition may depress the effect of a targeted boost in resource. In 2015, the UK Parliament's Public Accounts Committee noted that the gap between disadvantaged pupils and their peers had reduced (House of Commons Committee of Public Accounts, 2015) and in 2016 the Social Mobility Commission said: "there is some evidence that the Pupil Premium has had a positive effect on the attainment gap, but is not definitive, because it cannot definitively say what would have happened to attainment had it not been introduced" (p. 81). Further doubt has been raised regarding the efficacy of this policy by a report published by the Education Policy Institute which showed that while there has been some progress on the closing of the attainment gap for disadvantaged pupils on average since 2007, it is closing at an unpredictable rate (Andrews, Robinson, & Hutchinson, 2017).

3.4.6 *"What Works" and the Education Endowment Foundation*

One way in which the government has attempted to narrow the attainment gap is through its increased emphasis on funding research into "what works" in educational attainment. This has come with a particular focus on providing evidence about changes teachers and schools can make to improve attainment among those from disadvantaged backgrounds. In 2011, the Department for Education provided the funding for the establishment of the Education Endowment Foundation (EEF)[10] with the specific remit of funding robust research in this area and disseminating its findings to teachers, particularly through its "Teaching and Learning Toolkit" and, increasingly, guidance reports focused on specific issues.

Some issues explored by the Toolkit to raise the quality of teaching and learning include the impact of mentorship and digital technologies, and making best use of teaching assistants, for example, and are assessed in terms of cost-effectiveness, evidence strength and impact. Moreover, they aim to provide an accessible summary of existing international data analyses for schools and teachers to navigate the evidence-base. Since 2011, up to two-thirds of all senior leaders in schools reporting having used the Teaching and Learning Toolkit to inform decision making and over 10,000 schools, nurseries and colleges have taken part in a trial

---

[10]The EEF is an independent charity governed by The Sutton Trust and the Impetus-Private Equity Foundation.

funded by the EEF. The most encouraging interventions tested through this process have accelerated student progress by 3 months in a year and an independent evaluation has estimated that the lifetime gains for students taking part in EEF trials amounting to three times the cost of delivering and evaluating them (EEF, 2017).

This approach has not been without controversy, with some researchers arguing that the kinds of approaches needed to improve the performance of disadvantaged pupils are not best addressed by asking "what works?", instead advocating alternative approaches such as "realist evaluation" that ask "What works for whom in what circumstances and in what respects, and how?" (Pawson & Tilley, 1997). However, we believe these should be seen as complementary, rather than competitive, and seek ways to integrate elements as proposed with approaches such as "realist RCTs" (Bonell et al., 2012) and approaches combining improvement science with experimental approaches (Peterson, 2016). The best designed experimental evaluations already include such elements, for example by being part of an embedded mixed methods design also incorporating an implementation and process evaluation (Anders et al., 2017). Nevertheless, there is doubtless more that can be done in this respect, as highlighted by Connolly et al. (2018) in their systematic review of experimental evaluations in education.

3.5 Conclusion

This chapter has outlined key characteristics of English students and attainment inequalities associated with these, and discussed recent policies introduced to address these inequalities, including discussion of the extent to which there is evidence that these have been successful in their stated aims. Because it is always difficult to isolate the effects of policy changes that occur on a national basis, our conclusions on this last point are particularly tentative.

In international terms, England is a country with low levels of disadvantage. However, there are sizeable differences in educational attainment by SES and we see little evidence of substantial or sustained narrowing in these attainment gaps in recent years. There are also concerns that well-intentioned policies will fail to narrow the attainment gap due to the ways they have been implemented.

For example, while the introduction of academies may have helped to improve the performance of some schools, the evidence on their efficacy is mixed and suggests performance improvements have come from those at the top of the attainment distribution, not the bottom. Changes to school funding to increase resources for those with more disadvantaged pupils through the Pupil Premium have not included sufficient accountability to ensure they are used to improve the attainment of disadvantaged pupils. Likewise, the introduction of curricular reforms aimed at widening access to "powerful knowledge" may be hampered by lack of consideration of the need to tailor this curriculum for pupils from all backgrounds. Meanwhile, there are also signs that some policy changes are likely to be detrimental for those from disadvantaged backgrounds, most notably the mooted expansion of selective schooling, which is highly likely to widen the gap between the top and the bottom of the attainment distribution.

As such, it is far from clear that many of England's recent reforms hold lessons for other countries wishing to reduce their attainment gaps. However, this is not the case across the board. Notable exceptions include the increased investment in widening access to high-quality pre-school education and increased focus on delivering and disseminating robust evidence on school- and classroom-level interventions that will narrow the attainment gap.

References

Anders, J. (2012). The link between household income, university applications and university attendance. *Fiscal Studies, 33*(2), 185–210. https://doi.org/10.1111/j.1475-5890.2012.00158.x.

Anders, J. (2017). The influence of socioeconomic status on changes in young people's expectations of applying to university. *Oxford Review of Education, 43*(4), 381–401. https://doi.org/10.1080/03054985.2017.1329722.

Anders, J., Brown, C., Ehren, M., Greany, T., Nelson, R., Heal, J., Groot, A., Sanders, M., & Allen, R. (2017). *Evaluation of complex whole-school interventions: Methodological and practical considerations*. Report to the Education Endowment Foundation.

Anders, J., Henderson, M., Moulton, V., & Sullivan, A. (2018a). Incentivising specific combinations of subjects—Does it make any difference to university access? *National Institute Economic Review, 243*(1), R37–R52. https://doi.org/10.1177/002795011824300113.

Anders, J., Henderson, M., Moulton, V., & Sullivan, A. (2018b). The role of schools in explaining individuals' subject choices at age 14. *Oxford Review of Education, 44*(1), 75–93. https://doi.org/10.1080/03054985.2018.1409973.

Anders, J., & Jerrim, J. (2017). The socio-economic gradient in educational attainment and labour market outcomes: A cross-national comparison. In I. Schoon & R. K. Silbereisen (Eds.), *Pathways to adulthood: Social inequalities, structure and agency and social change* (pp. 25–50). London, UK: UCL IOE Press.

Andrews, J., Hutchinson, J., & Johnes, R., (2018). *Grammar schools and social mobility*. London, UK: Education Policy Institute. Retrieved from https://epi.org.uk/wp-content/uploads/2018/01/Grammar-schools-and-social-mobility_.pdf.

Andrews, J., Robinson, D., & Hutchinson, J. (2017). *Closing the gap? Trends in educational attainment and disadvantage*. London, UK: Education Policy Institute. Retrieved from https://epi.org.uk/publications-and-research/closing-gap-trends-educational-attainment-disadvantage/.

Bernardinelli, D., Rutt, S., Greany, T., & Higham, R. (2018). *Multi-academy trusts: Do they make a difference to pupil outcomes?*. London, UK: UCL IOE Press.

Boliver, V. (2013). How fair is access to more prestigious UK universities? *The British Journal of Sociology, 64*(2), 344–364. https://doi.org/10.1111/1468-4446.12021.

Bonell, C., Fletcher, A., Morton, M., Lorenc, T., & Moore, L. (2012). Realist randomized controlled trials: A new approach to evaluating complex public health interventions. *Social Science and Medicine, 75*(12), 2299–2306.

Burgess, S., Dickson, M., & Macmillan, L. (2014). *Selective schooling systems increase inequality* (DoQSS Working Paper 14-09). London, UK: UCL Institute of Education. Retrieved from https://ideas.repec.org/s/qss/dqsswp.html.

Chowdry, H., Crawford, C., Dearden, L., Goodman, A., & Vignoles, A. (2013). Widening participation in higher education: Analysis using linked administrative data. *Statistics in Society, Series A, 176*(2), 431–457. https://doi.org/10.1111/j.1467-985X.2012.01043.x.

Connolly, P., Keenan, C., & Urbanska, K. (2018). The trials of evidence-based practice in education: A systematic review of randomised controlled trials in education research 1980–2016. *Educational Research, 60*(3), 276–291. https://doi.org/10.1080/00131881.2018.1493353.

Crawford, C., Macmillan, L., & Vignoles, A. (2017). When and why do initially high-achieving poor children fall behind? *Oxford Review of Education, 43*(1), 88–108. https://doi.org/10.1080/03054985.2016.1240672.

Department for Education. (2010). *Provision for children under five years of age in England—January 2010.* London, UK: Author. Retrieved from https://data.gov.uk/dataset/d3954344-470b-4e5d-8bf4-6b4f77c0f6c4/provision-for-children-under-five-years-of-age-in-england.

Department for Education. (2014). *Measuring disadvantaged pupils' attainment gaps over time* (Statistical Working Paper SFR 40/2014). London, UK: Author. Retrieved from https://www.gov.uk/government/statistics/measuring-disadvantaged-pupils-attainment-gaps-over-time.

Department for Education. (2015). *Education provision: Children under 5 years of age, January 2015.* London, UK: Author. Retrieved from https://www.gov.uk/government/statistics/provision-for-children-under-5-years-of-age-january-2015.

Department for Education. (2017a). *Destinations of key stage 4 and key stage 5 students, England, 2015/16.* London, UK: Author. Retrieved from https://assets.publishing.service.gov.uk/government/uploads/system/uploads/attachment_data/file/651012/SFR56_2017_Main_Text.pdf.

Department for Education. (2017b). *National curriculum assessments at key stage 2 in England, 2017* (revised). London, UK: Author. Retrieved from https://www.gov.uk/government/uploads/system/uploads/attachment_data/file/667372/SFR69_2017_text.pdf.

Department for Education. (2017c). *Participation rates in higher education: Academic years 2006/2007–2015/2016 (provisional).* London, UK: Author. Retrieved from https://assets.publishing.service.gov.uk/government/uploads/system/uploads/attachment_data/file/648165/HEIPR_PUBLICATION_2015-16.pdf.

Department for Education. (2017d). *Schools, pupils and their characteristics: January 2017* (SFR 28.2017). London, UK: Author. https://www.gov.uk/government/uploads/system/uploads/attachment_data/file/650547/SFR28_2017_Main_Text.pdf.

Department for Education. (2018a). *Pupil premium: Funding and accountability for schools.* London, UK: Author. Retrieved from https://www.gov.uk/guidance/pupil-premium-information-for-schools-and-alternative-provision-settings#funding-for-financial-year-2016-to-2017.

Department for Education. (2018b). *Revised 2018 GCSE and equivalent results in England, 2016 to 2017* (SFR01/2017). London, UK: Author. Retrieved from https://assets.publishing.service.gov.uk/government/uploads/system/uploads/attachment_data/file/676596/SFR01_2018.pdf.

Department for Work and Pensions. (2017a). *Households below average income: 1994/95 to 2015/16.* London, UK: Author. Retrieved from https://www.gov.uk/government/statistics/households-below-average-income-199495-to-201516.

Department for Work and Pensions. (2017b). *Households below average income: 1994/95 to 2016/17.* London, UK: Author. Retrieved from https://www.gov.uk/government/uploads/system/uploads/attachment_data/file/691899/directory-of-tables-hbai-2016-17.ods.

Dewey, J., Husted, T. A., & Kenny, L. W. (2000). The ineffectiveness of school inputs: A product of misspecification? *Economics of Education Review, 19*(1), 27–45. https://doi.org/10.1016/S0272-7757(99)00015-1.

Education Endowment Foundation. (2017). *The attainment gap//2017.* Retrieved from https://educationendowmentfoundation.org.uk/public/files/Annual_Reports/EEF_Attainment_Gap_Report_2018_-_print.pdf.

Eyles, A., & Machin, S. (2015). *The introduction of academy schools to England's education.* London, UK: Centre for Economic Performance, London School of Economics.

Eyles, A., Machin, S., & Silva, O. (2015). *Academies 2: The new batch* (CEP Discussion Paper No. 1370). London, UK: Centre for Economic Performance, London School of Economics. Retrieved from http://cep.lse.ac.uk/pubs/download/dp1370.pdf.

Gibbons, S., McNally, S., & Viarengo, M. (2017). Does additional spending help urban schools? An evaluation using boundary discontinuities. *Journal of the European Economic Association*, 1–51. https://doi.org/10.1093/jeea/jvx038.

Greany, T., & Higham, R. (2018). *Hierarchy, markets and networks: Analysing the "self-improving school-led system" agenda in Britain and the implications for schools.* London, UK: UCL IOE Press.

Hanushek, E. A. (1997). Assessing the effects of school resources on student performance: An update. *Educational Evaluation and Policy Analysis, 19*(2), 141–164. https://doi.org/10.3102/01623737019002141.

Henderson, M., Sullivan, A., Anders, J., & Moulton, V. (2017). Social class, gender and ethnic differences in subjects taken at age 14. *The Curriculum Journal*. https://doi.org/10.1080/09585176.2017.1406810.

Holmlund, H., McNally, S., & Viarengo, M. (2008). *Impact of school resources on attainment at key stage 2* (DCSF Research Report No. RR043). London, UK: Department for Children, Schools and Families.

House of Commons Committee of Public Accounts. (2015). *Funding for disadvantaged pupils: Third Report of Session 2015–16.* London, UK: The Stationery Office Limited. Retrieved from https://publications.parliament.uk/pa/cm201516/cmselect/cmpubacc/327/327.pdf.

Ilie, S., Sutherland, A., & Vignoles, A. (2017). Revisiting free school meal eligibility as a proxy for pupil socio-economic deprivation. *British Educational Research Journal, 43*(2), 253–274. https://doi.org/10.1002/berj.3260.

Jerrim, J. (2012). The reliability of trends over time in international education test scores: Is the performance of England's secondary school pupils really in relative decline? *Journal of Social Policy, 42*(2), 259–279. https://doi.org/10.1017/S0047279412000827.

Jerrim, J., & Micklewright, J. (2014). Socio-economic gradients in children's cognitive skills: Are cross-country comparisons robust to who reports family background? *European Sociological Review, 30*(6), 766–781. https://doi.org/10.1093/esr/jcu072.

Jerrim, J., & Sims, S. (2018, March). *Why do so few low and middle-income children attend a grammar school? New evidence from the Millennium Cohort Study.* Retrieved from https://johnjerrim.files.wordpress.com/2018/03/working_paper_nuffield_version_clean.pdf.

Lupton, R., & Thomson, S. (2015). Socio-economic inequalities in English schooling under the Coalition Government 2010–2015. *London Review of Education, 13*(2), 4–20.

Lupton, R., Thomson, S., & Obolenskaya, P. (2016). Schools. In R. Lupton, T. Burchardt, J. Hills, K. Steward, & P. Vizard (Eds.), *Social policy in a cold climate: Policies and their consequences since the crisis* (pp. 59–79). Bristol, UK: Policy Press.

Machin, S., & Silva, O. (2013, March). *School structure, school autonomy and the tail* (CEP Special Paper No. 29). Retrieved from http://cep.lse.ac.uk/pubs/download/special/cepsp29.pdf.

Machin, S., & Vernoit, J. (2012). *Changing school autonomy: Academy schools and their introduction to England's education* (CEE Discussion Paper No. 123). Retrieved from http://cee.lse.ac.uk/ceedps/ceedp123.pdf.

McDool, E. (2016). *The effect of primary converter academies on pupil performance* (Sheffield Economic Research Paper Series No. 2016013). Retrieved from https://www.sheffield.ac.uk/polopoly_fs/1.670238!/file/paper_2016013.pdf.

McGuinness, F. (2018). *Poverty in the UK: Statistics* (House of Commons Library Briefing Paper No. 7096). Retrieved from http://researchbriefings.files.parliament.uk/documents/SN07096/SN07096.pdf.

Moulton, V. G., Sullivan, A., Henderson, M., & Anders, J. (2018). Does what you study at age 14–16 matter for educational transitions post-16? *Oxford Review of Education, 44*(1), 94–117. https://doi.org/10.1080/03054985.2018.1409975.

Nicoletti, C., & Rabe, B. (2014). *Spending it wisely: How can schools use their resources to help poorer pupils?* Colchester, UK: Institute for Social and Economic Research. Retrieved from https://www.iser.essex.ac.uk/files/news/2014/spending-it-wisely.pdf.

Office of National Statistics. (2017). *Statistical bulletin: Families and households: 2017*. Retrieved from https://www.ons.gov.uk/peoplepopulationandcommunity/birthsdeathsandmarriages/families/bulletins/familiesandhouseholds/2017.

Organisation for Economic Co-operation and Development. (2012). *PISA 2012 results: What makes schools successful? Resources, policies and practices (Vol. IV)*. Paris, France: OECD Publishing. Retrieved from https://www.oecd.org/pisa/keyfindings/pisa-2012-results-volume-IV.pdf.

Pawson, R., & Tilley, N. (1997). *Realistic evaluation*. Thousand Oaks: Sage.

Peterson, A. (2016). Getting 'What Works' working: Building blocks for the integration of experimental and improvement science. *International Journal of Research & Method in Education, 39*(3), 299–313. https://doi.org/10.1080/1743727X.2016.1170114.

Roberts, N. (2018). *The school curriculum in England* (House of Commons Library Briefing Paper No. 06798). Retrieved from http://researchbriefings.files.parliament.uk/documents/SN06798/SN06798.pdf

Schneider, S. L. (2008). The application of the ISCED-97 to the UK's educational qualifications. In S. L. Schneider (Ed.), *The International Standard Classification of Education (ISCED-97): An evaluation of content and criterion validity for 15 European countries* (pp. 281–300). Mannheim, Germany: MZES. Retrieved from https://www.mzes.uni-mannheim.de/publications/misc/isced_97/schn08e_the_application_of_the_isced-97_to_the_uks_educat.pdf.

Sibieta, L., Chowdry, H., & Muriel, A. (2008). *Level playing field? The implications of school funding* (CfBT Education Trust Research Paper). Retrieved from https://www.ifs.org.uk/docs/level_playing.pdf.

Social Mobility Commission. (2016). *State of the nation 2016: Social mobility in Great Britain*. Retrieved from https://assets.publishing.service.gov.uk/government/uploads/system/uploads/attachment_data/file/569410/Social_Mobility_Commission_2016_REPORT_WEB_1.pdf.

Stewart, K., & Obolenskaya, P. (2016). Young children. In R. Lupton, T. Burchardt, J. Hills, K. Stewart, & P. Vizard (Eds.), *Social policy in a cold climate: Policies and their consequences since the crisis* (pp. 35–58). Bristol, UK: Policy Press.

Strand, S. (2016). Do some schools narrow the gap? Differential school effectiveness revisited. *Review of Education, 4*(2), 107–144. https://doi.org/10.1002/rev3.3054.

The Sutton Trust. (2012). *NFER Teacher Voice Omnibus 2012: The use of the Pupil Premium*. Slough, UK: National Foundation for Educational Research. Retrieved from https://www.nfer.ac.uk/publications/91062/91062.pdf.

Wakeling, P., & Laurison, D. (2017). Are postgraduate qualifications the "new frontier of social mobility"? *The British Journal of Sociology, 68*(3), 533–555. https://doi.org/10.1111/1468-4446.12277.

Whitty, G. (2010, July). *Who you know, what you know or knowing the ropes? New evidence in the widening participation debate*. Paper presented at the Festival of Education, Wellington College, Crowthorne, UK.

Whitty, G., & Anders, J. (2017). "Closing the achievement gap" in English cities and towns in the twenty-first century. In W. Pink & G. Noblit (Eds.), *Second international handbook of urban education* (pp. 1079–1101). Dordrecht, The Netherlands: Springer.

Williams, M., & Grayson, H. (2018). *School funding in England since 2010—What the key evidence tells us*. Slough, UK: NFER.

Young, M. (2010). Alternative educational futures for a knowledge society. *European Educational Research Journal, 9*(1), 1–12. https://doi.org/10.2304/eerj.2010.9.1.1.

Chapter 4
Socioeconomic Inequality and Student Outcomes in German Schools

Horst Entorf and Maddalena Davoli

Abstract The poor performance of Germany in PISA 2000, in terms of both average and dispersion, stimulated a heated public debate and a strong policy response. The government reacted to the low average and remarkable disparities registered by the test and spurred reforms that led to a significant improvement in the country's educational performance and to a reduction of the gap between children from advantaged and disadvantaged educational backgrounds. Still, between-group achievement inequalities persist within the country. This chapter first discusses the relative development of PISA scores since 2000, and gives a description of existing socioeconomic characteristics and inequalities, with particular attention paid to migratory backgrounds. We also analyze the importance of SES backgrounds, language deficits, and cultural possessions and further explain the characteristics of students' achievements. Second, the chapter provides an overview of the national educational system and addresses important policy reforms following the PISA shock in 2000. We focus on specific features of the country, namely, the large proportion of students with an immigration background and the early selection of pupils into secondary school tracks, and we discuss the role of school streaming as a driver of inequality at school.

Keywords Student achievement · Socioeconomic status · Inequality · Germany

4.1 Introduction

Newspaper headlines dating back to the release of the first Germany PISA results provide a clear idea of the outcry raised in the public opinion because of the poor performance in the PISA 2000 test: "Abysmal Report Card for Obsolete School System" (SZ, 2001); "The Bill for Our Outdated Education System" (Lehmann,

---

H. Entorf (✉) · M. Davoli
Goethe University, Frankfurt, Germany
e-mail: entorf@wiwi.uni-frankfurt.de

© Springer Nature Singapore Pte Ltd. 2019
L. Volante et al. (eds.), *Socioeconomic Inequality and Student Outcomes*, Education Policy & Social Inequality 4,
https://doi.org/10.1007/978-981-13-9863-6_4

2001); "Outcome Could Not Have Been Worse" (Schubert, 2001); "A Disaster in Almost Every Respect" (TAZ, 2001).

The first warning signs appeared already in 1995 when Germany participated in the Trends in International Mathematics and Science Study (TIMMS) and also performed quite poorly. However, it was only with the release of PISA 2000, in December 2001, that the general public became fully aware of the low results of German students, as compared to international standards. The news had a "tsunami-like impact" on the educational discourse in Germany and occupied the headlines of German newspapers for several weeks (Waldow, 2009).

The shock generated by the PISA results was motivated by the fact that Germany had quite a strong perception of its educational apparatus, believed to be an efficient and highly performing system that reflected the generally strong and efficient structure of the country's economy. The results of the first international comparison that Germany took part in—PISA 2000—revealed a different story.

In order to understand German pupils' educational outcomes and the spike in debates that sprang from PISA 2000, a short overview of the most unique characteristics of German education is needed. A first important element of the German system is the great heterogeneity existing across states. The 16 German *Länder* are the sole authority in charge of educational decisions at the state level, so that sizeable differences exist in terms of organization and efficiency, and hence in terms of students' educational outcomes across *Länder* (see Wössmann, 2007, for evidence on cross-state variation in educational policies in Germany). The 16 states, as we will better explain at the end of the paper, present differences in terms of tracking age, central exit examinations, and per-student expenditures, with some of these differences being a consequence of changes implemented after the so-called 2000 PISA shock. Such heterogeneity makes it difficult to analyze educational outcomes in a unified framework, without taking into account regional differences. A second crucial aspect is the early tracking, which characterizes the German system. At the age of 10 (or 12, in some *Länder*), after a common elementary school, each student is placed in one of the three existing school tracks, giving different access to higher tertiary education and to the labor market. The decision on the type of secondary school to attend is based on teachers' recommendations and pupils' performance in earlier classes. *Hauptschule* and *Realschule*, the least theoretically oriented secondary schools, provide education up to grade 9 and 10, allowing students to proceed to vocational training or to nonacademic careers, whereas *Gymnasium* provides education up to grade 12 or 13, preparing students to access university formation. The *Gymnasium* gives access to a standardized central examination, the *Abitur*—the only gateway to university access. Some *Länder* integrates all three tracks in a comprehensive school (*Gesamtschule*), making it easier to access the higher ability tracks.

The three-tiered system was devised as a means to help all students develop their individual abilities already from an early age, preparing them to enter the labor market in a way that best takes into account their inclinations. Instead, as it was revealed quite clearly to the German public by the PISA 2000 results, the tracking system had a rather segregating effect from a very early age (Odendahl, 2017).

The PISA shock brought to light several concerns. First, German students performed poorly, as compared to other OECD countries, with average test scores well below international averages in all three areas measured. Besides, the results of these tests revealed a great inequality existing within the system: students' socioeconomic status and social background were largely related to educational success or failure in German schools. Having or not having a migratory background shaped enormously the differences in test achievements, and the gap between low and high achievers was particularly marked in Germany as compared to other countries. In addition, because students in *Gymnasiums* scored higher than those in other tracks, and because the attendance of *Gymnasium* rather than *Hauptschule* or *Realschule* is greatly determined by pupils' socioeconomic background, the socioeconomic selectivity imposed by the tracking system translated into a selectivity in terms of educational outcomes (Ertl, 2006). A great heterogeneity in mean test scores emerged as well across different *Länder*.

The intense debate initiated thanks to PISA 2000 caused some major policy changes and a shift in the idea of education, as we will explain at the end of the paper. The strong reaction to the negative news about the educational system made it possible to implement a series of reforms aimed at reducing inequalities and enhancing the achievement of disadvantaged students. Since 2000, Germany's PISA results have exhibited a steady increase, reverting the trend of the beginning of the century. As can be seen in Figure 4.1, now the country performs well above the OECD averages in all tested areas, and the country scores have been growing from 2003 onwards.

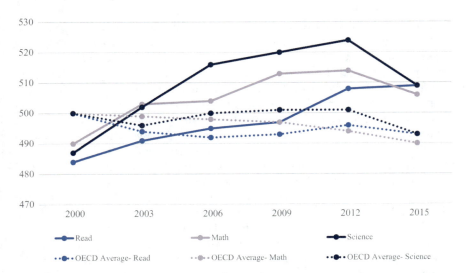

Fig. 4.1 Average test scores (2000–2015). *Notes* Data Source: Organisation for Economic Co-operation and Development (2015, 2016b, 2018). Test scores were normalized to have a mean of 500 and variance equal to 100. Authors' own calculations

The rest of the chapter is organized as follows. The next section presents the characteristics of the student population in Germany and informs about students' education outcomes, using the latest release of the PISA assessment, PISA 2015. Following this, the chapter uses some regression analyses to assess the importance of explaining factors, where we focus on immigrant students and pupils coming from families with low parental educational achievement. The final part of the chapter highlights the main educational policy initiatives and changes spurred by the PISA debate in Germany.

4.2 Key Characteristics of the National Student Population

In order to provide the reader with an overview of disadvantaged students in German secondary schools, we present some descriptive statistics focusing on pupils with a low socioeconomic and/or migration background. For this purpose, we make use of the most recent available wave of PISA, PISA 2015. The dataset of PISA 2015 on Germany contains information on about 6,000 students, mostly from the 8th and 9th grade in 256 different schools.

As a measure of students' socioeconomic background, we employ parental educational achievement, since in the case of Germany previous studies have provided evidence of a particularly low intergenerational mobility with respect to educational attainment (see Entorf & Minoiu, 2005; Heineck & Riphahn, 2009). Children from poorly educated families face considerably more difficulties compared to those with highly educated parents, this being particularly true for students having a migratory background. Recent evidence (Organisation for Economic Co-operation and Development, 2018) finds some intergenerational progress in educational attainment, in particular for the native-born children of Turkish immigrants. However, the OECD report also concludes that due to persistent intergenerational transmission mechanisms, the educational attainment of migrant children coming from families with a low parental status still lags behind that of Germans of native descent. Also, Italian immigrants, despite exhibiting high intergenerational mobility, still display lower educational achievement as compared to native Germans, a sign that the assimilation process is not yet completed (Bönke & Neidhöfer, 2018).

In this chapter, we want to shed more light on the size and development of the gap between children from high and low educated parents, analyze potential reasons for persistent disadvantages such as language proficiency, and study the performance heterogeneity based on nationality, gender, school type, etc. The empirical analysis of our chapter follows the classification suggested by the Organisation for Economic Co-operation and Development (2016a), so that highly educated parents (one or both) have reached at least ISCED 5A (theoretically oriented tertiary and postgraduate qualifications) and poorly educated parents have reached at most ISCED level 2 (lower secondary qualifications). As a large share of the disadvantaged children have a migration background, the focus will be on children and parents with non-German roots. Again, following the classification suggested by the PISA assessment, a student is classified as non-German if both parents were born abroad and she or he was born either abroad (first-generation immigrant) or in Germany (second-generation immigrant). Table 4.1 displays the composition of subgroups of interest of the student population according to this parental background typology. All statistics are weighted and clustered according to PISA sampling methodology (i.e., at school level). Furthermore, results relative to PISA test scores are standardized to have a mean of zero and a variance of one, and only the first of the 10 available plausible values was employed.

Table 4.1 Composition of student population

	Low parental education (%)	High parental education (%)	In whole PISA sample (%)
All students	22.1	34.4	
Native	36.7	63.3	84.5
With migration background	51.5	48.5	15.5
–Other Nationalities	35.9	64.1	11.7
–Ex-Yugoslavia	54.7	45.3	1.8
–Italy	48	51.9	1.5
–Poland	33.5	66.5	2.9
–Former USSR	44.5	55.5	4.7
–Turkey	64.9	35.1	5.6
–Born in Germany (II gen)	56.5	43.5	12.3
–Born abroad (I gen)	65.5	34.5	3.3
Language other than German at home	49.2	50.8	10.5
Male	37.7	62.3	48.9
Female	40.6	59.4	51.1
Low performers: math	59.7	40.3	14.4
Low performers: read	54.5	45.5	12.4
Low performers: science	62.4	37.6	13.9
Gymnasium	16.8	83.2	36.7
More than 100 books at home	19.4	80.6	48.5
Single-parent households	41.4	58.6	13.7

Source PISA 2015, 2012, Germany. Results are weighted and only the first plausible value for PISA scores has been employed. Information on single-parents family comes from PISA 2012, as the information was not available in PISA 2015

Native students have at least one parent born in Germany. Students are classified as being from a certain origin country if either the mother, the father, or the student was born in the specified country. Low parental education is defined as either of the parents having achieved at most level ISCED 1 or 2 of education; high parental education if ISCED 5a or 6 was achieved by either of the parents. Low performers are defined according to OECD guidelines: students that achieved a test score lower than 420, 407, and 410 points in math, reading, and science, respectively

Germany has been the destination country of sizeable migration flows since the beginning of the twentieth century. On the one hand, a sizeable group of migrants came to Germany as temporary guest workers from 1955 to 1973, mostly from Turkey, Italy, and former Yugoslavia. Although originally supposed to only temporarily work and live in Germany, they ended up bringing their families and raising most of the students who now form the group of second-generation immigrants. A second group of immigrants, mostly first-generation students, came from the former Yugoslavian countries and Eastern Europe following the dissolution of socialism (Carey, 2008; Fertig & Schmidt, 2001). This composite population is also reflected in the school system, where a migratory background characterizes a considerable proportion of the students. Following the PISA definition, students are defined as native if at least one of their parents were born in Germany; they are defined as an immigrant if either they or both of their parents were born outside of Germany. In PISA 2015, we observe roughly 16% of the students with a migratory background (Table 4.1), of which the majority is formed by second-generation pupils (i.e., children born in Germany with foreign parents).

It is striking to see the differences in the parental background for some of the subgroups of interest. First, we observe how the majority of natives have parents who achieved high qualifications in education, whereas among students with a migratory background the distribution is more balanced. The situation within the immigrant group, however, is far from being homogeneous. In order to take into account such heterogeneity, we classify a student as having, for example, a Polish background if either the father, the mother, or the student was born in Poland (the same applies for the other countries of origin in the sample). While a student with a Polish background is comparable with a native German in terms of parental education, the same does not apply for all other countries of origin. Pupils from Turkey and from former Yugoslavia face a particularly disadvantaged situation at home, with 55–65% of them having parents who achieved only up to ISCED 2 qualifications. Turkish pupils, amounting to 6% of the entire PISA sample and, thus, representing the largest share among foreign students in German schools, start their educational career with the strongest disadvantage relative to native students.

Differences in parental educational backgrounds matter and persist to the next generation. Proficiency in PISA assessment is divided into six levels and low-performing students are defined as those who score below 420 points in math, 407 points in reading, and 410 points in science (Organisation for Economic Co-operation and Development, 2016a). Below such thresholds, students are believed to lack basic competencies required at their age level. Considerably high percentages of low performers show up in the low parental education category. Not surprisingly, on the opposite side of the spectrum, students attending *Gymnasium* and having more than 100 books at home (a proxy for cultural possession) are mostly from families with highly educated parents.

Living in a family with a single parent (in most cases the mother) is not necessarily associated with a poorer family background; on the contrary, in both categories, more students belong to the high parental education classification. The same holds true for speaking a foreign language at home.

4.3 Factors Associated with Students' Outcomes in Secondary School

The descriptive statistics presented in Table 4.1 clearly show a positive relation between test scores and socioeconomic characteristics of the family, particularly with the educational level of parents. Figures 4.2 and 4.3, plotting the change in the average test score gaps between native and immigrant students (Figure 4.2) and between students with high and low parental education (Figure 4.3), show that the country has considerably reduced the gaps that emerged in the first PISA surveys. The difference in performances of students whose parents are highly or poorly educated has reduced by about 40 points on average in all subject areas, becoming even smaller than the OECD average gap. However, despite improving their performance over time, immigrants in Germany still achieve between 60 and 70 points less than natives, while the OECD gap is of about 40 points on average. According to OECD guidelines—one school year of competences corresponds to about 35–40 points in the PISA tests—immigrants' performance is behind that of natives by about 1.5 years of schooling. Hence, although there has been a remarkable decrease in inequality originating from a heterogeneous parental background, considerable gaps do still exist.

In order to better identify factors associated with students' school performance, we employ multivariate linear regressions and estimate the partial correlation between students' characteristics and PISA test results, conditioning on other relevant variables. Marginal effects from OLS estimation are presented in Table 4.2: Columns (1),

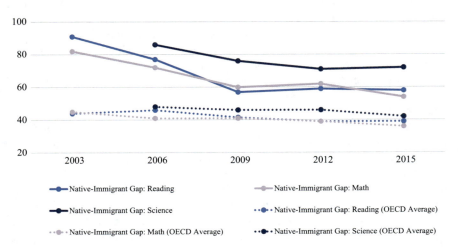

Fig. 4.2 Average native–immigrant gap (2003–2015). *Notes* Data source: Organisation for Economic Co-operation and Development (2015, 2016b, 2018). Test scores were normalized to have a mean of 500 and variance equal to 100. Authors' own calculations

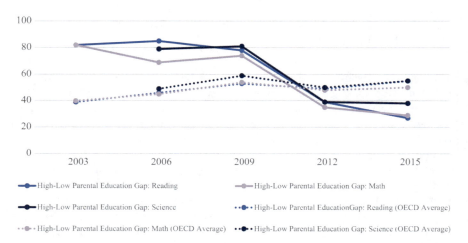

Fig. 4.3 Average high–low parental education gap (2003–2015). *Notes* Data source: Organisation for Economic Co-operation and Development (2015, 2016b, 2018). Test scores were normalized to have a mean of 500 and variance equal to 100. Authors' own calculations

(3), and (5) report estimates for all relevant variables; columns (2), (4), and (6) have a more direct focus on parental education (by omitting variables that depend on the influence of parents). The gap of students with a migratory background becomes obvious throughout all six models of Table 4.2. Immigrant students, no matter whether born abroad or in Germany, score significantly worse than native Germans with at least one parent born in Germany. Pupils born abroad (i.e., first-generation students) are the ones who experience the biggest disadvantage, and they do so the later they arrive in Germany, as can be seen from the estimated coefficients associated with age at arrival. We also observe that important differences in performance relate to the country of origin: when at least one of the parents (or the child) is born in Turkey, the average student has a malus of 0.3–0.6 standard deviations in her test score, with math and science being especially affected by such disadvantage. Also, pupils of Italian origin experience a disadvantage, whereas Polish origin positively correlates with test scores, although not always significantly.

Students' characteristics representing parental economic background and education are highly correlated with students' assessments. Because we want to analyze the strength of the intergenerational educational correlation, we provide a closer look at the particular role of parents' education in columns (2), (4), and (6). Here, we omit "Gymnasium" and "Books at Home" (a proxy for family's wealth and cultural capital), as these characteristics might already be the result of parents' educational background (see Angrist & Pischke, 2009, for an in-depth discussion of the concept of "bad control" variables). Once parental education is the only proxy for students' socioeconomic background, we observe a very strong influence of low parental education on school performance of children. In all three subject areas, the difference between performance levels amounts to about 0.4 standard deviation when compared to non-low educated parents.

Table 4.2 Student performance: OLS

Variables	Read		Math		Science	
	(1)	(2)	(3)	(4)	(5)	(6)
First generation	−0.279*	−0.398**	−0.265**	−0.388***	−0.115	−0.249
	(0.141)	(0.158)	(0.115)	(0.132)	(0.134)	(0.153)
Second generation	−0.110*	−0.159**	−0.057	−0.109**	−0.155***	−0.218***
	(0.055)	(0.061)	(0.051)	(0.054)	(0.051)	(0.055)
Italian origin	−0.116	−0.174*	−0.253**	−0.313**	−0.173*	−0.232**
	(0.100)	(0.103)	(0.114)	(0.123)	(0.097)	(0.099)
Polish origin	0.164**	0.156*	0.081	0.072	0.046	0.036
	(0.068)	(0.081)	(0.074)	(0.091)	(0.082)	(0.096)
Ex-USSR origin	0.143*	0.126	0.038	0.020	0.019	0.004
	(0.072)	(0.079)	(0.062)	(0.065)	(0.070)	(0.070)
Turkish origin	−0.269***	−0.421***	−0.457***	−0.615***	−0.432***	−0.595***
	(0.072)	(0.080)	(0.061)	(0.074)	(0.056)	(0.061)
Ex-Yugoslavia origin	0.023	−0.002	−0.122	−0.148	−0.251**	−0.279***
	(0.103)	(0.110)	(0.098)	(0.099)	(0.098)	(0.104)
Other origin	−0.132***	−0.184***	−0.196***	−0.250***	−0.152***	−0.205***
	(0.041)	(0.053)	(0.042)	(0.052)	(0.041)	(0.054)
Female	0.100***	0.137***	−0.301***	−0.262***	−0.208***	−0.165***
	(0.024)	(0.026)	(0.021)	(0.023)	(0.022)	(0.025)
Age	0.228***	0.178***	0.325***	0.273***	0.256***	0.206***
	(0.046)	(0.053)	(0.045)	(0.051)	(0.043)	(0.051)
Low parental education	−0.063**	−0.347***	−0.112***	−0.407***	−0.094***	−0.405***
	(0.027)	(0.030)	(0.026)	(0.032)	(0.027)	(0.032)
More than 100 books	0.262***		0.275***		0.367***	
	(0.023)		(0.024)		(0.026)	
Gymnasium	0.898***		0.926***		0.892***	
	(0.034)		(0.037)		(0.037)	

(continued)

Table 4.2 (continued)

Variables	Read		Math		Science	
	(1)	(2)	(3)	(4)	(5)	(6)
Other language at home	−0.262***	−0.317***	−0.249***	−0.306***	−0.271***	−0.335***
	(0.050)	(0.061)	(0.048)	(0.057)	(0.043)	(0.056)
Age at arrival: 4–6 years	0.140	0.182	0.261	0.305	−0.045	−0.016
	(0.207)	(0.235)	(0.202)	(0.226)	(0.216)	(0.246)
Age at arrival: 7–9 years	−0.218	−0.367	−0.234	−0.388*	−0.178	−0.336
	(0.219)	(0.248)	(0.204)	(0.227)	(0.197)	(0.228)
Age at arrival: 10–12 years	−0.425	−0.617*	−0.399*	−0.598***	−0.315*	−0.522**
	(0.365)	(0.344)	(0.202)	(0.213)	(0.183)	(0.199)
Age at arrival: 13–15 years	−0.784***	−0.849***	−0.154	−0.222	−0.589***	−0.667***
	(0.217)	(0.259)	(0.226)	(0.264)	(0.214)	(0.252)
Constant	−3.909***	−2.579***	−5.250***	−3.875***	−4.222***	−2.840***
	(0.723)	(0.837)	(0.715)	(0.808)	(0.674)	(0.808)
N	5317	5317	5317	5317	5317	5317
R-squared	0.345	0.108	0.378	0.138	0.398	0.142

Source PISA 2015, Germany. Table reports the results of OLS regressions. First plausible value employed. All results are weighted and replication weights are taken into account. Test scores were normalized to have a mean of 0 and variance equal to 1. Errors are robust and clustered at the school level. Standard errors in parentheses. ***$p < 0.01$, **$p < 0.05$, *$p < 0.1$

Native students have at least one parent born in Germany. Students are classified as having a certain origin country if either the mother, the father, or the student was born in the specified country. Low parental education is defined as either of the parents having achieved at most level ISCED 1 or 2 of education

Clearly, many factors that correlate with students' performances are missing in the estimation model, which is why our estimates represent partial correlations rather than causal effects. However, the multivariate model confirms the descriptive results of the previous section: pupils' migratory and socioeconomic background can negatively affect the test score of disadvantaged students. Students with some foreign background, fewer books, and a non-German language spoken at home, and with parents who themselves have achieved low levels of education, on average achieve scores that range between 0.2 and 0.6 standard deviations below the average performance of their respective counterparts.

4.4 Education Policies Designed to Address Socioeconomic Disadvantaged Students

The disappointing "shock" of the first PISA results in 2000 has been a wake-up call for the German educational system. Germany's children performed significantly below the OECD average, and a broad group was identified as "functional illiterate" because their cognitive competences, reading, and writing skills were inadequate for everyday needs. Only a decade later, Germany has managed a turnaround. As shown in Figure 4.1, scores in reading, mathematics, and science have significantly increased and are well above the OECD average after 2012. At the same time, the impact of socioeconomic background has decreased. As noted by the Organisation for Economic Co-operation and Development (2015), Germany is one of only three member countries where both mathematics scores and equity indicators have improved since 2003. Moreover, an increasing percentage of the German student population is "resilient"—meaning that pupils, despite their disadvantaged socioeconomic background, score among the top 25% of students around the world (Organisation for Economic Co-operation and Development, 2016b). The share of resilient students in Germany has increased by 9 percentage points since 2006, which is by far exceeding the OECD average increase of 2 percentage points during the same period. The increasing performance of students with a disadvantaged socioeconomic background becomes even more remarkable when we distinguish between high and low educated parents by using the ISCED level (low parental education: at most level ISCED 1 or 2; high parental education: ISCED 5a or 6, achieved by either of the parents). As shown in Figure 4.3, the performance gap between advantaged and disadvantaged students used to be more than 70 PISA score points (roughly equivalent to 2 years of schooling) and still high above the OECD average in 2009; it is down to less than 40 points and well below the average in 2015.

So, what educational policies and reforms, if any, have caused these improvements? A first relevant remark to make is that the intense debate following PISA 2000 caused a major shift in the idea of education. Neumann, Fischer, and Kauertz (2010) thoroughly explain how one of the core elements of the reform of the educational system following PISA 2000 was the passage from the German *Bildung*, an idea of education based on the development of the individual rather than on specific functional abilities, to the notion of Anglo-American literacy, where educational standards and assessment of students' achievements are central. PISA contributed to the development of an empirically based framework for research in education, previously not very developed in Germany, somehow more practically oriented and based on competences (Ertl, 2006; Neumann et al., 2010). National Education Standards (NES), common across all *Länder*, were introduced by the Ständige Konferenz der Kulturminister to define ability levels that all pupils should reach by the end of grade 4, ability levels which represent clear, assessable goals to be achieved within a specific age.

In addition, as Waldow (2009) points out, one should be aware of the fact that many of the changes to the educational system following PISA 2000 were already underway before the public release of the results, and were not uniquely determined by the test results, as many people believe. The introduction of educational standards and centralized examinations, the creation of all-day schools (*Ganztagsschule*) and the changes in the structure of lower secondary schools were elements already in place in some of the Federal States and in a discussion phase across the country. However, the PISA shock was employed as a legitimization tool to implement many long-needed changes in educational policy measures and to create consensus among the population for such changes (Waldow, 2009).

When having a closer look at the reforms carried out in Germany, it needs to be stressed at the outset that it is difficult to characterize the national educational system because education is regulated by the individual federal states (*Bundesländer*), and every state has its own peculiarities. However, according to educational research and discussions among practitioners, seven major points have contributed to the improvement, which are given as follows:

1. Rethinking streaming children at the age of 10
2. Softening segregation
3. Standardization of curricula
4. Monitoring and ensuring comparability
5. Introduction of central examinations
6. Increasing school autonomy
7. Expanding and strengthening the educational content of pre-primary schools.

4.4.1 Streaming

The findings of 2000 have brought about strong arguments against tracking students into differing-ability schools as early as age 10 (compared to the OECD average of 14) because it significantly increases educational inequality (Entorf & Lauk, 2008; Hanushek & Wössmann, 2006). A few states (*Länder*) have introduced policies to reduce the potentially negative effects of early tracking on equity. In Berlin and

Brandenburg, all primary schools are comprehensive until grade 6 (age 12), and in Hesse students can choose between 4-year and 6-year primary schools. Nevertheless, a large majority of secondary students, particularly in the Western part of Germany, still undergo some early tracking. However, the downsides of the early tracking into different-ability schools have been alleviated by reforms that changed the German school system to a more comprehensive and less segregated approach in which students with greater heterogeneity of abilities are admitted to the same school.

4.4.2 Segregation

Perhaps the most significant change has been the merging of the two lower level tracks (*Realschule* and *Hauptschule*) into one school, called *Regionalschulen* ("regional schools") in several states. The change improved the general education level and it has taken away a lot of stigma because *Hauptschulen* were and are still characterized as places for children with (very) poor prospects. The previously dominating non-comprehensive school system was found to magnify the prevailing educational inequality between students with a low parental socioeconomic background, particularly those with a migration background, and children from more privileged families (Entorf & Lauk, 2008). Closing *Hauptschulen*, again, does not apply to all states. Baden-Württemberg, Bavaria, Hesse, Lower Saxony, and North Rhine-Westphalia maintain the traditional three-tier education system. However, *Hauptschulen* in Baden-Württemberg and Bavaria are still considered less segregated than elsewhere because in these states the share of pupils attending the lowest level track is still relatively large, and the system facilitates considerable upward mobility to higher ability tracks (Bellenberg, 2012). As a matter of fact, PISA scores variation within schools was greater in 2015 (56%) than in 2006 (46%) (Organisation for Economic Co-operation and Development, 2016b). Thus, the pre-reform ability grouping between schools has been partly replaced by ability grouping within schools. According to the Organisation for Economic Co-operation and Development (2015), only 32% of students have been in schools without grouping, whereas this number was 54% in 2003.

PISA results revealed poor performance of students with a migration background. One of the key problems for their underperformance and lacking integration into German society has been language problems. The Kultusministerkonferenz (KMK; The Standing Conference of the Ministers of Education and Cultural Affairs of the *Länder* in the Federal Republic of Germany) showed a prompt response and announced a series of policy responses, including language training for migrant children starting already from preschools, and a concept called *Deutsch als Zweitsprache* ("German as second language"), which is now practiced in most kindergartens (KMK, 2002).

4.4.3 Standardization

The PISA shock prompted a debate about missing standards for education in Germany. Therefore, the KMK decided on cross-border educational standards for all federal states of Germany, which were introduced in 2003 and 2004. In 2004, a new Institute for Educational Quality Improvement (*Institut zur Qualtitätsentwicklung im Bildungswesen* [IQB]) has been founded. Its key objectives are development, operationalization, standardization, and examination of educational standards, including the design of national tests across *Länder*. These tests address standards for basic school graduates at all school levels. The first implementation took place in 2009 in German, English, and French languages, followed by Mathematics and German in 2011, and by 2012 educational standards were introduced for all school types (Gemeinsame Wissenschaftskonferenz [GWK], 2014). Therefore, contrary to pre-PISA times, students are now preparing for German and international standard tests such as PISA, IGLU (Internationale Grundschule-Lese-Untersuchung), and TIMSS.

4.4.4 Monitoring

Differently from other OECD countries such as England, results from IQB evaluations are not publicly available. IQB only publishes the ranking of states, and participating schools receive a summary about the performance of their students. This kind of monitoring is associated with less pressure on teachers and pupils than in countries where league tables are available at the individual school level. It has the advantage of informing schools about local problems and deficiencies, without inducing a circle of stigmatization of less successful schools.

4.4.5 Centralization of Exams

Most *Länder* introduced the *Zentralabitur* (central upper secondary school leaving examination) during the years 2005 and 2008. As of today, all states except Rhineland-Palatinate have a centralized examination. Before 2000, it was in place in Bavaria and in Eastern states of the former GDR. The reform improved comparability, and it has put some pressure on schools, perhaps even stronger than that induced by other means of monitoring. However, contrary to a widespread belief, examinations are not standardized at the national but rather at the state level. Therefore, not surprisingly, there is still an ongoing demand for high and low-quality standards, and for comparability between states.

4.4.6 School Autonomy

Standardization, comparability, and central exams can only be successful when school leaders have enough autonomy for school-specific changes and improvements. Indeed, Wössmann and Fuchs (2007) point out that school performance is positively correlated with school autonomy. The Organisation of Economic Co-operation and Development (2015) reports that in recent years German school leaders have benefited from increasing autonomy, and their use of instructional leadership approaches is above the OECD average.

4.4.7 Preschools

Attendance of kindergarten used to be relatively low in Germany, particularly for children with migration background. This has changed fundamentally. In 2012, 96% of the 4-year-old German children (OECD average: 82%) and 91% of all 3-year-olds (OECD average: 70%) attended kindergarten (GWG, 2014). As preschool is a place that offers the opportunity for leveling out social and cultural differences, the general acceptance of kindergarten has led to a decrease of the gap between children from high and low educated parents at the start of school.

In conclusion, the PISA shock has acted as a spur to the German educational system. Many reforms have been implemented that eventually led to a schooling system which has become more standardized and centralized, more closely monitored, and perhaps most importantly, less segregated than at the time before PISA 2000. The result of this change can be seen when looking at the performance difference of PISA scores between children from high-educated and those from low-educated parents (ISCED 5a or 6, compared to ISCED 1 or 2). Whereas the disadvantage was significantly above the OECD average in 2009, it fell well below the average after 2012. Still, children with a migratory history lag behind. Despite some improvements, the gap between native and immigrant children has remained above the OECD level. When analyzing the reasons for this persistent disadvantage, language problems can easily be identified as one of the major obstacles. In this respect, the common practice of early tracking restricts integration, as many of those with a poor command of the German language end up in *Hauptschulen*, where their peers continue to speak their mother tongue.

Finally, although the OECD's PISA tests seem to be very successful, particularly in Germany, it should be noted that PISA itself has also been criticized. For example, in an open letter to PISA director Dr. Andreas Schleicher, many educational scientists from around the world expressed their concern about a potentially misleading impact of PISA tests (Andrews et al., 2014). Among other matters, they worried about a bias in favor of the economic role of public schools. They emphasized that preparing children for gainful employment "is not the only, and not even the main goal of public education" (Andrews et al., 2014, para. 6). Instead, students should be prepared for participation in democratic self-government, moral action, and well-being. This critique is certainly an opinion that is not shared by the majority of German citizens and researchers working on education, but it represents the voice of a significant number of practitioners and educational scientists.

References

Andrews, P., Atkinson, L., Ball, S., Barber, M., Beckett, L., Berardi, J., ... Zhao, Y. (2014, May 6). OECD and Pisa tests are damaging education worldwide. *The Guardian*. Retrieved from https://www.theguardian.com/education/2014/may/06/oecd-pisa-tests-damaging-education-academics.

Angrist, J. D., & Pischke, J. S. (2009). *Mostly harmless econometrics: An empiricist's companion*. Princeton, NJ: Princeton University Press.

Bellenberg, G. (with Forell, M.). (2012). *Schulformwechsel in Deutschland. Durchlässigkeit und Selektion in den 16 Schulsystemen der Bundesländer innerhalb der Sekundarstufe* [School form change in Germany. Permeability and selection in the 16 school systems of the federal states within secondary education]. Gütersloh, Germany: Bertelsmann Stiftung.

Bönke, T., & Neidhöfer, G. (2018). Parental background matters: Intergenerational mobility and assimilation of Italian immigrants in Germany. *German Economic Review, 19*(1), 1–31. https://doi.org/10.1111/geer.12114.

Carey, D. (2008). *Improving education outcomes in Germany*. Paris, France: OECD Publishing. https://doi.org/10.1787/241675712618.

Entorf, H., & Lauk, M. (2008). Peer effects, social multipliers and migrants at school: An international comparison. *Journal of Ethnic and Migration Studies, 34*(4), 633–654. https://doi.org/10.1080/13691830801961639.

Entorf, H., & Minoiu, N. (2005). What a difference immigration policy makes: A comparison of PISA scores in Europe and traditional countries of immigration. *German Economic Review, 6* (3), 355–376. https://doi.org/10.1111/j.1468-0475.2005.00137.x.

Ertl, H. (2006). Educational standards and the changing discourse on education: The reception and consequences of the PISA study in Germany. *Oxford Review of Education, 32*(5), 619–634. https://doi.org/10.1080/03054980600976320.

Fertig, M., & Schmidt, C. M. (2001). *First-and second-generation migrants in Germany—What do we know and what do people think?* (CEPR Discussion Paper No. 2803). Retrieved from https://ideas.repec.org/p/cpr/ceprdp/2803.html.

Gemeinsame Wissenschaftskonferenz. (2014). *Aufstieg durch Bildung—Die Qualifizierungsinitiative für Deutschland. Bericht zur Umsetzung 2014* [Advancement through education—The qualification initiative for Germany. Implementation Report 2014]. Bonn, Germany: Author. Retrieved from https://www.gwk-bonn.de/fileadmin/Redaktion/Dokumente/Papers/Qualifizierungsinitiative-Umsetzungsbericht-2014.pdf.

Hanushek, E. A., & Wößmann, L. (2006). Does educational tracking affect performance and inequality? Differences- in-differences evidence across countries. *The Economic Journal, 116* (510), C63–C76. https://doi.org/10.1111/j.1468-0297.2006.01076.x.

Heineck, G., & Riphahn, R. T. (2009). Intergenerational transmission of educational attainment in Germany—The last five decades. *Jahrbücher für Nationalökonomie und Statistik, 229*(1), 36–60. https://doi.org/10.1515/jbnst-2009-0104.

Kultusministerkonferenz. (2002). *PISA 2000—Zentrale Handlungsfelder. Zusammenfassende Darstellung der laufenden und geplanten Maßnahmen in den Ländern. Beschluss der 299* [PISA 2000—Central fields of action. Summary of the current and planned measures in the countries. Resolution 299]. Retrieved from https://www.kmk.org/fileadmin/Dateien/veroeffentlichungen_beschluesse/2002/2002_10_07-Pisa-2000-Zentrale-Handlungsfelder.pdf.

Lehmann, A. (2001, February 12). Die Quittung für unser veraltetes Bildungssystem [The receipt for our outdated education system]. *Der Tagesspiegel*. Retrieved from https://www.tagesspiegel.de/kultur/deutsche-schulen-die-quittung-fuer-unser-veraltetes-bildungssystem/274662.html.

Neumann, K., Fischer, H. E., & Kauertz, A. (2010). From PISA to educational standards: The impact of large-scale assessments on science education in Germany. *International Journal of Science and Mathematics Education, 8*(3), 545–563. https://doi.org/10.1007/s10763-010-9206-7.

Odendahl, W. (2017). *Bildungskrise—PISA and the German educational crisis. IAFOR Journal of Education, 5*(1), 209–226. https://doi.org/10.22492/ije.5.1.11.

Organisation for Economic Co-operation and Development. (2015). Germany. In *Education policy outlook 2015: Making reforms happen*. Paris, France: OECD Publishing. https://doi.org/10.1787/9789264225442-24-en.

Organisation for Economic Co-operation and Development. (2016a). *PISA 2015 low-performing students: Why they fall behind and how to help them succeed Paris*. France: OECD Publishing. https://doi.org/10.1787/9789264250246-en.

Organisation for Economic Co-operation and Development. (2016b). *Germany. Country note—Results from PISA 2015*. Paris, France: OECD Publishing.

Organisation for Economic Co-operation and Development. (2018). *Catching up? Country studies on intergenerational mobility and children of immigrants*. Paris, France: OECD Publishing.

Schubert, B. (2001, March 12). Schlimmer hätte es nicht kommen können [Outcome could not have been worse]. *Der Tagesspiegel*. Retrieved from https://www.tagesspiegel.de/weltspiegel/gesundheit/schlimmer-haette-es-nicht-kommen-koennen/275076.html.

SZ. (2001, April 12). Miserables Zeugnis für überholtes Schulsystem [Abysmal report card for obsolete school system]. *Süddeutsche Zeitung*, p. 8.

TAZ. (2001, May 12). Fast in jeder Hinsicht ein Desaster [A disaster in almost every respect]. *Die Tageszeitung*. Retrieved from http://www.taz.de/!1137421/.

Waldow, F. (2009). What PISA did and did not do: Germany after the "PISA-shock". *European Educational Research Journal, 8*(3), 476–483. https://doi.org/10.2304/eerj.2009.8.3.476.

Wössmann, L. (2007). *Fundamental determinants of school efficiency and equity: German states as a microcosm for OECD countries* (IZA Discussion Paper No. 2880). Retrieved from https://ideas.repec.org/p/iza/izadps/dp2880.html.

Wössmann, L., & Fuchs, T. (2007). What accounts for international differences in student performance? A re-examination using PISA data. *Empirical Economics, 32*(2–3), 433–464. https://doi.org/10.1007/s00181-006-0087-0.

Chapter 5
Socioeconomic Inequality and Student Outcomes in Italy

Nicola Pensiero, Orazio Giancola and Carlo Barone

Abstract This chapter assesses inequalities in educational outcomes in Italy linking their evolution to changes in the Italian educational system. We analyze how to track choice and performance in PISA tests among 15-year olds are influenced by social origins. We consider how inequalities by social origins are intertwined with inequalities by immigrant status and area of residence. We detect a small reduction of inequalities in participation in the academic track and a reduction of inequality in achievement limited to the northern regions, but overall our results show high inertia in the reproduction of social inequalities. These results are observed during a period where the reduction of inequalities in education has remained a marginal issue in the policy debate as well as a marginal target of educational policies.

Keywords Student achievement · Socioeconomic status · Inequality · Italy

5.1 The Italian Educational System: An Overview

This chapter assesses the evolution of social inequalities in compulsory education for the period 2000–2015 in Italy. Drawing on PISA data corresponding to track choices and student skills in three domains, we analyze recent trends in the disadvantage of students from low-educated families and the interplay between family background, immigrant status, and territorial inequalities, which are particularly pronounced in this country. In this section, we quickly sketch the main characteristics of the Italian educational system, while in Sect. 5.2 we summarize the key

---

N. Pensiero (✉)
Institute of Education, University College London, London, UK
e-mail: n.pensiero@ucl.ac.uk

O. Giancola
Sapienza University of Rome, Rome, Italy

C. Barone
Sciences Po, Paris, France

© Springer Nature Singapore Pte Ltd. 2019
L. Volante et al. (eds.), *Socioeconomic Inequality and Student Outcomes*, Education Policy & Social Inequality 4,
https://doi.org/10.1007/978-981-13-9863-6_5

findings of empirical research concerning the educational disadvantages of low-SES students in Italy. In Sect. 5.3, we present fresh evidence concerning the evolution of these educational inequalities over the past two decades, and in Sect. 5.4 we relate these results to the evolution of the policy context. Section 5.5 provides some concluding remarks.

In Italy, compulsory education starts at the age of 6, but pre-primary education for children aged 3–5 is quasi-universalistic since attendance rates are above 90% (Organisation for Economic Cooperation and Development, 2017a). Primary and lower secondary education is comprehensive and takes 8 years to complete, from the age of 6–14. Lower secondary school leavers have three main options in high school: academic (*licei*), technical (*istituti tecnici*), or vocational schools (*istituti professionali*). All of these tracks take 5 years to complete and open access to higher education in any field, regardless of previous school performance. Ability grouping within tracks is highly uncommon. Three-year vocational training courses represent a fourth option at the upper secondary level, which is chosen by a small percentage of students. Teachers formulate a formal track recommendation in grade 8, which is not binding. In Italy, students have very limited choice regarding school subjects once they have chosen a track. The private education sector enrols only 6.5 and 4.5% of the high school and junior school students, respectively. Adult education is highly underdeveloped in Italy.

The Italian school system thus presents an intermediate level of educational stratification: students are tracked at the age of 14, but track assignment is not binding for access to higher education; the differences between tracks in their school curricula are substantial, but the vocational track is mainly school-based and has weak connections with firms and employer associations. Upper-class students are strongly overrepresented in the academic track, whose students display much higher rates of university enrolment to and completion of higher education than students attending the other two tracks. Conversely, working class, immigrant, low-performing students are significantly overrepresented in the vocational track and, to a lesser extent, in the technical track (Azzolini & Barone, 2013). Compulsory education lasts until the age of 16. Dropout rates are comparatively high in the first 2 years following high school and university enrolment, and again they are strongly patterned by students' socioeconomic and immigrant background (Triventi & Trivellato, 2015).

Overall, from the post-WWII years until the present day, the educational system in Italy, as in many other countries in the OECD, has been characterized by reform processes to increase its inclusiveness and to reduce phenomena of social exclusion. International data (Organisation for Economic Cooperation and Development, 2017a) have shown that as far as the inclusion capacity of various types of studies is concerned, the possession of lower and upper secondary school diplomas has become increasingly widespread. This trend has been accompanied by a significant reduction of inequalities of educational opportunity by social origins in the postwar decades (Barone, Luijkx & Schizzerotto, 2010), as well as by growing gender equality in participation in the educational system (De Vita & Giancola, 2017).

The level of centralization of the Italian school system is traditionally high. From the end of the 1990s to the present, with a notable acceleration in the last 10 years (2005–2015), the Italian educational system has become the object of several reforms seeking to promote decentralization and school autonomy. This dynamic was produced on the one hand by exogenous factors (broader reform processes aiming at increasing the efficiency of the public administration, pressures towards a rationalization of public spending, the need for integration between the various national educational systems) and, on the other, by factors endogenous to school systems (new conceptions of learning processes promoting a more flexible and targeted view of educational processes) (Giancola, 2010). The opening of the European Education area and the role of supranational agencies (Giancola & Viteritti, 2014) have pushed the educational system simultaneously towards an increasing role of local governance and a growing similarity with the other European educational systems (Benadusi & Giancola, 2016).

These reforms to foster school autonomy and decentralization have produced contradictory effects (Grimaldi & Serpieri, 2012). These processes have transferred some tasks to the schools (the organization of part of the student curriculum, the development of extracurricular projects, etc.), but school autonomy concerning teachers' recruitment and career advancement is still quite limited, and the weight of the central bureaucracies is preponderant also with respect to school budgets. Some recent school reforms have tried to increase the rights of school principals in relation to the selection of teachers and their remuneration, but this process has been controversial, and its outcomes currently remain uncertain. Hence, despite these reform efforts, the Italian school system is still characterized by a high level of uniformity and rigidity (Giancola & Fornari, 2011). Several studies show that the characteristics of the student, the school, and the school context are not independent from each other but rather overlap and influence students' performances (Giancola, 2010; Triventi, 2014).

The degree of standardization and centralization of exams and assessments is low in Italy. Grading standards vary considerably across regions and school tracks (Argentin & Triventi, 2015). The national bureau for school testing (INVALSI) carries out regular standardized assessments of students' skills at grades 2, 5, 8, and 10, but their individual-level results are not communicated to the teachers, or to the students and their families.[1] Since 2017, the school-level results of these assessments are in principle made accessible to families via a website, which may increase in the future the competition between schools, but currently the impact of this mild form of quasi-market model seems rather limited. Since 2014, Italy has a national system of school quality assessment. Each school receives an annual set of 51 performance indicators (such as average scores on the INVALSI assessments, dropout rates, teacher turnover, etc.) at the school level, with comparisons along

---

[1]The only exception was the test administered at the lower secondary final examinations, which contributed to the final grade. However, due to the limited external control during this test, cheating at this test was common practice (INVALSI, 2017). Since 2017, the test has no longer any consequence for the final grade.

these indicators with other schools in the same area. The school uses this information to prepare a self-evaluation report, which forms the basis for a school improvement plan. An external evaluation committee may visit the school to assess the reliability of this self-evaluation report, but in practice this external control occurs only in a very small minority of schools. This mild form of evaluation involves only the schools and there is no standardized mechanism of teachers' performance assessment. If the school fails to reach the goals of the school improvement plan, there is no sanction in terms of school resources or teachers' salaries; the school principal may face some negative consequences in terms of career development, but this still remains unclear, as the system is new and schools have just begun to implement the improvement plans. Overall, the pressures towards increasing school accountability are still quite limited in Italy as compared to other European countries, such as England or the Netherlands, but the direction of recent reforms marks a significant change towards more pressure concerning school performances. Unfortunately, the focus is largely on school-level averages in educational output indicators, while the objective of fostering equal opportunities by promoting the educational success of disadvantaged students remains quite marginal in the current understandings of what makes a "good school".

Finally, higher education virtually coincides with university courses comprising 3-year bachelor and 2-year master courses. Postsecondary vocational education remains marginal. Access to university education is formally open to all high school diploma holders, although in fact entry examinations based on standardized tests are increasingly common. Universities enjoy much larger autonomy than schools with regards to the management of human and financial resources. Accountability dynamics are also more pronounced at this level, since the scientific output and the teaching practices of each university are routinely evaluated.

5.2 Family Background and Educational Success in Italy

Italy displays comparatively low levels of educational attainment in tertiary education and, to a lesser extent, in upper secondary education. Moreover, educational achievement as measured in PISA and TIMSS surveys is also comparatively low among secondary-aged children. These low levels of educational success go hand in hand with strong social inequalities in educational participation. It is well-documented that parents' educational and occupational position exerts a strong influence on their children's educational opportunities in Italy. Family background is associated with student grades and scores in standardized tests in primary (INVALSI, 2017; Raimondi, Barone, & De Luca, 2013), lower secondary (Fondazione Giovanni Agnelli, 2011; INVALSI, 2017; Mullis, Martin, Foy, & Hooper, 2016), and upper secondary education (Benadusi, Fornari, & Giancola, 2010; Giancola & Fornari, 2011).

Moreover, a low-SES family background is associated with higher chances of enrolment in the vocational track and with higher dropout risks. Controlling for performance in standardized tests, low-SES students get lower grades (Triventi & Trivellato, 2015), and controlling for test scores, grades, and school-based measures of behavioral problems, these students are less likely to get a teacher recommendation for the general track (Argentin, Barbieri, & Barone, 2017), possibly because teachers anticipate lower family support for these students (Romito, 2016). In turn, track choice impacts considerably on their chances to enrol at university and to achieve bachelor and master degrees.

The influence of family background on track choices and high school completion is comparatively very strong in Italy, which ranks among the most unequal countries in Europe (Barone & Ruggera, 2018; Braga, Checchi, & Meschi, 2015). It is also remarkable that this influence is less mediated than elsewhere by school performance. For instance, school results mediate less than half of the association between social origins and track choice (Azzolini & Contini, 2016; Contini & Scagni, 2013). The influence of family background on educational attainment has declined significantly in the birth cohorts schooled in the 1950s and 1960s, while in recent cohorts it shows a high degree of persistence (Ballarino & Schadee, 2008; Barone, Schizzerotto, & Luijkx, 2010; Shavit & Westerbeek, 1997). The relationship between social class and track choice displays a considerable degree of stability in the long run (Ballarino & Panichella, 2014). At the same time, it should be noted that the incidence of students from low-educated families has declined sharply. For instance, between 2000 and 2015, their share declines from 31 to 19%, as reported in Table 5.1.

In Italy, inequalities by family background are strongly intertwined with inequalities by immigrant status and area of residence. In this country, immigration is a relatively recent phenomenon and the presence of immigrant students was quite negligible until the mid-1990s. Since then, their share has started to increase, as reported in Table 5.1, and research has documented that these students are systematically overrepresented among low-achievers, dropouts, and students in the vocational track (Azzolini & Contini, 2016). Because immigrant parents are strongly overrepresented in unskilled, low-income, precarious jobs (even when they

Table 5.1 Trend in the distribution of parents' education and migrant status (PISA) (column proportions)

	2000	2003	2006	2009	2012	2015
ISCED 2 or less	0.31	0.29	0.28	0.24	0.20	0.19
ISCED 3/4	0.46	0.36	0.46	0.43	0.43	0.42
ISCED 5/6	0.23	0.35	0.26	0.33	0.38	0.40
Total	1.00	1.00	1.00	1.00	1.00	1.00
N	1085	11336	21554	28916	28599	10069
Native	0.98	0.98	0.96	0.96	0.94	0.93
Non-native	0.02	0.02	0.04	0.04	0.06	0.07
Total	1.00	1.00	1.00	1.00	1.00	1.00
N	1094	11153	21260	29030	28285	10003

have high-level qualifications), social class correlates with immigrant status and mediates about half of the gap between non-natives and natives in track choice and dropout risks (Azzolini & Barone, 2013). This gap declines substantially in the second generations and is weakest among Eastern European and Southern American nationalities and strongest among Northern African nationalities (Azzolini & Contini, 2016).

The socioeconomic gap between the rich regions of Northern and Central Italy and the poor regions of the South is a core social divide (Benadusi et al., 2010). Relative poverty rates are more than three times higher in Southern Italy (Istat, 2018), youth unemployment risks are two times as high, and the net income per household is 37% higher in Northern Italy than in the South (Istat, 2015). Hence, the incidence of low-SES families is higher in Southern Italy. Southern students underperform substantially in the achievement tests and are exposed to higher dropout risks (Bratti, Checchi, & Filippin, 2007).

Finally, it should be noted that male low-SES students are substantially more at risk of low test scores and school grades than their female counterparts. They are also more likely to enrol into vocational tracks and to leave the education system early. For PISA test scores, it is well-documented that female students enjoy a strong advantage in reading and a moderate disadvantage in math, while gender differences in science are negligible (Organisation for Economic Co-operation and Development, 2017b).

It should be noted that while the results that we have summarized in this section are well-established in the literature concerning the Italian case, we lack trend analyses concerning the evolution of social inequalities in compulsory education for the more recent years (2000–2015). This research gap partly reflects a lack of suitable data, since national register data are not yet accessible and no repeated, nationwide survey is available to analyze the longitudinal evolution of educational careers in primary and secondary education. We have thus decided to resort to the PISA data to analyze the evolution of the social gradients in student skills and track choices.

5.3 The Evolution of Social Inequalities in Italian Upper Secondary Education: Methods and Results

For the analyses, we use the 2000–2015 waves of PISA data.[2] In Italy, students aged 15 years attend the first or the second year of upper secondary school. We exclude from the analytical sample students attending lower secondary education or vocational training courses (approximately 3% of the total).

---

[2]Results obtained from the 2000 survey should be interpreted with caution because a relatively large proportion of students did not provide enough information to impute an achievement score. Excluding the cases that have a non-imputable score in at least one domain, the resulting sample is

The outcome variables are the student scores in reading, mathematics, and science based on the five plausible values used in PISA, and the attendance of the academic track (*liceo*) at age 15. Unfortunately, no reliable data source is available to measure social inequalities in student dropout risks.

The main independent variable is parental education, coded into three categories of the ISCED classification: primary or lower secondary (ISCED 1–2), upper secondary (ISCED 3–4), and tertiary (ISCED 5–6). We will present results concerning the gaps between children from low-educated families and from a tertiary education background. In some control analyses that we comment below, we have replaced parental education with the ESCS index commonly used in the analyses of the PISA data. For both measures of family background, we apply the dominance criterion, which selects the highest educational or occupational level of the parents.

Our covariates are gender, country of birth (Italy vs. abroad), and area of residence (North, Centre, South). We have also estimated models that incorporate the upper secondary track (general, technical, vocational), which is recognized in the literature as a major mediator of family background effects. We take into account the complex survey design of PISA using the PISA replicate weights. In estimating the uncertainty associated with the plausible values of achievement scores, we consider both the sampling error and the imputation error deriving from the testing procedures. We adjust the standard errors of the regression estimates to take into account school-level clustering. The graphs show the marginal values of the regression models.

As reported in Fig. 5.1, which plots the imputed values extrapolated from the OLS models, the gap in the attendance rates of the academic track by parental education at age 15 has narrowed over the period under consideration. In 2003, less than a fifth (18%) of children from low-educated families (ISCED 1–2) attended the academic track, while in 2015 this proportion increased to almost one-third (29%), which is a larger increase than that experienced by children from a high ISCED background, which moved from a 57% to a 63% attendance rate. The difference in the trend between the two groups expressed in terms of log odds is significant at the 5% level. Despite this reduction in the gap between the two groups (−5%), the gap itself remains substantial (34%).

The 2010/2011 reform of the academic track, which created new curricula in the academic track, and most notably some curricula that do not involve the study of Latin and philosophy, may have contributed to this limited equalization, since these school subjects are taken more often by upper-class students, and thus represents a highbrow cultural barrier to enrolment in the academic track for low-SES students.

---

reduced from almost 5000 to slightly more than 1000 cases. Assuming that the missing cases are missing at random, as the Organisation for Economic Cooperation and Development (OECD) and INVALSI do, those numbers are probably sufficient for the main, aggregate analysis, yet they are less reliable for the subgroup analysis. For this reason, when we test the significance of the changes in educational inequality over time, we use the 2003 survey as the starting point of the time series. The inclusion or exclusion of the 2000 wave does not substantially affect our main conclusions concerning the evolution of educational inequalities in Italy.

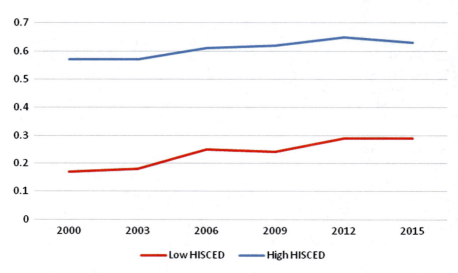

Fig. 5.1 Academic track attendance gap by parents' ISCED (estimates obtained from PISA)

However, it should be noted that the trend starts before this reform, in the early years 2000s.

The achievement gaps by parents' education did not change over time, except possibly for science. As can be seen from Fig. 5.2 concerning math achievement, the trends for the two groups move perfectly in parallel, and the same applies for reading achievement (Fig. 5.3). For science (Fig. 5.4), the gap is significantly reduced from almost 40–30 points, thanks to the skills improvements of children from low-educated families; yet the reduction of social inequalities is only

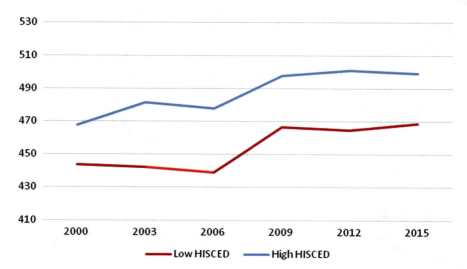

Fig. 5.2 Math achievement gap by parents' ISCED (estimates obtained from PISA plausible values)

5 Socioeconomic Inequality and Student Outcomes in Italy

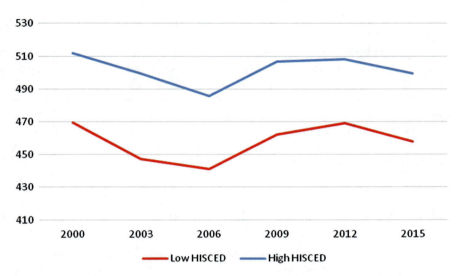

Fig. 5.3 Reading achievement gap by parents' ISCED (estimates obtained from PISA plausible values)

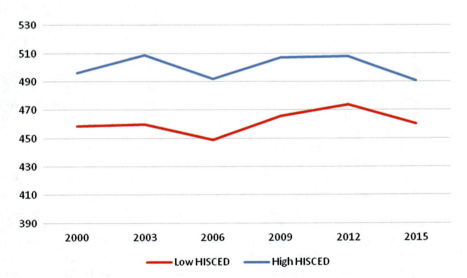

Fig. 5.4 Science achievement gap by parents' ISCED (estimates obtained from PISA plausible values)

significant at the 13% level when comparing the achievement gap by parents' education in 2003 with that of 2015.

In some additional analyses (available upon request), we have considered the evolution of these educational gaps separately for female and male students and for natives and non-native students, and the broad picture does not change. The only notable change in the achievement gap is the one occurring in the Northern regions, where the gap in reading scores by parental education shrunk from 48 to 25 and this reduction is highly significant ($p < 0.01$). Similar patterns occur for the other domains. At the same time, the gap is stable in the Central and Southern regions (results available upon request).

5.4 The Evolution of the Policy Context

The evolution of the Italian socioeconomic and institutional context in the period under consideration has not been particularly favorable to a reduction of educational inequalities. After an initial period of slow economic growth in the early 2000s, Italy has faced a strong and prolonged economic recession between 2008 and 2015. The marked income inequalities that characterize this country, with a Gini index only slightly lower than those observed in the U.S. and the U.K., have continued to increase since the mid-1980s (Brandolini, 2017), parallel to a substantial growth of precarious jobs and unemployment risks (Reyneri, 2014). Due to the crisis of public finances, welfare coverage of unemployed and low-income families has remained at extremely low levels in this period, despite the growing risks of economic insecurity.

The institutional architecture of the educational system has remained largely unchanged (Benadusi & Giancola, 2014). Indeed the fundamental structure of a tripartite model with tracking age at 14 and strong differences in the curricula, prestige, selectivity, and social profiles of the three tracks has persisted in Italy since 1942; that is, it dates back to the Fascist regime. As mentioned above, since the late 1990s Italian schools have enjoyed an increasing level of curricular and organizational autonomy, but the centralistic and bureaucratic control of the national level has remained largely prevalent.

Moreover, the funding of the school system has been substantially reduced in the period under consideration (Organisation for Economic Co-operation and Development, 2017a, 2017b). Income support for low-SES students is negligible in primary and secondary education. Affirmative action policies and interventions to redirect resources towards the most disadvantaged school contexts are virtually absent—and actually not even debated—in Italy. Educational support programmes for disadvantaged students (low-educated parents, immigrant families) are extremely scant and they are largely developed on the initiative of single schools or teachers, in the absence of a nationwide policy framework. More generally, the reduction of social inequalities in education is a marginal issue in public debates, as well as in the agenda of policymakers. In the period under consideration, the initiatives to reduce the cultural, social and economic barriers that hinder school success for disadvantaged students have been very limited in scope.

Within this highly inertial situation, two significant changes in the institutional structure of the Italian school system in the period under consideration can be mentioned. First, compulsory education has been raised from 14 to 15 in 1999 and then to 16 in 2006. These reforms have been implemented in a context where the objective of reducing early high school dropouts and increasing upper secondary completion rates has become a priority in the agenda, also following some pressures from the European institutions. As explained above, due to data limitations we are unfortunately unable to analyze the evolution of social inequalities in dropout rates. Second, the curricular differences between academic and technical schools have been softened in 2009, thanks to the introduction of some intermediate curricula in the academic track that do not comprise Latin and philosophy.

5.5   Concluding Remarks

Overall, socioeconomic inequalities in education have been broadly stable in Italy during the period under consideration. On one hand, inequalities by parental education in track choice, which impact so heavily on inequalities in higher education, are comparatively strong and have diminished very slowly. To illustrate, a decline of only five percentage points over the 12 years out of an initial gap of 39 points means that, if we plot for the future the linear trend that we have detected between 2003 and 2015, it would take more than 80 years to erase these educational inequalities. We cannot wait that long. These results are in line with the relatively strong influence of family background on track choices and high school completion found in previous research (Barone & Ruggera, 2018; Braga, Checchi, & Meschi, 2015). However, the small decline in inequality in participation in the academic track is a significant finding in the light of the high degree of persistence of intergenerational inequalities found in recent cohorts (Ballarino & Schadee, 2008; Barone, Schizzerotto, & Luijkx, 2010). The 2010/2011 reform of the academic track which created new curricula in the academic track that do not involve the study of Latin and philosophy might also have played a role in this equalization, but it should be born in mind that the trend started in the early years 2000s, that is, before the reform was introduced. Moreover, it should be borne in mind that we currently do not know whether students who take these less selective academic tracks enjoy similar opportunities in higher education than students in the traditional academic tracks.

On the other hand, socioeconomic inequalities in skill development are overall unchanged across domains for both male and female students. Only the Northern regions show a mild reduction of inequality in achievement by social origins. It should be noted that these skill gaps are not very pronounced in comparison with those observed in other OECD countries, but also that inequalities in skill development are not a high-stake issue in Italy (Sestito, 2016). As explained above, student scores in standardized tests have no direct implication for grade advancement or for track decisions, and the final exam in upper secondary education does not involve any standardized testing of student skills. At the same time, the credentialist nature of the Italian labor market implies that the possession of relevant educational qualifications is far more relevant than the actual skill levels. The incentives to develop high skill levels are undermined in an economic context characterized by a remarkably low share of skilled occupations, and where informal connections play a major role in job search processes. Credentials and social networks, more than skills, are the key drivers of social competition in education in Italy. Unsurprisingly, in Italy, the average levels of student skills as measured in PISA are far below the OECD average.

The strong social inequalities characterizing educational attainment in the Southern and Central regions are a longstanding issue. There is a large economic and social divide between the richer Northern regions and the other regions, where the incidence of low-SES families is higher and students underperform in the achievement tests. Conversely, students in the Northern regions perform well above the cross-country average in PISA tests (Bratti, Checci, & Filippin, 2007).

Overall, the inertia of educational inequalities in Italy is unsurprising in light of our analysis of the structural and institutional context that characterizes this country. In a context of economic stagnation and increasing socioeconomic insecurity, where financial and educational support to disadvantaged students is remarkably weak, the fact that educational inequalities at the upper secondary level have not increased may be even regarded as a "partial success".

References

Argentin, G., Barbieri, G., & Barone, C. (2017). Origini sociali, consiglio orientativo e iscrizione al liceo: un'analisi basata sui dati dell'Anagrafe Studenti [Social origin, educational counseling and high school enrollment: An analysis based on enrollment data]. *Italian Journal of Social Policy/Rivista delle politiche sociali, 4*(1), 53–74. https://doi.org/10.7389/86412.

Argentin, G., & Triventi, M. (2015). The North-South divide in school grading standards: New evidence from national assessments of the Italian student population. *Italian Journal of Sociology of Education, 7*(2), 157–185. https://doi.org/10.14658/pupj-ijse-2015-2-7.

Azzolini, D., & Barone, C. (2013). Do they progress or do they lag behind? Educational attainment of immigrants' children in Italy. *Research in Social Stratification and Mobility, 31*, 82–96. https://doi.org/10.1016/j.rssm.2012.11.002.

Azzolini, D., & Contini, D. (2016). Performance and decisions: Immigrant–native gaps in educational transitions in Italy. *Journal of Applied Statistics, 48*(1), 98–114. https://doi.org/10.1080/02664763.2015.1036845.

Azzolini, D., & Schnell, P. (2015). The academic achievements of immigrant youths in new destination countries: Evidence from southern Europe. *Migration Studies, 3*(2), 217–240. https://doi.org/10.1093/migration/mnu040.

Ballarino, G., & Schadee, H. (2008). La disuguaglianza delle opportunità educative in Italia, 1930–1980: Tendenze e cause [The inequality of educational opportunities in Italy, 1930-1980: Trends and causes]. *Polis, 22*(3), 373–402. https://doi.org/10.1424/28282.

Ballarino, G., & Panichella, N. (2014). Origini familiari, scuola secondaria e accesso all'università dei diplomati italiani, 1995–2007 [Family origins, secondary school and access to the university of Italian graduates, 1995–2007]. *Scuola Democratica: Strategie Educative e Territorio, 5*(2), 365-392. https://doi.org/10.12828/77422.

Barone, C., & Ruggera, L. (2018). Educational equalization stalled? Trends in inequality of educational opportunity between 1930 and 1980 across 26 European nations. *European Societies, 20*(1), 1–25. https://doi.org/10.1080/14616696.2017.1290265.

Barone, C., Schizzerotto, A., & Luijkx, R. (2010). Elogio dei grandi numeri: Il lento declino delle disuguaglianze nelle opportunita di istruzione in Italia [Praise of big numbers: The slow decline in inequality in education opportunities in Italy]. *Polis, 24*(1), 5–34.

Benadusi, L., Fornari, R., & Giancola, O. (2010). Così vicine, così lontane. La questione dell'equità scolastica nelle regioni italiane [So close, so far: The question of school equity in Italian regions]. *Scuola Democratica: Learning for Democracy, 1,* 52–79.

Benadusi, L., & Giancola, O. (2014). Saggio introduttivo: sistemi di scuola secondaria comprensivi versus selettivi. Una comparazione in termini di equità [Introductory essay: Secondary school systems including selective versus. A comparison in terms of equity]. *Scuola Democratica: Learning for Democracy, 2,* 461–482.

Benadusi, L., & Giancola, O. (2016). Per una valutazione bilanciata nel sistema educativo italiano [For a balanced assessment in the Italian educational system]. In P. Ladri & A. Maccarini (Eds.), *Uno specchio per la valutazione della scuola: paradossi, controversie, vie di uscita* (pp. 49–64). Milan, Italy: Franco Angeli.

Braga, M., Checchi, D., & Meschi, E. (2015). *Institutional reforms and educational attainment in Europe: A long run perspective* (IZA Discussion Paper No. 6190). Retrieved from ftp.iza.org/dp6190.pdf.

Brandolini, A. (2017). *Income inequality in Italy: Facts and measurement* (pp. 55–87). XLIV Riunione Scientifica, CLEUP, Padova. Retrieved from http://www.sis-statistica.org/old/htdocs/files/pdf/atti%20pubblicati%20da%20Cleup_55-77.pdf.

Bratti, M., Checci, D., & Filippin A. (2007). Territorial differences in Italian students' mathematical competencies: Evidence from PISA 2003 (IZA Discussion Paper No. 2603). Retrieved from ftp.iza.org/dp2603.pdf.

Contini, D., & Scagni, A. (2013). Social origin inequalities in educational careers in Italy: Performance or decision effects? In M. Jackson (Ed.), *Determined to succeed? Performance versus choice in educational attainment* (pp. 149–184). Stanford, CA: Stanford University Press.

De Vita, L., & Giancola, O. (2017). Between Education and Employment: Women's Trajectories in STEM Fields. *Polis, 31*(1), 45–72.

Fondazione Giovanni Agnelli. (2011). *Rapporto sulla scuola in Italia* [Report on schools in Italy]. Rome, Italy: Laterza.

Giancola, O. (2010). *Performance e disuguaglianze nei sistemi educativi Europei. Un tentativo di spiegazione del "caso" italiano* [Performance and inequality in European education systems: An attempt to explain the Italian "case"]. Rome, Italy: Aracne Editrice.

Giancola, O., & Fornari, R. (2011). Policies for decentralization, school autonomy and inequalities in educational performance among the Italian regions: Empirical evidence from Pisa 2006. *Italian Journal of Sociology of Education, 8*(2), 150–172. https://doi.org/10.14658/pupj-ijse-2011-2-8.

Giancola, O., & Viteritti, A. (2014). Distal and proximal Vision: A multi-perspective research in sociology of education. *European Educational Research Journal, 13*(1), 47–57. https://doi.org/10.2304/eerj.2014.13.1.47.

Grimaldi, E., & Serpieri, R. (2012). The transformation of the education state in Italy: A critical policy historiography from 1944 to 2011. *Italian Journal of Sociology of Education, 10*(1), 146–180. https://doi.org/10.14658/pupj-ijse-2012-1-7.

INVALSI. (2017). *Rilevazioni nazionali degli apprendimenti 2016–2017* [National surveys of 2016-2017 learning]. Retrieved from https://invalsi-areaprove.cineca.it/docs/file/Rapporto_Prove_INVALSI_2017.pdf.

Istat. (2015). *Condizioni di vita e di reddito* [Living and income conditions]. Rome, Italy: Author.

Istat. (2018). *Noi-italia*. Rome, Italy: Author. Retrieved from http://noi-italia.istat.it/.

Mullis, I. V. S., Martin, M. O., Foy, P., & Hooper, M. (2016). *TIMSS 2015 international results in mathematics*. Chestnut Hill, MA: TIMSS & PIRLS International Study Center, Boston College.

Organisation for Economic Co-operation and Development. (2017a). *Education at a glance*. Paris, France: OECD Publishing. Retrieved from https://www.oecd-ilibrary.org/education/education-at-a-glance-2017_eag-2017-en.

Organisation for Economic Co-operation and Development. (2017b). *PISA country report: Italy*. Paris, France: OECD Publishing.

Organisation for Economic Co-operation and Development. (2018). *Education at a glance*. Paris, France: OECD Publishing. Retrieved from https://www.oecd-ilibrary.org/education/education-at-a-glance-2018_eag-2018-en.

Panichella, N., & Triventi, M. (2014). Social inequalities in the choice of secondary school: Long-term trends during educational expansion and reforms in Italy. *European Societies, 16* (5), 666–693. https://doi.org/10.1080/14616696.2014.939685.

Raimondi, E., Barone, C., & De Luca, S. (2013). Origini sociali, risorse culturali familiari e apprendimenti nelle scuole primarie: Un'analisi dei dati Pirls 2006 [Social origins, family cultural resources and learning in primary schools: An analysis of PIRLS 2006 data]. *Quaderni di Sociologia, 61*, 34–49. Retrieved from https://journals.openedition.org/qds/481.

Reyneri, E. (2014). *Sociologia del mercato del lavoro* [Sociology of the labor market]. Bologna, Italy: Mulino.

Romito, M. (2016). *Una scuola di classe: Orientamento e disuguaglianza nelle transizioni scolastiche* [A school of class: Orientation and inequality in school transitions]. Milan, Italy: Guerini.

Shavit, Y., & Westerbeek, K. (1997). Educational Stratification in Italy: Reforms, expansion and equality of opportunity. *European Sociological Review, 14*, 33–47.

Sestito, P. (2016). *La scuola imperfetta: Idee per spezzare un circolo vizioso* [The imperfect school: Ideas to break a vicious circle]. Bologna, Italy: Mulino.

Triventi, M. (2014). Le disuguaglianze di istruzione secondo l'origine sociale. Una rassegna della letteratura sul caso italiano. *Scuola Democratica: Learning for Democracy, 2*, 321–342. https://doi.org/10.12828/77420.

Triventi, M., & Trivellato, P. (Eds.). (2015). *L'istruzione superiore: Caratteristiche, funzionamento e risultati* [Higher education: Characteristics, function and results]. Milan, Italy: Carocci.

Chapter 6
Socioeconomic Inequality and Student Outcomes in Spanish Schools

Álvaro Choi and Jorge Calero

Abstract International assessments show that the performance of Spanish students in core cognitive competencies is close to the international average and its socioeconomic gradient is below the mean of Organisation for Economic Co-operation and Development (OECD) countries. Additionally, the performance gap between students in socioeconomically advantaged and socioeconomically disadvantaged schools is relatively small. While these may be seen as remarkable facts, given the comparatively low socioeconomic level of Spanish families and the depth of the scars of the economic crisis, a closer look uncovers a more complex reality. For example, the likelihood of low performance and grade repetition among socioeconomically disadvantaged students relative to non-disadvantaged students is high and important differences across regions still prevail. In this chapter, we describe the recent evolution and situation of socioeconomic inequalities of school-aged Spanish students and discuss the policies that have been applied to tackle the socioeconomic-based performance gap. These policies have been developed within the framework of changing state-level general education acts and designed and applied at the regional level.

Keywords Student achievement · Socioeconomic status · Inequality · Spain

6.1 Introduction

The Spanish education system establishes compulsory education for children between 6 and 16 years of age. However, schooling in the earlier stage—that corresponding to pre-primary education between the ages of 3 and 5—has grown rapidly so that it is now practically universal (in 2015, 94.9% at 3 years old and 97.9% at 5 years old). In fact, since the application of the General Law of the

---

Á. Choi (✉) · J. Calero
Universitat de Barcelona, Barcelona, Spain
e-mail: alvarochoi@ub.edu

© Springer Nature Singapore Pte Ltd. 2019
L. Volante et al. (eds.), *Socioeconomic Inequality and Student Outcomes*, Education Policy & Social Inequality 4,
https://doi.org/10.1007/978-981-13-9863-6_6

Education System (LOGSE) in the 1990s, the choice of school for compulsory education, in most cases, is made at 3 years old. Knowing that priority is granted to students already enrolled in the school at the time of opting for a place in the first year of primary education, families enroll students at 3 years of age in the school where they wish them to remain during primary education. Moreover, since 2008, education for children between 3 and 5 years of age is free for families, since it is financed by the public sector.

Compulsory education is divided into two stages in Spain. Primary education covers 6 years, starting at 6 years of age, while lower secondary education (Compulsory Secondary Education, ESO) is completed in 4 years, beginning at age 12. The system is comprehensive, with no possibility of choosing alternative itineraries until the 4th year of lower secondary education. In the 4th year, itineraries are introduced, which vary across the different regions (autonomous communities).

The share of students in public schools in the Spanish primary and lower secondary education is low with only 67.7% (the European Union average is 86.7%) and 65.8% (the European Union average is 77.4%), respectively.[1]

Many of the privately owned schools cover most of their costs with public financing, in a system that is rare in the rest of European countries. In this system, private schools (religious and lay) can sign an agreement (in Spanish, *concierto*) with the Educational Administration by which they commit themselves to schooling the students in conditions of gratuity and to admit them according to the same criteria as public schools. On the other hand, the schools receive public transfers to cover current expenses (essentially, personal expenses). The system of public financing of private schools was formalized in 1985, as a system designed to guarantee families' capacity of choice. It was initially oriented to facilitate schooling in the schools of the Catholic Church, In fact, it has configured an educational quasi-market in which public financing "follows" the demand made by families—28.5% of the Spanish students of primary education are enrolled in private charter schools, a percentage that reaches 30.7% in lower secondary. The rest of the students (3.8% in primary education and 3.5% in lower secondary) attend independent private schools, which do not receive public funding.

To understand the evolution of students in Spanish compulsory education, it is necessary to focus on two variables that have changed markedly in recent decades. We refer, on the one hand, to the fertility rate and, on the other, to changes in the immigrant population. The fertility rate in Spain is among the lowest in the world, with a value of 1.32 children per woman in 2016, and it has always remained below 1.5 since 1990 (it was 2.80 in 1976). On the other hand, the rapid arrival of immigrant populations started in Spain at the end of the 1990s, coinciding with a period of economic growth that continued until 2007. During these years, the rate of incorporation of immigrant students into the Spanish education system was among

---

[1]For the distribution of students according to the ownership of the school, see Ministerio de Educación, Cultura y Deporte (MECD, 2017) and Eurostat on-line database.

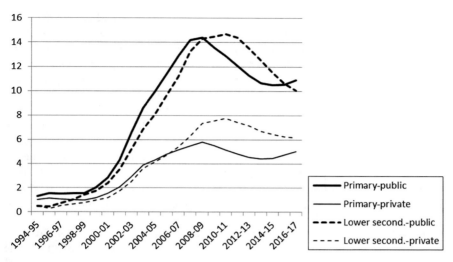

Fig. 6.1 Percent of immigrants enrolled in the Spanish compulsory schools over time and by school type. *Source* Own elaboration from student's statistics of *Ministerio de Educación y Formación Profesional*

the highest in Europe, leading to a visible strain on the system. The sociocultural and economic educational segregation increased, since a far greater than proportional number of immigrant students enrolled in the public schools of popular neighborhoods. Figure 6.1 shows the evolution of the enrollment of foreign students in compulsory education in the last two decades.

The Great Recession, which lasted far longer in Spain than in any other OECD countries, led to a sudden halt of new immigrant students. Since 2015, however, the incoming migrant flow has started to grow again.

An extremely important characteristic of education programs in Spanish compulsory education is the high incidence of repetition of the academic year. In 2015, 31.3% of 15-year-old Spanish students had repeated 1 or more years (compared to an 11.3% average for other OECD countries). In the case of primary school students, repetition affected 12.8% of Spanish students (6.4% in the OECD average). The incidence of repetition is very diverse in the different regions, ranging from 21% in the case of the region of Catalonia to 40% in the Balearic Islands at 15 years of age (OECD, 2016a, 2016b). It is a choice of action in schools that is largely detached from the skills acquired by students, since it can be seen how, with equal cognitive skills, Spanish students tend to fail and repeat years more frequently than their counterparts in other European countries.

The repetition of academic years during compulsory education anticipates another problem that is most important in the Spanish educational system—early school leaving. At the end of compulsory education, a very high proportion of young Spaniards do not continue studying. In 2017, this proportion stood at 18.3%, while the average of the European Union-28 was 10.6%. Only Malta, with 18.6%, had a higher value for this indicator in Europe. Early school leaving had reached 31.7% in 2008,[2] but it dropped rapidly during the Great Recession, due to the drop in the opportunity cost of studies, derived from the enormous youth unemployment that arose during those years. In recent years, the recovery of employment has slowed down the drop in the early school leaving rate, which started to pick up slightly in the second half of 2017 and the first quarter of 2018.[3] The reduction in early abandonment, which was good news for the Spanish educational system, may have had an important short-term component, corresponding to the evolution of the labor market during the Great Recession, rather than to any structural change in how Spanish youth value post-compulsory education as a long-term investment. The post-Great Recession labor market, with a rebound in the creation of jobs with low added value (and very low salaries) for young people, may once again constitute a "trap" for the training trajectories of young Spaniards.

We will finish this section with a brief reference to how public spending allocated to the education system has been substantially reduced since 2010. The austerity policies imposed since that year have led to a total reduction of 7000 million Euros per year in public education spending, comparing the figures for 2016 and 2010. This cut, equivalent to 0.7 percentage points of GDP, has affected public schools much more intensely. The private education sector has enjoyed a slight increase in its total funding, as some regional governments have favored the creation of government-subsidized private schools. Budget cuts have particularly affected the availability of regular teachers and support staff in public schools.

6.2 The Socioeconomic Profile of Spanish Students

Socioeconomic status (SES) may be proxied through different variables. Throughout this chapter, we have selected parental education as our preferred SES-proxy as it is less likely to change across time than alternative variables, such as books at home or occupational status. More specifically, we define low-SES students as those living in a household where the maximum educational level of parents is below level 3 in the ISCED 1997 scale; that is, for the Spanish case, students whose parents have not completed post-compulsory secondary education. High-SES students are defined as those whose parents have completed at least level ISCED 5A (Bachelor's or equivalent level).

Applying this definition to data from the OECD's 2015 Programme for International Student Assessment (PISA), 24.9, 36.5, and 38.6% of Spanish

---

[2]Source: Retrieved from the EUROSTAT Database: http://ec.europa.eu/eurostat/tgm/table.do?tab=table&plugin=1&language=en&pcode=t2020_40.

[3]Source: Retrieved from the INE (*Instituto Nacional de Estadística*) Database: http://www.ine.es/dyngs/INEbase/es.

15-year-old students come from low, middle, and high-SES backgrounds, respectively. The analogous figures for the OECD average were 16.7, 46.3, and 37.7%. Indeed, while the share of low-SES households is higher in Spain, the percentage of high-SES ones is very similar to the OECD average. This is congruent with the hourglass structure of the educational endowment of the Spanish adult population, where a high percentage of university graduates coexist with a small share of adults who have completed, at most, intermediate studies (ISCED 3 and 4 levels), and a large proportion of adults who have completed, at most, compulsory education. At the same time, the progressive expansion of the education system has led to a significant improvement in the SES of Spanish households during the last decade— the percentage of students from low, middle, and high-SES backgrounds were, according to PISA 2006 microdata, 36.3, 38.1, and 25.6%, respectively.

The distribution of Spanish students by SES is however heterogeneous across regions and subgroups such as immigrants and the Roma community. The SES background of students varies widely across Spanish regions (*Comunidades Autónomas*). In regions such as the Basque Country or Madrid, less than 15% of students come from disadvantaged backgrounds, while approximately half of the students live in high-SES households. In contrast, in Andalucía and Extremadura, around 38% of children come from low-SES backgrounds, and only around 30% from high-SES ones.

As has been described in the introduction, one of the main challenges faced by the Spanish education system during the 2000 decade was the arrival of students from abroad. The socioeconomic composition of first and second-generation immigrant students differs from that of the native students. According to PISA 2015, 24.7% of the latter were low-SES households; the respective figures for first- and second-generation immigrant households were 22.6 and 33.2%. While 39.2% of 15-year-old native students had a high-SES profile, only 35.9 and 30.4% of first- and second-generation immigrant households came from highly educated backgrounds. The existence of heterogeneous situations across the immigrant collective must, however, be acknowledged.[4]

Most studies highlight the low SES of families from some specific ethnic groups. For example, applying our SES definition to the data provided by the Ministry of Education, Science and Sports (MECD, 2013), 95.8% of Roma students come from low-SES backgrounds. Although there has been a progressive inclusion of Roma students in the education system, early school dropout rates for this group are still above 60%.

It is worth mentioning at this point, as we will come back to this in the last section, that socioeconomic background is a key variable for understanding student segregation across schools in Spain. Students from disadvantaged backgrounds are predominantly enrolled in public schools (84.5%, at age 15). This percentage is

---

[4]For Spain, the selected definition of SES underestimates the socioeconomic differences between natives and immigrants. The use of alternative definitions, such as occupational category or the ESCS index provided by PISA, increases these differences.

53.1% for high-SES students. Consequently, only 15.5% of low-SES students are enrolled in private schools (14% in publicly funded private schools and 1.5% in private independent schools), while 46.9% of high-SES students attend privately owned schools. Geographical segregation of the population by SES and—although legally banned—student selection by publicly funded private schools are possible explanatory factors.

6.3   Educational Inequalities by Socioeconomic Status

There is a strong positive association between high-SES and educational success in Spain (Table 6.1). By age 15, high-SES students outperform their low-SES counterparts in all the indicators presented in Table 6.1. In Spain, the gap in performance between high- and low-SES students is below the OECD average for the three competencies assessed by PISA. However, the size of the raw SES gaps in the three competencies is still remarkable—approximately 60 points in the PISA metrics, which may be translated into 1.5 academic years. At this point, it is important to stress that the distribution of scores in Spain is more compressed than in most OECD countries (i.e., students concentrate around the mean; OECD, 2016a). This is also visible in Table 6.1, which shows Spain has neither many top performers in the three competencies, nor many poor performers—these being defined as performing above level 4 and below level 2 in PISA, respectively. Thus, although the absolute SES performance gap is low in Spain, it has a large capacity for explaining overall inequalities in educational outcomes.

Grade repetition is widely applied in Spain. By age 15, almost one-third of students have repeated at least one academic year, which is about three times more than students in other OECD countries on average. Half of the low-SES 15-year-old Spanish students have repeated at least 1 year; this figure is 17.1% for high-SES students. Striking as these figures may be, it is also worth underlining that the application of grade repetition in Spain is more SES biased than in other countries— the ratio of the percentage of the repetition rates of low- and high-SES students is larger for Spain (2.95) than in most OECD countries (2.54, on average). This ratio is especially high at the lower secondary school level (3.27). Thus, this should be a matter of concern for Spanish policymakers for obvious equity reasons, but also for efficiency ones, as previous research has consistently described the pernicious effect of grade repetition on academic performance (Choi, Gil, Mediavilla, & Valbuena, 2017; Manacorda, 2012).

Indeed, the previous discussion uncovers a paradox in the Spanish educational system, while 15-year-old students perform relatively well according to international standards and, even more importantly, only a small proportion has a very poor performance—Schleicher (2007) argues that students below level 2 in PISA may be considered to be at risk of early school dropout as there is a high percentage of students with low educational expectations in this group—the percentage of Spanish students with low educational expectations is comparatively high. This may translate, some

6 Socioeconomic Inequality and Student Outcomes …

Table 6.1 Educational outcomes of 15-year-old Spanish students, by socioeconomic status, year 2015

	Average		Low-SES		High-SES	
	ESP	OECD	ESP	OECD	ESP	OECD
Average score in mathematical competencies	486	490	455	435	512	512
Average score in scientific competencies	493	493	460	434	518	519
Average score in reading competencies	496	493	463	434	521	517
Low achievers in the three competencies (%)	11.0	14.1	19.5	31.3	3.1	6.7
High achievers in the three competencies (%)	1.7	3.7	0.6	0.6	6.0	9.9
Students who have repeated at least one year (%)	31.3	11.3	50.5	21.9	17.1	8.6
– In primary education (%)	12.8	6.4	21.9	14.1	7.0	4.7
– In lower secondary education (%)	26.6	5.4	44.9	11.1	13.7	4.2
Students with low educational expectations (%)	13.0	6.1	24.6	12.2	6.2	4.2
Students with high educational expectations (%)	51.0	44.2	44.6	26.2	68.5	57.1

Note Low-SES: students whose parents have completed, at most, lower secondary education; high-SES: students whose parents have completed at least an undergraduate degree. Low achievers: students who perform below level 2 in PISA; high achievers: students who perform above level 4 in PISA. Low educational expectations: students who do not expect to complete post-compulsory education. High educational expectations: students who expect to obtain at least an undergraduate degree. Calculations were derived from the source http://www.oecd.org/pisa/data/2015database/
Source Authors' own elaboration from PISA 2015 microdata

years later, into early school dropout decisions (Ou & Reynolds, 2008). As can be seen in Table 6.1, in Spain, the difference in educational expectations by SES level is also larger than in most developed countries. Thus, while different theories—such as the rigidity and hardness of the educational system and the structure of the labor market, where low-skilled job places had, until the Great Recession, traditionally been abundant—have been put forward as factors to explain the high early school dropout rates (Aparicio-Fenoll, 2016; Guio, Choi, & Escardíbul, 2018), SES inequalities, as Choi and Calero (2013) pointed out, also seem to play an important role in this process. It is remarkable that the percentage of low SES Spanish students with high educational expectations (24.6) is similar to the percentage of high-SES students with high educational expectations for the OECD (26.2).

Among the different subgroups, the situation of immigrant students in Spain seems to be especially complex. Table 6.2 shows that the educational outcomes of immigrant students are systematically lower than those of native students. The educational outcomes of high-SES immigrant students are very similar to those obtained by low-SES native students in Spain. Immigrant students perform worse in the three competencies assessed by PISA, and face higher risks of early school dropout and grade repetition. They are also more extreme in their educational expectations. While the SES of immigrants is lower than that for natives, the educational gaps by SES seem to be lower for the former.

The raw performance gap between low-SES and high-SES students is wider for native students. For native students, the probability of being a low achiever in the three competencies (i.e., having a high risk of early school dropout) is four times larger for low-SES students; for immigrant students, this probability is around 1.7. The same happens when focusing on grade repetition—low-SES native students have a 3.5 higher probability of having repeated at least 1 year by age 15 than their high-SES counterparts. This ratio is 1.5 for immigrant students. Also, the expectations of immigrant students seem to be less affected by their SES than for natives. Interestingly, the educational expectations of low-SES students are similar for immigrant and native students. The same does not hold for high-SES students. As it may be seen, multivariate analyses are needed to disentangle the effects linked to the place of birth and SES. Thus, we performed the following analyses, comprising two sets of regressions. In the first set, using the entire PISA 2015 sample of 15-year-old Spanish students we estimate a model where the score in mathematical

Table 6.2 Educational outcomes of 15-year-old Spanish students, by socioeconomic and immigrant status, year 2015

	Average		Low-SES		High-SES	
	Native	Immig	Native	Immig	Native	Immig
Average score in mathematical competencies	492.01	448.55	460.63	424.41	519.39	462.07
Average score in scientific competencies	499.03	456.80	465.85	424.86	525.05	471.22
Average score in reading competencies	501.52	461.14	468.17	433.31	527.74	472.01
Low achievers in the three competencies (%)	9.39	19.76	17.85	29.66	4.32	17.19
High achievers in the three competencies (%)	1.87	0.82	0.73	0	3.23	2.39
Students who have repeated at least one year (%)	28.52	50.92	66.27	48.18	13.85	44.63
– In primary education (%)	10.46	28.67	18.61	44.58	5.22	22.61
– In lower secondary education (%)	24.61	39.18	43.46	51.63	11.14	35.41
Students with low educational expectations (%)	12.41	15.54	24.26	21.45	5.32	12.64
Students with high educational expectations (%)	34.83	43.59	31.56	31.51	71.07	50.22

Note Low-SES: students whose parents have completed, at most, lower secondary education; high-SES: students whose parents have completed at least an undergraduate degree. Low achievers: students who perform below level 2 in PISA; high achievers: students who perform above level 4 in PISA. Low educational expectations: students who do not expect to complete post-compulsory education. High educational expectations: students who expect to obtain at least an undergraduate degree

Source Own elaboration from PISA 2015 microdata

competencies (which is replicated for the other two competencies, obtaining similar results) depends only on two dummy variables—being a first- and a second-generation immigrant, respectively; thus, the reference category is being a native. Both coefficients are negative, especially for first-generation immigrants, and statistically significant, indicating that native students outperform immigrants. We then add two additional variables controlling for SES. Strikingly, coefficients for the variables flagging immigrant students are not significantly different from the unconditional ones. This indicates that immigrant students face educational issues that are independent of their SES.

In the second set of analyses, we calculate the socioeconomic gradient—defining it as the average distance, measured in PISA points, between high-SES and low-SES students—and split the sample into three—native students, first-generation immigrant students and second-generation immigrant students. This should enable us to determine whether SES has heterogeneous effects depending on immigrant status. The results show that while the socioeconomic gradient for natives and second-generation immigrants are very similar (59 and 57 points, respectively), the gradient for first-generation immigrants is considerably lower (38 points). SES does not affect immigrant and native students equally. Identifying the factors behind these results is beyond the scope of this chapter and remains open to different interpretations. At the same time, any interpretation of the former issue should bear in mind that the definition of our SES variable—based on completed educational levels—does not take into account the quality of education and the heterogeneous composition, by country of origin, of the Spanish immigrant community.

Besides students' family SES, socioeconomic inequalities may affect academic performance through additional channels. For example, the influence of the SES of peers on educational careers has been well documented (Berkowitz, Moore, Astor, & Benbenishty, 2017) and, in some countries, low-SES students may attend schools with less or lower quality resources than high-SES students. While the latter does not seem to hold for the Spanish case (student–teacher ratios and the teachers' level of qualifications are similar in public and private schools, teacher quality measures being similar in both types of schools (Calero and Escardíbul, 2017)), there is a clear concentration of low-SES students in public schools. Thus, low-SES students are facing double jeopardy due to their socioeconomic background. Figure 6.2 confirms this point; it presents the performance gap in mathematics between students enrolled in public schools, students in publicly subsidized private schools, and students in independent private schools. Beginning from the left, the first two bars display the raw performance gap between students by school type. As can be seen, in Spain, students enrolled in private schools outperform those in public schools.

The two central bars show that once we condition on the effect of individual SES using OLS regressions, the advantage of students in publicly subsidized private schools halves, and that for students in independent private schools falls by more

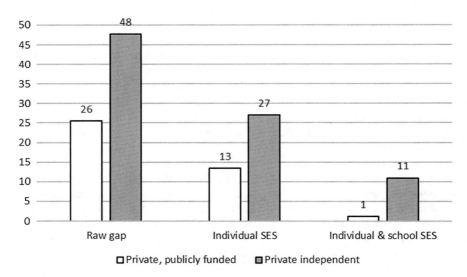

Fig. 6.2 Average performance gap in mathematics between 15-year-old Spanish students enrolled in public schools and students in private, publicly funded and private independent schools before and after controlling for individual and school SES. *Note* The graph displays the results of hierarchical linear models (OLS regressions) that include the following controls: for the raw gap, two dummy variables identifying public funded privately owned schools (the control group are children in public schools); for the third and fourth columns (individual SES), two additional dummies controlling for the SES of students are incorporated. The final model (individual & school SES) adds two dummies that control for the modal SES of the schools. All analyses have incorporated the whole set of plausible values, weights, and replicate weights provided by PISA. Only performance gaps for the first four bars are statistically significant at the 5% level

than 40%. Finally, once we take into account the effect of the SES of schools, measured as the modal level of education of parents in that school, the advantage of publicly subsidized private schools disappears and that for independent private schools shrinks to 11 points approximately. Moreover, the two bars on the right-hand side of Fig. 6.2 are statistically not significant; that is, once we control for the individual and school SES, we cannot state that the difference in performance between public and private schools is different from zero. In other words, in Spain, the main reason why private schools outperform public schools is the different composition by SES of their students. It is worth mentioning too that the above results hold with the independence of the analyzed competency assessed by PISA.

6.4 Education Policies Designed to Address Socioeconomic Disadvantages

Since the 1970s, the orientation of educational policies in Spain has been marked to a large extent by the ideological positions of the parties in government. We refer not only to central governments but also to regional governments. These positions have been translated into a succession of basic educational legislation, which has been aimed at boosting families' ability to choose and the ability of the private sector to generate educational provision autonomously, in the case of conservative governments, and to promote equal access and trajectories in the case of school–left governments. In both cases, policies aimed at promoting equity in the education system have been based more on general principles of design and financing of the system, such as the promotion of universal access to compulsory education or quasi-gratuity, up to 2012, of higher education, than on specific programs aimed at populations at risk of suffering inequalities and/or exclusion from the education system. Specific programs of this type have usually been of a modest magnitude and, very frequently, with serious problems stemming from their lack of continuity and their deficits in terms of evaluation and design. Scholarship programs in Spain, for example, have the characteristics that we have described, designed in 1983, they have reached the present with very little funding, a low coverage rate, and serious design problems. Regarding the level of coverage, Spain is among the European countries where the percentage of expenditure allocated to scholarships and grants is lowest, only 4.9% of the total public education expenditure is allocated to scholarships at pre-university levels (11.4% at the higher education level).

One element that generates important educational inequalities in Spain and which is difficult to resolve through educational policies is the link between urban segregation, educational segregation, and the reproduction of inequalities. Urban segregation is intense and students tend to group in schools according to their sociocultural and economic origin. These segregation processes intensified in the 1999–2008 period as a result of the arrival of the immigrant population (Zinovyeva et al. 2014). In these processes, it has been the public schools that have endured the greatest difficulties derived from the schooling of the immigrant population.

The Spanish educational system also has an important problem related to the access and initial training of its teachers. The teaching profession has little recognition and social prestige and it is not among the priorities of the best students of secondary education to dedicate themselves to it. In addition, students with fewer sociocultural and economic resources attend schools in which the effect of school teachers on performance is lower (see Calero & Escardíbul, 2017). This situation suggests the need for in-depth changes regarding the training and assignment of teachers in compulsory education in Spain.

The situation described above reflects a complex problem for which education policies have yet to find an efficient response. In the last few years, there have been two attempts to overcome the ideological difference between the biggest political parties using extensive negotiations to reach an Education Pact. The first of these attempts was aborted by the *Partido Popular* (conservative) in 2010[5] and the second by the school–left, left-wing, and nationalist parties in 2018—in both cases after several months' work in the parliamentary chambers.

Bearing in mind all of the above, the rest of this section will briefly outline a series of education policy instruments that we consider to be potentially useful for addressing the equity problems of the Spanish education system.

6.4.1 Reduction in Repetition of Academic Year

This intervention is perhaps the most urgent and involves the most immediate consequences for the reduction of educational inequalities in Spain. The repetition of the academic year is a practice that is too deeply rooted in Spanish schools and, also, too arbitrary. It especially harms students with fewer resources. The policies that can be most effective in this regard have been discussed in Choi et al. (2017) and are based on the double principle of individualized treatment and early intervention. The latter is especially relevant if we take into account that Spanish students are left behind before the rest of the students from OECD countries. In fact, Choi and Jerrim (2016) provide robust evidence showing that SES inequality in Spain does not decline between the end of primary and secondary school, thus concluding that SES-based educational inequalities are generated before ages 9/10.

6.4.2 Gratuity of Children's Education from 0 to 3 Years Old

We have seen that after 3 years of age, schooling in children's education is practically universal, despite not being compulsory, and it has been free since 2008. The first cycle of pre-primary education (between 0 and 3 years), however, is not free and has important inequalities in terms of access depending on the region and the ability of families to pay. The now well-established importance of this educational level for future educational and labor trajectories would make it desirable to ensure equal access, through the expansion of the public supply and, in any case, the financial coverage of costs by the public sector.

---

[5]The MECD published in 2010 a document with a series of possible agreements, entitled *Pacto social y político por la educación*. Some of these possible agreements concern the following areas: evaluation of education, promotion of Professional Training, use of ICTs, promotion of plurilingualism, modernization and internationalization of the universities, scholarships and study aids, professional and social recognition of teachers and inclusive education, diversity and interculturality.

6.4.3 Universalization of Upper Secondary Education

As we have mentioned before, the main problem of the Spanish education system is the high level of early school leaving. This is a problem that reflects the socio-cultural and economic inequalities in compulsory education and which, in turn, generates enormous inequalities throughout life, since young people (especially men) who abandon education at age 16 have a high probability of getting jobs with low added value and low wages throughout their lives. The proposal for the universalization of upper secondary education was raised from various positions during the discussions on the Education Pact in 2017 and 2018. In Spain, this universalization would contribute to modifying, gradually, a highly anomalous structure of qualifications, which currently has many people with high and low qualifications and few people with intermediate qualifications. Consider that in 2016 only 24% of employed Spanish adults had upper secondary education (this percentage is twice as high with 48.3% in the European Union); 33.9% of employed persons had a very low level of education (as a maximum lower secondary education), while this percentage is around half with 17.6%in the European Union. The shape of the hourglass is completed with a large group of the population with higher education (42.1% as opposed to 33.9% of the European Union).[6]

The universalization of upper secondary education as an educational policy objective should be accompanied by a substantial increase in the number of students in the vocational branch of this educational level (in Spain, CFGM [*Ciclos Formativos de Grado Medio*]: Middle-Grade Vocational Training). Vocational studies have traditionally had very limited implantation in Spain. Consider that, in 2017, only 33.2% of high school students enrolled in CFGM. The prestige of this type of study is still low; its rate of return in terms of wages and the probability of unemployment are also low. During the Great Recession, the CFGM graduates were the most affected by unemployment. On the other hand, higher vocational education (CFGS [*Ciclos Formativos de Grado Superior*]: Higher Level Vocational Training) has been met with a growing demand in the last 15 years, becoming more widely known among young people who see this qualification more widely accepted by employers.

At the same time, a boost in vocational studies that allows a greater percentage of students from families with few resources to be retained in the education system is a good protection against changes in the productive system, where a great number of low value-added jobs will disappear in the next few years, jobs currently occupied by workers with few qualifications. The extension of Dual Vocational Training may be one of the factors that could contribute to increasing the participation of young people in the education system beyond compulsory education. The Dual FP in Spain, established in 2012, only accounted in 2017 for 3% of upper

---

[6]All of the data referring to the distribution of the population by education level come from the *European Union Labour Force Survey*. Retrieved from the EUROSTAT Database: http://ec.europa.eu/eurostat/web/microdata/european-union-labour-force-survey.

secondary vocational students and presents important problems. Its share should continue to grow and the system should be reformed to improve relationships with companies. However, it should be borne in mind that its implementation in Spain is difficult, due, among other things, to the small average size of companies.

6.4.4 Reduction in School Segregation

The decoupling of the strong relationship between urban segregation and school segregation is not easy since the relationship between them is affected by a variety of economic and sociocultural factors. Among them, one of the most important is the immigrant status of the students. An important factor generating segregation is that groups with fewer resources face more difficulties to access private schools financed with public funds. These, in many cases, have managed to "shield" themselves against the arrival of a low-income immigrant population. Strict compliance with current regulations, which for the time being is circumvented by many schools, would make it possible to guarantee that the gratuity demanded by the regulation should be put into effect. A larger program of travel grants would also help to de-link the place of residence from the possibilities of access to schools.

6.4.5 Modification of Access System and Allocation of Teachers in Compulsory Education

The Spanish health system has excellent access and training procedure for its professionals (doctors and pharmacists). This procedure (MIR in its acronym in Spanish) includes a centralized access test and a training period as a resident in hospitals accredited for training. After several decades of application, it has achieved great prestige and ability to attract talent. We believe that the application of a similar procedure to the education system would improve the prestige of the teaching profession and act, in the medium and long term, as a factor for improving the quality of the education system. Along with such a reform in the access procedure, it would be desirable to establish mechanisms that allow the best teachers to work in the schools where they are most needed; that is, in those where students have fewer sociocultural and economic resources. This would reverse the current trend, which reinforces the processes of reproduction of inequalities.

6.5 Conclusions

The socioeconomic level of the home is one of the main factors that condition the academic performance of Spanish students. Although there is a substantial heterogeneity of situations by groups and by Autonomous Communities, the relevance of the socioeconomic background is around the average of the developed countries. This is reflected in issues such as the breadth of the gap in achievement between students with a high and low socioeconomic level, both in primary and secondary education, and in the probability of having a very low academic performance, of repeating the course—the application of which is highly SES biased in Spain—and of abandoning the educational system prematurely. In fact, the reduction in this last problem, the biggest one facing the Spanish educational system, is limited by the low levels of ascending educational intergenerational mobility for students from low-educated households (OECD 2018).

While it is true that the economic crisis, deeper in Spain than in most OECD countries, has limited the capacity of intervention of the Spanish public sector to combat educational inequalities for socioeconomic reasons, some interventions have contributed to exacerbate them. For example, cuts in the education budget have not been distributed proportionally between public and publicly funded private schools, these cuts affecting the former with greater intensity—students enrolled in public schools have, on average, a lower socioeconomic level. In parallel, there is scope for greater control in the selection processes of students by the publicly funded private schools. Both issues contribute to the creation of two parallel educational systems, financed with public funds, in which the socioeconomic variable constitutes one of the main axes of school segregation.

In addition, the high levels of school repetition, the rigidity of the criteria for accessing upper secondary education and the underdevelopment of the vocational training system have contributed to widening the educational gap by socioeconomic level and perpetuating early school leaving. Changes in the policies described above, as well as the recovery of educational spending levels prior to the crisis, paying special attention to targeted grants and scholarships, would allow the reduction of educational inequalities due to socioeconomic reasons. The evidence for the Spanish case seems to indicate that the policies implemented in the initial educational levels will be more effective for reducing SES-based educational inequalities. The introduction of free education in education from 0 to 3 years appears to be one of the most promising policies in this regard.

References

Aparicio-Fenoll, A. (2016). Returns to education and educational outcomes: The case of the Spanish housing boom. *Journal of Human Capital, 10*(2), 235–265. https://doi.org/10.1086/686154.

Berkowitz, R., Moore, H., Astor, R. A., & Benbenishty, R. (2017). A research synthesis of the associations between socioeconomic background, inequality, school climate, and academic achievement. *Review of Educational Research, 87*(2), 425–469. https://doi.org/10.3102/0034654316669821.

Calero, J., & Escardíbul, J. O. (2017). *La calidad del profesorado en la adquisición de competencias de los alumnos. Un análisis basado en PIRLS-2011*. Madrid, Spain: Fundación

Ramón Areces, Fundación Europea Sociedad y Educación. Retrieved from https://issuu.com/efse/docs/la-calidad-del-profesorado.

Choi, Á., & Calero, J. (2013). Determinantes del riesgo de fracaso escolar en España en PISA-2009 y propuestas de reforma. *Revista de Educación, 362,* 562–593. https://doi.org/10.4438/1988-592X-RE-2013-362-242.

Choi, Á., Gil, M., Mediavilla, M., & Valbuena, J. (2017). The evolution of educational inequalities in Spain: Dynamic evidence from repeated cross-sections. *Social Indicators Research, 138*(3), 853–872. https://doi.org/10.1007/s11205-017-1701-6.

Choi, Á., & Jerrim, J. (2016). The use (and misuse) of PISA in guiding policy reform: The case of Spain. *Comparative Education, 52*(2), 230–245. https://doi.org/10.1080/03050068.2016.1142739.

Guio, J., Choi, Á., & Escardíbul, J.-O. (2018). Labor markets, academic performance and school dropout risk: Evidence for Spain. *International Journal of Manpower, 39*(2), 301–318. https://doi.org/10.1108/IJM-08-2016-0158.

Manacorda, M. (2012). The cost of grade retention. *Review of Economics and Statistics, 94*(2), 596–606. https://doi.org/10.1162/REST_a_00165.

Ministerio de Educación, Cultura y Deporte. (2010). *Pacto social y político por la educación.* Madrid, Spain: Author. Retrieved from http://www.apega.org/attachments/article/254/pacto-educativo-final-22-abril.pdf.

Ministerio de Educación, Cultura y Deporte. (2013). *El alumnado gitano en secundaria. Un estudio comparado.* Madrid, Spain: Author. Retrieved from https://www.gitanos.org/upload/92/20/EstudioSecundaria.pdf.

Ministerio de Educación, Cultura y Deporte. (2017). *Sistema estatal de indicadores de la educación. Edición 2017.* Madrid, Spain: Author. Retrieved from http://www.mecd.gob.es/dctm/inee/indicadores/2017/2017-seie-final-21-julio-2017.pdf?documentId=0901e72b8260b0e1.

Organisation for Economic Co-operation and Development. (2016a). *PISA 2015 results (Volume I): Excellence and equity in education.* Paris, France: OECD Publishing. https://doi.org/10.1787/9789264266490-en.

Organisation for Economic Co-operation and Development. (2016b). *PISA 2015 results (Volume II): Policies and practices for successful schools.* Paris, France: OECD Publishing. https://doi.org/10.1787/9789264267510-en.

Organisation for Economic Co-operation and Development. (2018). *Education at a Glance 2018: OECD Indicators.* Paris, France: OECD Publishing. https://doi.org/10.1787/eag-2018-en.

Ou, S.-R., & Reynolds, A. J. (2008). Predictors of educational attainment in the Chicago longitudinal study. *School Psychology Quarterly, 23*(2), 199–229. https://doi.org/10.1037/1045-3830.23.2.199.

Schleicher, A. (2007). Can competencies assessed by PISA be considered the fundamental school knowledge 15-year-olds should possess? *Journal of Educational Change, 8*(4), 349–357. https://doi.org/10.1007/s10833-007-9042-x.

Zinovyeva, N., Felgueroso, F., & Vazquez, P. (2014). Immigration and student achievement in Spain: Evidence from PISA. *SERIEs—Journal of the Spanish Economic Association, 5*(1), 25–60.

Chapter 7
Socioeconomic Inequality and Student Outcomes in the Netherlands

Jaap Scheerens, Anneke Timmermans and Greetje van der Werf

Abstract In this chapter, we address the educational outcomes of students with low socioeconomic status (SES), both Dutch and with an immigrant background. We indicate how these outcomes have developed over time, and how this development might be related to educational policy measures that seek to enhance the educational opportunities for students with a disadvantaged background. We start with a description of the Dutch school structure and note that the highly tracked secondary school level and high school autonomy are significant features. Next, we provide a short description of the share of low SES parents and primary school students, and how these have evolved over time during the period 2008–2017, while distinguishing between Dutch and immigrant background. The main body of the chapter provides an overview of the outcomes of low SES and immigrant students in primary and secondary education. Finally, we critically comment on the effectiveness and efficiency of the Dutch educational equity policy.

Keywords Student achievement · Socioeconomic status · Inequality · The Netherlands

---

J. Scheerens (✉)
University of Twente, Enschede, The Netherlands
e-mail: j.scheerens@utwente.nl

A. Timmermans · G. van der Werf
University of Groningen, Groningen, The Netherlands

© Springer Nature Singapore Pte Ltd. 2019
L. Volante et al. (eds.), *Socioeconomic Inequality and Student Outcomes*, Education Policy & Social Inequality 4,
https://doi.org/10.1007/978-981-13-9863-6_7

7.1 Introduction: The Dutch School System[1]

7.1.1 The School Structure

Figure 7.1 depicts the school structure in the Netherlands. There are perhaps two features that are particularly worth mentioning. The first is that there is a strong vocational strand, manifested by specialized vocational schooling at the junior and senior secondary level (vmbo and mbo). The second related feature is the strong structural differentiation or tracking at the secondary level combined with a relatively early selection moment for a particular track at the end of primary school.

Full-time education is compulsory from the age of 5 to the age of 16, but pupils can (voluntary) enter primary education at the age of 4. Students who have not acquired a start qualification for the labor market when they leave full-time education are required to follow part-time education until the age of 18. The Dutch education system is divided into three levels: primary, secondary, and tertiary education. Primary schools in the Netherlands cater for children from 4 to 12 years of age. Schools are usually arranged into 8-year groups. Grade retention during primary education is possible and whether a child is retained a grade is decided by the school the child attends. Children in need of special care and attention can attend special schools. Depending on the type of special educational needs, a child can be admitted to specialized schools.

Secondary education is divided into the following:

- Practical education (pro), 12–16 years, for students with special educational needs
- Junior vocational education (vmbo), 12–16 years. This type of education consists of four different tracks: the basic vocational track, preparing students for the lowest levels of senior vocational education (mbo), and the advanced vocational, the theoretical, and the mixed track, each of which prepares students for the two highest levels of senior vocational education. Students who have completed the theoretical or mixed track also can continue in senior general secondary education (havo, see below)
- Senior general secondary education (havo), 12–17 years, preparing for higher professional education or universities for applied sciences (hbo)
- Pre-university education (vwo), 12–18 years, preparing students for university.

Evidently, the system of secondary education is strongly stratified, both within and between schools. After primary education, pupils are selected into one or sometimes two adjacent tracks described above (Korpershoek, Naaijer, & Bosker, 2016). Selection is currently only informed by the primary school teachers' track

---

[1]This section is based on Scheerens, Ehren, Sleegers, and De Leeuw (2012) and Nusche, Braun, Halasz, and Santiago (2014). The latter study is a review of educational evaluation and assessment in the Netherlands by the Organisation for Economic Co-operation and Development (OECD); the former study is a national pre-study to the OECD review.

7 Socioeconomic Inequality and Student Outcomes ...

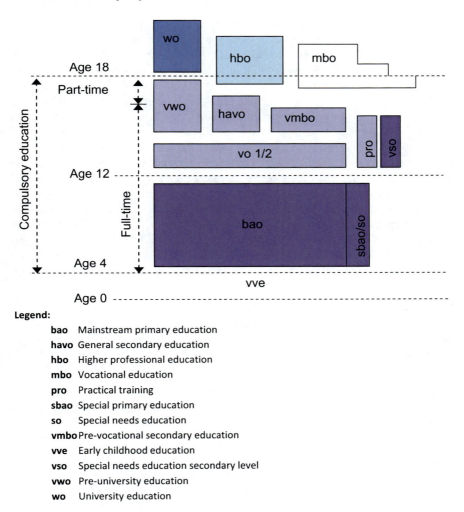

Legend:

bao	Mainstream primary education
havo	General secondary education
hbo	Higher professional education
mbo	Vocational education
pro	Practical training
sbao	Special primary education
so	Special needs education
vmbo	Pre-vocational secondary education
vve	Early childhood education
vso	Special needs education secondary level
vwo	Pre-university education
wo	University education

Fig. 7.1 The Dutch school system

recommendation. Before 2015, track selection was informed by student performance during primary education and the teachers' track recommendation (Timmermans, Kuyper, & van der Werf, 2013). The brightest students attend havo and vwo; the others go to vmbo schools. For many students, the track in which they were selected is decisive for their educational careers; however, grade retention and intermediate upward and downward mobility are possible.

From 1993 onwards, a shared curriculum for students during the first 3 years of secondary education was the official policy (the so-called *Basisvorming* or basic general education). The introduction of basic general education could be seen as an attempt to introduce comprehensive schooling. Despite this attempt, the reality in most schools is streaming in which the differentiation at the upper secondary level is already "foreshadowed." In this respect, the attempt to introduce comprehensive schooling was not successful. The failure of the *Basisvorming* is documented in the 2008 report of the 'Parliamentary Inquiry Committee Educational Innovations' (Ministry of Education, 2008).

At the upper secondary level, the differentiation consists of a havo, a vwo, and a vocational stream of upper secondary education (see below). Diplomas from the havo and vwo track are considered a basic qualification for entering the labor market. In these differentiations/tracks, students choose a particular set of school subjects (or profiles) at the end of grade 3, when the students are approximately 15 years old. In the vmbo tracks, the decision about school subjects is already made at the end of grade 2, when the students are approximately 14 years of age. This latter choice is very decisive as the choices in senior secondary vocational education are highly restricted by the set of school subjects chosen in vmbo (Vugteveen, Timmermans, Korpershoek, van Rooijen, & Opdenakker, 2016). For the havo and vwo tracks, the choice of profiles is, although important, less restrictive for further choices.

Senior vocational education, 16–20 years, is divided into four levels of training:

Level 1: training to assistant level, 6 months–1 year
Level 2: basic vocational training, 2–3 years
Level 3: professional training, 2–4 years
Level 4: middle-management training, 3–4 years, or specialist training, 1–2 years
Adult Education

The purpose of adult education, unlike vocational education, is not to train students for a particular occupation but rather to provide a solid foundation for vocational and secondary education courses and to enable adults to participate in society (social and life skills).

Tertiary education is divided into the following:

- higher professional education (hbo)
- university education (wo)
- open higher distance education (Open University).

Given the scope of this chapter, no further details about adult education and tertiary education will be provided.

7.1.2 Governance

7.1.2.1 School Autonomy and Freedom of Education

The Netherlands has one of the OECD's most devolved education systems, with schools enjoying a high degree of autonomy. Responsibility for education is shared almost entirely between schools and the central government, with no significant intermediate level of educational administration. With regard to ensuring teaching quality, the Dutch Government describes the distribution of responsibilities for educational reform as follows: "the government will establish the objectives of the policy measures (what) while the field itself will decide how best to pursue those objectives (how)."

School autonomy is grounded in the principle of "freedom of education," which is guaranteed by the Dutch Constitution since 1917. Freedom of education gives the right to any natural or legal person to set up a school, to organize teaching, and to determine the (educational, religious, or ideological) principles on which teaching is based. This constitutional arrangement puts public and private schools on an equal footing, with all schools receiving public funding provided that they meet the requirements for schools in their sector. Parents have free school choice, and funding "follows the student," which lays the foundation for potentially strong competition among schools (Nusche et al., 2014, pp. 20–21).

7.1.2.2 Central Steering and Support

The Ministry of Education, Culture and Science has the responsibility for the overall education system, but it does not interfere with the organization of individual schools. The Ministry's responsibilities relate mainly to setting legislation and determining the structure and funding mechanisms of the education system. It can also control the system by setting quantitative or qualitative standards, attainment targets, and examinations. The Minister of Education is also responsible for the evaluation of the quality of education, which is carried out by the Dutch Inspectorate of Education.

Schools and school boards are responsible for ensuring quality at the school level, and the Inspectorate of Education checks that they do so effectively by means of monitoring student performance and school visits. There is also a large intermediary structure of organizations originally created to serve the interests of pressure groups that used to be organized according to religious denominations. In the 1990s, several of these bodies were secularized and merged into Councils for each of the educational sectors. The Council for Primary Education (PO-raad), the Council for Secondary Education (VO-raad), and the Council for Senior Vocational Education (MBO-raad) represent the employers (school boards) of their respective sectors and offer support services to schools, such as a team of "flying brigades" that work with schools identified by the Inspectorate as weak or very weak (Nusche et al., 2014, p. 22).

7.2 Distribution of Socioeconomic Status (SES) Among the Dutch Population and the Students in Primary Education

Parents' educational level is the regular indicator for SES that is used in the Netherlands by researchers, the Central Bureau of Statistics, and the Inspectorate and is usually operationalized as the highest level of education completed by one or both of the students' parents. Because the data that we will present in this chapter are mainly based on secondary sources, we will only use the parental level of education as an indicator of SES. Unfortunately, there is no consistency in the categorization of the level of education based on SES among the different sources. For this reason, we will, where appropriate, explain the details of the different categories of SES when discussing the tables. Also, because the category of low SES students includes a very substantial number of students with a migrant background, who—until very recently—were explicitly one of the most important target groups of the Dutch educational equity policy, we will present the data separately for Dutch students and students with a immigrant (Western and non-Western) background as often as possible.

Table 7.1 shows the distribution of the level of education in the Dutch population across the period from 2010 until 2017, in proportions of the total number of 15–65-year olds belonging to the inhabitants of the Netherlands with respectively a Dutch, a Western, or non-Western immigration background. The data are derived from population data available at Statistics Netherlands, which uses the following categorization of SES: Low = primary education, vmbo, junior havo, or junior vwo (grade 1–3) or mbo1 (no start qualification); Middle = senior havo or vwo, or mbo level 2, 3, or 4 (start qualification); High = Bachelor or Master from higher professional education or university, or a Ph.D. The data show that in all three groups (Dutch, Western, and non-Western background), the share of low SES people in the population is declining over time. The decline is strongest among the people with a non-Western background, from 46.4% in 2010 to 36.6% in 2017, and smallest among inhabitants with a Dutch background, from 31.8% in 2010 to 28.2% in 2017. Nevertheless, the share of low SES people in the population remains the largest among the people with a non-Western migration background.

Table 7.2 shows the distribution of students in kindergarten and primary school across the three levels of SES and migration background across the period 2008 through 2014, in percentages of the total number of students in each year in kindergarten, grade 3, and grade 6 classes, respectively. The data are based on the COOL[5–18] cohort study reported in Driessen, Mulder, Ledoux, Roeleveld, and Van der Veen (2009), Driessen, Mulder, and Roeleveld (2012), and Driessen, Elshof, Mulder, and Roeleveld (2015). COOL[5–18] is a large-scale cohort study monitoring student's educational career from age 5 (kindergarten) to age 18. Data collection took place every 3 years (in 2008, 2011 and 2014), in kindergarten, grade 3 and grade 6 of primary school and Grade 9 of secondary school. SES categories were defined in COOL[5–18] as follows: Low = both parents have completed at the highest

7 Socioeconomic Inequality and Student Outcomes … 117

Table 7.1 Educational level of the Dutch population between 15- and 65-year-olds from 2010 to 2017

Migration background	SES	2010	2011	2012	2013	2014	2015	2016	2017
Dutch	Low	0.318	0.324	0.321	0.303	0.300	0.296	0.295	0.282
	Middle	0.403	0.400	0.397	0.398	0.401	0.400	0.398	0.398
	High	0.273	0.269	0.275	0.286	0.292	0.299	0.302	0.312
Western	Low	0.310	0.316	0.296	0.262	0.266	0.256	0.247	0.248
	Middle	0.368	0.362	0.364	0.403	0.406	0.395	0.399	0.398
	High	0.314	0.314	0.330	0.304	0.304	0.323	0.327	0.329
Non-Western	Low	0.464	0.443	0.416	0.375	0.398	0.400	0.390	0.366
	Middle	0.335	0.345	0.366	0.404	0.380	0.368	0.366	0.379
	High	0.191	0.199	0.202	0.177	0.182	0.189	0.199	0.207

Source: Central Bureau voor de Statistiek (2008)

Table 7.2 Level of parental education for students in Dutch Kindergarten, Grade 3, and Grade 6 classes

SES	Migration background	Kindergarten			Grade 3			Grade 6		
		2008	2011	2014	2008	2011	2014	2008	2011	2014
Low	Dutch	12.2	9.5	8.5	13.4	9.9	8.4	16.7	11.8	9.0
	Non-Western	8.3	5.5	5.8	8.8	5.8	6.9	9.1	6.0	6.3
Middle	Dutch	40.2	38.6	37.6	40.1	38.9	39.6	39.2	39.9	40.3
	Non-Western	5.4	5.1	6.5	5.0	4.7	5.7	4.5	4.4	5.8
High	Dutch	31.0	37.5	37.4	30.4	37.7	35.7	28.1	35.2	35.5
	Non-Western	2.8	3.8	4.2	2.2	2.9	3.8	2.4	2.6	3.0

Note Numbers in the table are based on survey data with the following sample sizes
Kindergarten 2008 $N = 10069$; 2011 $N = 9261$; 2014 $N = 7279$
Grade 3 2008 $N = 9288$; 2011 $N = 10109$; 2014 $N = 7449$
Grade 6 2008 $N = 8545$; 2011 $N = 9444$; 2014 $N = 7909$
Sources Driessen et al. (2009, Table 4.4); Driessen et al. (2012, Table 4.4); Driessen et al. (2015, Table 4.4)

vmbo; Middle = one of the parents or both parents have completed at the highest havo, vwo or mbo; High = one of the parents or both parents have completed higher professional education or university. Furthermore, it is important to note that the minority status of the students is based on the country of birth of the parents. Migrant parents who were born in a Western country were included in the category Dutch. In a family with a mixed background, the country of birth of the mother was leading. In case of a one-parent family, the data of that parent was leading.

The data in Table 7.2 show that during the period 2008 through 2014, the SES level of the students in kindergarten and primary school increased, both among students with a Dutch (or Western migration) background and students with a non-Western immigration background. This is due to an increase in the percentage of higher educated and a decrease in the percentage of lower educated parents. For example, for the final grade of primary education (grade 6) the percentage of Dutch students with highly educated parents increased from 28.1% in 2008 to 35.5% in 2014. The percentage of students from middle SES families remained rather stable in this time frame.

7.3 Socioeconomic Background and Student Outcomes

The tables presented in this section illustrate the differences in educational outcomes of students according to the level of SES of their family, and when the data are available, also to their migration background. In the description, we focus on primary and secondary education, for which data on both attainment and achievement[2] indicators are available. In addition, for primary education only data on non-cognitive outcomes are reported. For senior vocational, higher professional, and university education we only present data on attainment indicators, like participation, drop-out, and graduation rates.

7.3.1 Student Outcomes in Primary Education

7.3.1.1 Cognitive Outcomes and Attainment in Grade 6

Table 7.3 shows the development of the performance of students in year 8 (comparable to U.S. grade 6) over the years 2008, 2011, and 2014, as well as the track recommendation students received at the end of primary school, separately for the three levels of SES and the categories Dutch and migrant students (see also Table 7.2). The data are based on the reference group of schools participating in the COOL$^{5-18}$ cohort studies in primary education, which is representative of the population of Dutch primary schools.

The performance scores include the composite score (range of scores 501–550) on the final school leaving test, a highly reliable high stakes test, consisting of the domains mathematics, Dutch language, and information processing. The table also presents student outcomes on the knowledge and skills part of a Citizenship Competence test, taken in the COOL$^{5-18}$ cohort studies (range of scores 0–1 and 1–4, respectively). The data on the track recommendation include the percentage of students who were recommended to one of the academic tracks—that is, recommendation for havo, vwo, or combined havo/vwo track in secondary education.

The data in Table 7.3 show that the scores on the final school leaving test of the Dutch students are almost stable over time. The difference between the lowest and

---

[2]Attainment indicators refer to formal levels of education; achievement indicators are based on test scores or examination marks.

Table 7.3 Student average performance scores and attainment (in percentages) in Grade 6 of primary education, 2008–2014

		Low SES				Middle SES				High SES			
		Dutch		Migrant		Dutch		Migrant		Dutch		Migrant	
		M	SD	M	SD	M	SD	M	SD	M	SD	M	SD
Final school leaving test	2008	529.1	10.2	527.6	10.1	534.1	9.5	531.8	10.1	539.1	8.3	532.9	10.4
	2011	530.7	9.4	528.8	9.2	534.2	8.8	531.9	10.2	539.4	7.7	536.7	8.7
	2014	528.5	10.3	528.7	10.6	533.2	10.0	531.8	10.5	538.5	9.1	536.5	9.9
Civic knowledge	2008	0.73	0.17	0.70	0.17	0.77	0.16	0.74	0.17	0.82	0.16	0.75	0.18
	2011	0.73	0.17	0.71	0.16	0.78	0.16	0.73	0.16	0.83	0.14	0.78	0.13
	2014	0.71	0.18	0.69	0.17	0.77	0.17	0.73	0.16	0.83	0.15	0.77	0.15
Civic skills	2008	2.96	0.40	3.13	0.40	2.99	0.39	3.16	0.42	3.05	0.38	3.08	0.42
	2011	2.95	0.42	3.12	0.41	2.97	0.39	3.13	0.43	3.04	0.37	3.10	0.41
	2014	2.93	0.45	3.17	0.45	2.99	0.40	3.16	0.42	3.05	0.38	3.17	0.40
Percentage havo/vwo recommendation	2008	20.8		17.8		39.1		37.5		64.3		40.1	
	2011	21.5		18.2		38.3		33.9		64.6		51.0	
	2014	20.9		23.6		36.1		33.7		63.3		55.1	

Note Numbers in the table are based on survey data with the following sample sizes: 2008 $N = 8545$; 2011 $N = 9444$; 2014 $N = 7909$
Sources Driessen et al. (2009, Tables 9.8, 10.4, 10.6); Driessen et al. (2012, Tables 10.8, 11.4, 11.6); Driessen et al. (2015, Tables 10.8, 11.4, 11.6)

highest SES group is around 10 points in every year, which is a difference of approximately one standard deviation. For the students with a migrant background, we see a similar picture over time. Comparing the data between Dutch and migrant students shows that for each SES category, the differences are very small. As regards the scores on the citizenship competences, we also see little changes over time. The higher the level of SES, the higher the scores are. A striking result is that the students with a migrant background score lower on civic knowledge, but higher in civic skills, which holds for each SES category.

Also, for track recommendation, we hardly see any changes over time with respect to the influence of SES, at least for the Dutch students. The percentages of students who receive a recommendation for the highest tracks in secondary education are similar in every year, with a difference between the highest and lowest level of SES of around 40%. In contrast, the percentage of students with a migrant background who receive a higher recommendation is increasing over time. However, this is only due to the migrant students in the highest SES category. As a consequence, the difference between low- and high-SES migrant students who receive a high track recommendation increased from around 20% in 2008 to 35% in 2014. Further studies of the track recommendations indicate that the differences in recommendations between high- and low-SES students remain existent, although more modestly, after taking the students' performance into account. These differences in track recommendations are very dependent on the particular primary school a student is attending (Timmermans, Kuyper, & van der Werf, 2015), and they cannot be explained by differences in the teachers' perceptions of work habit and engagement of these students (Timmermans, de Boer, & van der Werf, 2016). One of the most frequently mentioned explanations is that teachers take into account the parents' ability and resources to support their children (Ditton et al., 2005). Teachers deem parents from lower SES backgrounds to be less well equipped to assist their children with school work. Furthermore, parents from higher social classes exert more pressure on teachers to get academic track recommendations (e.g., Dronkers et al., 1998), while poorly educated parents rarely object to low track recommendations (Hillmert & Jacob, 2010).

7.3.1.2 Non-cognitive Outcomes

According to the Dutch Inspectorate of Education (Inspectie van het Onderwijs, 2014), Dutch students in primary and secondary education do like school very much but are on the other hand not very motivated to learn and to perform. This finding was confirmed by the Organisation for Economic Co-operation and Development (2016a) in its report about the Netherlands, which showed that the Dutch students score almost the lowest on motivation of all countries participating in the OECD studies. However, both the Inspectorate and the OECD did not present data about the relation with SES and how this relation developed over time. In Table 7.4, we present data from the COOL[5–18] cohort study collected in 2008, 2011, and 2014 on

Table 7.4 Student well-being with teachers and classmates and motivation (average score) in Grade 6 of primary education

		Low SES				Middle SES				High SES			
		Dutch		Minority		Dutch		Minority		Dutch		Minority	
		M	*SD*	*M*	*SD*	*M*	*SD*	*M*	*SD*	*M*	*SD*	*M*	*SD*
Well-being with the teacher	2008	3.66	0.64	3.64	0.68	3.67	0.65	3.67	0.71	3.66	0.65	3.61	0.75
	2011	3.72	0.65	3.68	0.70	3.73	0.65	3.68	0.73	3.76	0.63	3.65	0.69
	2014	3.69	0.66	3.70	0.73	3.73	0.66	3.68	0.73	3.73	0.66	3.68	0.76
Well-being with classmates	2008	4.13	0.67	4.22	0.58	4.18	0.64	4.18	0.64	4.15	0.63	4.15	0.64
	2011	4.14	0.65	4.24	0.64	4.19	0.65	4.24	0.66	4.19	0.65	4.21	0.65
	2014	4.16	0.69	4.25	0.64	4.21	0.67	4.22	0.64	4.19	0.65	4.24	0.64
Mastery motivation	2008	3.64	0.58	3.98	0.60	3.66	0.56	3.99	0.62	3.71	0.57	3.92	0.58
	2011	3.67	0.57	3.94	0.59	3.69	0.56	3.97	0.58	3.74	0.54	3.96	0.59
	2014	3.67	0.63	4.06	0.60	3.70	0.57	4.03	0.60	3.75	0.58	4.06	0.54
Performance motivation	2008	1.92	0.72	2.17	0.87	1.97	0.72	2.24	0.85	2.06	0.73	2.17	0.84
	2011	1.97	0.76	2.31	0.90	1.95	0.76	2.22	0.87	2.06	0.77	2.27	0.89
	2014	1.98	0.79	2.41	0.95	1.97	0.76	2.28	0.91	2.08	0.79	2.33	0.94

Note Numbers in the table are based on survey data with the following sample sizes: 2008 $N = 8545$; 2011 $N = 9444$; 2014 $N = 7909$
Sources Driessen et al. (2009, Tables 8.4, 8.5, 8.10); Driessen et al. (2012, Tables 9.4, 9.5, 9.10); Driessen et al. (2015, Tables 9.4, 9.5, 9.10)

grade 6 students' well-being and motivation, again differentiated according to level of SES and migration background. The data on well-being (Peetsma, Wagenaar, & de Kat, 2001) and motivation (Ali & McInerney, 2004) were collected by means of a student questionnaire (score range 1–5).

Students indicate a relatively high level of well-being with their teacher and an even higher level of well-being with their classmates. There is hardly any difference in well-being between the different SES groups and only a small difference between Dutch and migrant students, in the advantage of the last category. With respect to the two indicators of motivation, the data show clearly that both Dutch as well as migrant students are more intrinsically motivated (mastery motivated, willing to learn) than motivated to perform. Higher SES students, both migrant as well as Dutch, are a bit more motivated (mastery and performance) than low SES students. But the most striking is that in all categories of SES, minority students are much more motivated than their Dutch classmates.

7.3.2 Student Outcomes in Secondary Education

7.3.2.1 Attainment Indicators

In the following, we first present data on student attainment in secondary education, followed by data on their performance in PISA. Because of the highly tracked system of secondary education in the Netherlands, already at the stage of the transition from primary to secondary school socioeconomic inequality may develop or even increase. In Table 7.5 we present data from the Dutch Inspectorate on students' track placement in grade 1 in secondary education, distinguished according to the level of SES. The Inspectorate used the original data on parental education of Statistics Netherlands, which imply that five categories were distinguished instead of three. The levels 1 and 2 in Table 7.5 are in agreement with (see Table 7.1) low SES (no start qualification), level 3 is similar to middle SES (start qualification), and level 4 and 5 are similar to high SES (higher professional or university). The figures in the table include the percentages of students who were placed in the track that corresponded with their score on the final school leaving test, respectively, half or one track lower or higher.

Table 7.5 shows that, in general, there is a very clear relation between the level of parental education and the chance of being placed in a higher school track compared to the track that might be expected given the students' performance. For example, in 2016 only 10% of the students with parents in the lowest category of education (Senior vocational education level 1, low SES) was placed one track higher than expected compared to 21% of the students with the highest educated parents (higher professional or University education, high SES). Furthermore, the chance of a higher track placement than indicated by the score on the final school leaving test increased over time for each category of SES. Nevertheless, this increase is more substantial among the students from higher SES families than

7 Socioeconomic Inequality and Student Outcomes … 123

Table 7.5 Chance (in %) on being placed in a higher or lower track in secondary education compared to the expected track placement given the students' performance on the school leavers test

Parental education	Year	One track lower	Half track lower	Corresponding track	Half track higher	One track higher
Secondary vocational education level 1, low SES	2014	12	23	43	14	7
	2015	17	24	39	12	7
	2016	14	22	40	14	10
Secondary vocational education level 2 & 3, low SES	2014	11	22	43	15	9
	2015	14	22	39	14	10
	2016	11	20	40	17	12
Secondary vocational education level 4, middle SES	2014	9	21	42	17	11
	2015	12	21	39	15	13
	2016	9	19	40	18	15
Higher professional education, high SES	2014	6	18	43	19	13
	2015	8	19	41	17	16
	2016	6	16	39	20	19
University education, high SES	2014	3	14	49	20	19
	2015	4	14	45	20	17
	2016	2	12	43	22	21

Note Population data
Source Inspectie van het Onderwijs (2017)

among lower SES students. At the same time, the decrease in placement in lower tracks is higher for high SES students compared to students from lower SES families. All together, these data point to the conclusion that the already existing socioeconomic inequality due to the Dutch tracked system is increasing instead of decreasing. This is even more serious because track placement in the first grade of secondary school foreshadows the rest of the school career of students in secondary education in terms of promotion/degradation to a lower or higher track, drop-out, completed level of secondary education, and transition to senior vocational education and higher professional education and university. Figures of the Inspectorate (Inspectie van het Onderwijs, 2017) show that students in grade 9 of secondary education from the lowest SES categories have a much lower chance to be promoted to a higher track. Also, these students have a much higher chance of having to repeat a grade or to be referred to a lower track.

7.3.2.2 Student Performance

Table 7.6 includes the average performance scores of the Dutch students on the PISA assessment in 2015, for the domains mathematics, reading, and science. The level of education of the parents was based on students' reports (1% primary

Table 7.6 Results of Dutch students in the PISA 2015 assessment given the level of parental education

Parental education	Mathematics	Reading	Science
Primary education not completed	430	425	427
Primary education or vmbo	463	455	451
havo/vwo/mbo	501	488	492
hbo/wo	524	516	523
Migration background			
Dutch	520	510	517
Migrant second generation	474	470	462
Migrant first generation	452	434	438

Note Numbers are based on PISA data. $N = 5.385$
Source Feskens, Kuhlemeier, and Limpens (2016)

education not completed, 5% primary education or vmbo completed, 30% havo/vwo/mbo completed, and 64% higher professional education or university completed), as well as their migrant background, based on the country of birth of their parents.

Fifteen-year-old students originating from a high SES family (higher professional education/university completed) perform better in all three domains than students from lower educated parents. The differences are very large; the average difference between the lowest and highest SES category is around one standard deviation for all three domains.

The data regarding migration background in Table 7.6 show that immigrant students achieve less well than native Dutch students on all three domains of science, readings skills, and mathematics. The difference between native Dutch students and second-generation immigrants is very large: the largest for science (55 points), the smallest for reading (40 points), and mathematics in between (46 points). The differences between the second and third generation are not relevant, though it is interesting that the largest difference is for reading. Unfortunately, it is not possible to compare the data per SES category between Dutch students and students with a migration background. However, an interesting performance indicator developed in PISA is the performance gap between immigrant and non-immigrant students. Results for science performance, established in PISA 2015, indicate that the unadjusted performance gap for the Netherlands was 60 points on the PISA scale, above the OECD average gap of 43 points. When looking at this indicator after adjustment for socioeconomic background the Dutch gap reduced to 33 points, while the OECD average gap reduced to 31 (Organisation for Economic Co-operation and Development, 2016b, Table 1.7.4a, p. 427). These figures show the strong determination of performance differences by socioeconomic background (this is a finding that applies across OECD countries, but quite strongly in the Netherlands). In comparison to results from PISA 2006, which also had science performance as the focal subject matter domain, the gap in 2015 was 16 points lower than in 2006, for unadjusted performance, where the gap at the OECD average reduced by 9 points. When considering the results adjusted for socioeconomic background, the gap in the Netherlands was reduced by 10 points while the OECD average showed a 6-point decrease in the gap (Organisation for Economic Co-operation and Development, 2016b, Table 1.7.15a, p. 440).

The trends shown on the basis of PISA 2006 and 2015 for science performance —namely a slow decrease of the gap between immigrant and non-immigrant students over time, the important influence of SES on the estimate of the performance gap, and the Netherlands scoring close to the OECD average on the estimates adjusted for SES—are corroborated by the results from PISA 2003 and 2012 with respect to mathematics performance. Between 2003 and 2012 the performance gap in mathematics between immigrant and non-immigrant students decreased from 66 points in 2003 to 57 in 2012 for the unadjusted results, and from 41 to 35 for the adjusted results (Organisation for Economic Co-operation and Development, 2013, Tables II3.4a, II3.4b, pp. 228–229). The overall picture from these data is that the achievement differences between Dutch and immigrant students have declined over time, that a large part of the differences can be explained by the level of education of immigrant students' parents, but that the influence of immigrant background nevertheless remains important for student performance in secondary education. Also, the performance gap related to SES is still rather impressive although it slightly improved during the period 2003–2015.

Another way to determine whether countries and economies are moving towards more equitable school systems is to see how they have promoted student resiliency. Resilient students are disadvantaged students (those in the bottom quarter of a country's or economy's distribution of SES) who perform in the top quarter of performance in all countries, after accounting for SES (Organisation for Economic Co-operation and Development, 2013, p. 41). Countries and economies in which the proportion of students who are resilient is growing are those that are improving the chances for disadvantaged students to become high achievers.

In PISA 2003, 6.4% of students in OECD countries were resilient; by 2012, this share had decreased slightly to 6.1%. Only in Germany, Italy, Mexico, Poland, Tunisia, and Turkey did the share of resilient students increase by more than one percentage point. In 11 countries and economies, the share of resilient students shrank—meaning that in these countries/economies it became less likely that disadvantaged students will perform at a high level. The resiliency score for the Netherlands remained virtually unchanged between 2003 and 2015, at a level slightly above the OECD average.

7.3.3 Attainment in Senior Vocational Education, Higher Professional Education, and University

To conclude this section, we present population data on SES related attainment of students who transfer from lower secondary education (vmbo) to senior vocational education, as well as from students who, coming from the two highest levels of secondary education (havo/vwo), continue their education career in higher professional education or university. The former is the educational sector where students can attain their start qualification for the labor market, the latter prepares for the well-paid jobs.

As regards the first category of students, the Dutch Inspectorate of Education (2017) showed that in the academic year 2014/2015 students from low SES families have a higher drop-out rate in senior vocational education than students from higher SES families. More detailed analyses of the data, taking into account several background characteristics of the students, like family income and migration background, show that students with a migrant background drop-out more often than Dutch students. Among Dutch students, the chance of getting a diploma is higher when their parents have a higher level of education or income.

Table 7.7 includes the percentages of students with a secondary school degree (havo, vwo, or senior vocational education level 4) who registered in higher professional education or university, distinguished by the level of education (SES) of their parents. The data are from the period 2008 through 2016. We see that there is a rather large SES related difference in the chance to continue the school career in higher education. The SES gap has become larger since 2015, which might be due to the fact that in that year the study grant for higher and university education was replaced by a study loan.

Table 7.7 Registration (in %) of students with a secondary school degree to higher professional and university education

Parental education	2008	2009	2010	2011	2012	2013	2014	2015	2016
Only primary education	65.7	66.2	63.9	62.3	60.9	62.2	59.0	57.3	58.0
Secondary vocational education level 1	66.2	64.3	61.9	60.5	59.8	60.8	58.7	54.3	55.4
Secondary vocational education level 2	65.4	65.7	61.5	62.5	60.2	59.6	59.1	55.6	56.6
Secondary vocational education level 3	70.2	71.6	69.0	68.2	67.4	67.7	67.5	63.2	62.1
Secondary vocational education level 4	75.8	75.7	75.3	74.5	73.7	74.5	72.3	69.9	70.2
Higher professional education	81.0	82.3	81.7	81.4	80.9	81.5	81.3	78.2	78.7
University education	87.4	87.7	87.1	86.1	86.5	88.0	87.6	85.1	85.2

Source Inspectie van het Onderwijs (2017)

7.4 Policy to Enhance Equity in Education in the Netherlands

Current and most recent developments in equity-oriented policies in Dutch primary and pre-primary education should be understood from a historical perspective spanning about 40 years.

The most constant policy instrument used in the Dutch equity-oriented policy has been the extra funding of schools based on school composition (Scheerens, 2014). Low SES and cultural minority students count as more than one student in the formulas for the school budget, which are based on the number of students enrolled. In the past (from 1986 to 2006) native Dutch students with low educated parents counted for 1.25 students and students with a non-Western immigrant background counted as 1.90. In the current "weights regulation", a distinction between native Dutch and non-Western immigrant students is no longer made. Only the level of education of the parents determines the weight factor. Students whose (both) parents have completed at maximum lower vocational education count as 1.3, students of whom one of the parents have just completed primary education and the other only preparatory lower vocational education count as 2.2. Schools are eligible for extra funding when they have a certain percentage of students meeting the selection criteria for educational priority (see above); and, since the 2006/2007 school year, the threshold has been lowered from 9 to 6%. Since 2010, eligible schools in the so-called Impulse areas, zip code areas that are determined as poverty areas, receive another increment in their budget over and above the student weight-based formula.

Schools are expected to spend the extra funding on measures that enhance the position of their disadvantaged learners, but they are free to decide how they do so; extra teaching and support staff, partly used for class-size reduction, and bringing in external support are the main "treatments" that schools are likely to choose. Driessen (2018) concludes that the extra funding is predominantly spent on class-size reduction, although precise information on these funding decisions is hard to come by because schools cannot be held accountable for how they spend their budget. Moreover, the effectiveness of limited class-size reduction is quite doubtful. Finally, there are no evaluation studies that can attribute results of equity-oriented policies to the actual treatments that schools implement on the basis of their extra funding, not only because of local control over the use of the funding, but also because of frequent refusals from schools to participate in research and evaluation studies. Thanks to a long tradition of cohort studies, outcomes that are most relevant to equity-oriented policies can be monitored quite well, but it is very difficult to find schools that are ready to cooperate in experimental or process-outcome evaluation studies (Scheerens & Doolaard, 2013).

The most recent development is a proposal from the Central Bureau of Statistics (Central Bureau voor de Statistiek) to compute a new composite indicator to determine the level of disadvantage of the school, including education levels of mother and father, country of origin of the mother, duration of stay in the

Netherlands, and being eligible for debt compensation. This proposal is contested because it no longer identifies disadvantaged students, but just provides a school level estimate, on which funding is based. Critics say that this further perils the proper and targeted use of extra funding (Driessen, 2018).

From 1998 onward, pre-school education (vve) became a second major target area for equity-oriented policy, next to regular primary education. The reason for this policy was that pre-school education was considered to be a good measure for preventing SES related educational inequality. The policy levers are exactly the same as described above: extra funding based on the "weights regulation," and pre-school institutions and schools free to choose treatments. Until now, the results of studies on the effectiveness of vve programs are not consistently positive and the effects on the longer term are still unknown (Centraal Planbureau, 2016).

Since 2010 extra measures have been stimulated by the government and key stakeholders, like employers of education. These involve different kinds of pull-out strategies, where special classes are formed of eligible students who get extra treatment like additional Dutch language education and extended learning time (longer school day, school week, or summer schools). Finally, equity stimulation more recently got an extra boost, when it was profiled as a dedicated component of more general educational policy that is aimed at enhancing quality and performance —known as *Basis voor Beter Presteren* (Driessen, 2013; Mulder & Meijnen, 2013).

7.5 Conclusion

When making up the balance on the position of low SES students in Dutch education, the strongly suppressing influence of low SES has been re-confirmed. This is also the case when concentrating on low SES students from immigrant groups. When considering student performance at the end of primary school, the influence is almost stable over time. The difference between the lowest and highest SES group is around 10 points every year. For the students with a migrant background, we see a similar SES related difference over time. Comparing the performance data between Dutch and migrant students shows that for each SES category, the differences are very small and almost stable over time.

As regards the performance in secondary education, also the SES influence is substantial and hardly decreasing over time. In comparison to other countries, the performance of both Dutch and immigrant students in secondary education depends on a relatively large share of their SES background. Taking the SES background into account, the performance difference between Dutch and immigrant students is slowly decreasing over time.

A similar picture regarding the influence of SES holds for the track recommendations students receive at the end of primary school and the actual track placement. Recommendations for higher track education are three times bigger for high than for low SES students. For Dutch students, the influence of SES on track recommendations has stayed stable as well. Only middle SES Dutch pupils have experienced a decline in their recommendations. In contrast, the percentage of students with a migrant background who receive a higher recommendation is increasing over time. Migrant students with high SES status experienced the highest increase, but are still 8 percentage points less likely to receive a recommendation than their Dutch counterparts. As a consequence, the difference between low and high SES migrant students who receive a high track recommendation increased from around 20% in 2008 to 35% in 2014, a finding which point at an increase of socioeconomic inequality among migrant students.

All together, the performance data of primary and secondary education show that the socioeconomic inequality in the Netherlands is very substantial and persistent, in contrast to inequality related to migration background, which is almost absent at the end of primary education and decreasing in secondary education. The same holds for track recommendation and track placement, i.e. stable large SES related differences and no or very small differences between Dutch and migrant students. Also regarding attainment indicators in secondary education (drop-out, continuation to tertiary education) the socioeconomic inequality is still rather substantial and most recent data on continuation to tertiary education even show that this inequality is increasing. Because data about difference over time between Dutch and immigrant students, taking SES into account, are not available, nothing can be yet concluded about migration-related inequality.

When it comes to an assessment of the effectiveness and efficiency of the equity-oriented policies in the Netherlands, there is a striking consensus among all evaluators and reviewers of these policies. They invariably point to the lack of coherence, clear planning frameworks, and limited evaluability of the way schools use extra funding and work towards the rather general policy objectives (Driessen, 2018; Driessen & Mulder, 1999; Mulder & Meijnen, 2013; Scheerens, 1987). The implicit message is that school autonomy has long gone over the edge in the Netherlands and is preventing policies that are effective and efficient. In the most recent evaluation study, Mulder and Meijnen (2013) are very explicit in their recommendations to have clearer targets from the center, more explicitly planned programs, stricter accountability requirements, and better conditions for program evaluation. The inefficiency in equity-oriented policy is part of a larger syndrome in Dutch education, in which innovation and reform are framed to be "bottom up," leading to many fragmented local initiatives in which the wheel is reinvented over and over again (Scheerens, 2013, 2014). Despite the recommendations in practically all evaluation studies, the counsel to make better use of evidence-based comprehensive school reform programs has never been followed up in a consistent way, so far (although there is a very recent initiative to implement the "Success for All" program in the Netherlands).

In summing up the basic situation of the Netherlands with respect to SES determinacy of educational outcomes, seen from an international perspective, the following points should be mentioned:

- Internationally, the Netherlands has an average position when the student level SES impact on performance is considered.
- The SES-related gap in student performance and attainment is substantial and persistent over time in primary and secondary education and increasing in tertiary education.
- The gap in student performance between migrants and Dutch students, taking into account the level of SES, is absent and stable over time in primary education, and declining over time in secondary education.
- The gap in student attainment between migrant and Dutch students, taking into account the level of SES, is absent and stable over time at the end of primary education (recommendation and track placement).
- The highly diversified structure of the secondary school system seems to reinforce inequalities, for instance when it comes to the high impact of SES on track placement and school drop-out. Another instance is the very high between-school variance in performance (Scheerens, 2014).
- Grossly inefficient educational policy to weaken SES determinacy of performance and increase equity (no demonstrable effects of very high financial investments).

References

Ali, J., & McInerney, D. M. (2004). Multidimensional assessment of school motivation. In H. W. Marsh, J. Baumert, G. E. Richards, & U. Trautwein (Eds.), *Self-concept, motivation and identity: Where to from here?* Sydney, Australia: SELF Research Centre, University of Western Sydney. Retrieved from https://www.researchgate.net/publication/314434491/download.

Central Bureau voor de Statistiek. (2018, August 14). *Statline: Bevolking; onderwijsniveau; geslacht, leeftijd en migratieachtergrond* [Population; education level; sex, age and migration background]. Retrieved from http://statline.cbs.nl/Statweb/publication/?DM=SLNL&PA=82275NED&D1=0&D2=0&D3=1&D4=1,4-5&D5=0-1,7,12,l&D6=39,44,49,54,59,64,69,74-75&HDR=T,G1,G5,G2&STB=G3,G4&VW=T.

Centraal Planbureau. (2016). *Kansrijk Onderwijsbeleid* [Promising education policy]. The Hague, The Netherlands: Author. Retrieved from https://www.cpb.nl/publicatie/kansrijk-onderwijsbeleid.

Ditton, H., Krüsken, J., & Schauenberg, M. (2005). Bildungsungleichheit – der Beitrag von Familie und Schule. *Zeitschrift für Erziehungswissenschaft, 8,* 285–304. https://doi.org/10.1007/s11618-005-0138-x.

Driessen, G. (2013). *De bestrijding van Onderwijsachterstanden* [Fighting educational inequality: A review of effective approaches]. Nijmegen, The Netherlands: ITS.

Driessen, G. (2018, April 1). Zo doorgaan met het onderwijsachterstandsbeleid [Should we carry on with the educational priority in this way?] [Web log post]. Retrieved from https://didactiefonline.nl/blog/blonz/zo-doorgaan-met-het-onderwijsachterstandenbeleid.

Driessen, G., Elshof, D., Mulder, L., & Roeleveld, J. (2015). *Cohortonderzoek COOL$^{5-18}$. Technisch rapport basisonderwijs, derde meting* [COOL$^{5-18}$ cohort study: Technical report primary education, third measurement]. Amsterdam, The Netherlands: Kohnstamm Instituut. Retrieved from https://www.bvekennis.nl/Bibliotheek/16-1106.pdf.

7 Socioeconomic Inequality and Student Outcomes … 131

Driessen, G., & Mulder, L. (1999). The enhancement of educational opportunities of disadvantaged children. In R. J. Bosker, B. P. M. Creemers, & S. Stringfield (Eds.), *Enhancing educational excellence, equity and efficiency*. Dordrecht, Boston, London: Kluwer.

Driessen, G., Mulder, L., Ledoux, G., Roeleveld, J., & Van der Veen, I. (2009). *Cohortonderzoek COOL$^{5-18}$. Technisch rapport basisonderwijs, eerste meting 2007/08* [COOL$^{5-18}$ cohort study: Technical report primary education, first measurement 2007/08]. Amsterdam, The Netherlands: SCO-Kohnstamm Instituut.

Driessen, G., Mulder, L., & Roeleveld, J. (2012). *Cohortonderzoek COOL$^{5-18}$. Technisch rapport basisonderwijs, tweede meting 2010/11* [COOL$^{5-18}$ cohort study: Technical report primary education, second measurement 2010/11]. Amsterdam, The Netherlands: Kohnstamm Instituut.

Dronkers, J., van Erp, M., Robijns, M., & Roeleveld, J. (1998). Krijgen leerlingen in de grote steden en met name in Amsterdam te hoge adviezen? *De relaties tussen taal- en rekenscores en advies binnen en buiten de Randstad onderzocht, Tijdschrift voor Onderwijsresearch, 23,* 17–30.

Feskens, R., Kuhlemeier, H., & Limpens, G. (2016). *Resultaten PISA 2015 in vogelvlucht. Kennis en vaardigheden van 15-jarigen.* [PISA 2015 results in bird's eye view: Knowledge and skills of 15-year-olds]. Arnhem, The Netherlands: Cito. Retrieved from https://www. lezenenschrijven.nl/uploads/editor/resultaten-pisa-2015-in-vogelvlucht.pdf.

Hillmert, S., & Jacob, M. (2010). Selections and social selectivity on the academic track: A lifecourse analysis of educational attainment in Germany. *Research in Social Stratification and Mobility, 28,* 59–76. https://doi.org/10.1016/j.rssm.2009.12.006.

Inspectie van het Onderwijs. (2014). *De Staat van het Onderwijs 2012/2013* [The state of education 2012/2013]. Utrecht, The Netherlands: Author.

Inspectie van het Onderwijs. (2017). *Technisch rapport hoofdstuk 1—Gelijke kansen. De Staat van het Onderwijs 2015/2016* [Technical report chapter 1—Equal opportunities. The state of education 2015/2016]. Utrecht, The Netherlands: Author.

Inspectorate of Education. (2017). *Technisch rapport Hoofdstuk 1 - Gelijke kansen. De Staat van het Onderwijs 2015/2016.* Utrecht: Author.

Korpershoek, H., Naaijer, H. M., & Bosker, R. J. (2016). *De inrichting van de onderbouw: Onderzoek naar de motieven en de beweegredenen van vo-scholen naar soort brugklas* [The layout of the substructure: Research into the motives of secondary schools by type of bridge class]. Groningen, The Netherlands: GION onderzoek/onderwijs.

Ministry of Education. (2008). *Parlementair onderzoek Onderwijsvernieuwingen* [Parliamentary study on educational innovations]. Kamerstukken II 2007–2008, 31 007, nr. 8.

Mulder, L., & Meijnen, W. (2013). *Onderwijsachterstanden in de BOPO-periode, 2009–2012. Een review* [Inequality in primary education in the period 2009- 2011. A review study]. Nijmegen, The Netherlands: ITS.

Nusche, D., Braun, H., Halasz, G., & Santiago, P. (2014). *OECD reviews of evaluation and assessment in education: Netherlands 2014.* Paris, France: OECD Publishing.

Organisation for Economic Co-operation and Development. (2013). *PISA 2012 results: Excellence through equity* (Vol. II). Paris, France: OECD Publishing.

Organisation for Economic Co-operation and Development. (2016a). *Netherlands 2016: Foundations for the future—Reviews of national policies for education.* Paris, France: OECD Publishing. https://doi.org/10.1787/19900198.

Organisation for Economic Co-operation and Development. (2016b). *PISA 2015 results: Excellence through equity* (Vol. I). Paris, France: OECD Publishing.

Peetsma, T. T. D., Wagenaar, E., & De Kat, E. (2001). School motivation, future time perspective and well-being of high school students in segregated and integrated schools in the Netherlands and the role of ethnic self-description. In J. K. Koppen, I. Lunt, & C. Wulf (Eds.), *Education in Europe: Cultures, values, institutions in transition* (pp. 54–74). New York, NY: Waxmann.

Scheerens, J. (1987). *Enhancing opportunities for disadvantaged learners: A review of Dutch research on compensatory education and educational development policy.* Amsterdam, The Netherlands: North-Holland Pub. Co.

Scheerens, J. (2013). *Educational Evaluation and Assessment in the Netherlands.* Addendum to the Country Background Report for the OECD Review on Evaluation and Assessment Frameworks for Improving School Outcomes. www.oecd.org/education/school/Netherlands%20CBR%20Update.pdf.

Scheerens, J. (2014). *Country report on The Netherlands, concerning equity oriented educational policies and programs.* Contribution to the network of experts on social aspects of education and training (NESET) under the auspices of the European Commission. Unpublished manuscript.

Scheerens, J., & Doolaard, S. (2013). *Review study on educational quality of Dutch primary schools.* Enschede, The Netherlands: GION/University of Twente.

Scheerens, J., Ehren, M., Sleegers, P., & De Leeuw, R. (2012). *Country background report for the OECD study on Evaluation and Assessment Frameworks for Improving School Outcomes.* Retrieved from http://www.sici-inspectorates.eu/getattachment/caf46482-5270-4bc6-b985-2bdf75b57e5f.

Timmermans, A. C., de Boer, H., Amsing, H. T. A., & van der Werf, M. P. C. (In press). Track recommendations bias: Gender, migration background and SES bias over a twenty-year period in the Dutch context. *British Educational Research Journal.* Retrieved from http://hdl.handle.net/11370/30914514-de3f-4388-93e8-1b64542d252b.

Timmermans, A. C., de Boer, H., & van der Werf, M. P. C. (2016). An investigation of the relationship between teachers' expectations and teachers' perceptions of student attributes. *Social Psychology of Education, 19*(2), 217–240. https://doi.org/10.1007/s11218-015-9326-6.

Timmermans, A., Kuyper, H., & van der Werf, G. (2013). *Schooladviezen en onderwijsloopbanen: Voorkomen, risicofactoren en gevolgen van onder- en overadvisering* [School recommendations and educational careers: Prevention, risk factors and consequences of under- and over-advice]. Groningen, The Netherlands: GION/RUG Onderwijskunde.

Timmermans, A. C., Kuyper, H., & van der Werf, G. (2015). Accurate, inaccurate, or biased teacher expectations: Do Dutch teachers differ in their expectations at the end of primary education? *British Journal of Educational Psychology, 85*(4), 459–478. https://doi.org/10.1111/bjep.12087.

Vugteveen, J., Timmermans, A. C., Korpershoek, H., van Rooijen, M., & Opdenakker, M.-C. (2016). *Overgangen en aansluitingen in het onderwijs: Deelrapportage 3: empirische studie naar de cognitieve en niet-cognitieve ontwikkeling van leerlingen rondom de vmbo-mbo overgang* [Transitions and connections in education: Partial report 3: empirical study on the cognitive and non-cognitive development of pupils around the vmbo-mbo transition]. Groningen, The Netherlands: GION onderzoek/onderwijs.

Chapter 8
Socioeconomic Inequality and Student Outcomes in Swedish Schools

Petra Löfstedt

Abstract This chapter outlines the current Swedish school system and also explains its governance and administrative processes. Then follows an overview of the study population in general and educational outcomes of socioeconomically disadvantaged students. The chapter highlights how the gap between the high and low performing and socioeconomically advantaged and disadvantaged students has increased in Sweden over the last decades referring mainly to PISA survey data and national population grades. Lastly, the chapter describes the extensive school reforms that have taken place since the 1990s, including decentralization and marketization. The chapter evaluates whether these extensive reforms have contributed to the decline in performances and whether they have resulted in increased segregation and weakened the school compensatory assignment (which aims at minimizing negative effects of student background on performance). The chapter concludes with recent policy responses to these continuing negative trends of increasing performance gaps between socioeconomically advantaged and disadvantaged students.

Keywords Student achievement · Socioeconomic status · Inequality · Sweden

8.1 The Current Swedish School System

The Swedish educational system comprises pupil education (preschools, preschool classes, comprehensive schools, upper secondary schools, Sami schools, special needs comprehensive, and upper secondary schools) and adult education (Organisation for Economic Cooperation and Development, 2015a).

P. Löfstedt (✉)
Department of Public Health and Community Medicine,
Sahlgrenska Academy, University of Gothenburg, Gothenburg, Sweden
e-mail: petra.lofstedt@folkhalsomyndigheten.se

© Springer Nature Singapore Pte Ltd. 2019
L. Volante et al. (eds.), *Socioeconomic Inequality and Student Outcomes*, Education Policy & Social Inequality 4,
https://doi.org/10.1007/978-981-13-9863-6_8

Children may attend preschool from the time they are one-year-old, and it is voluntary (Skolverket, 2018a). Preschool activities primarily are intended to assist in children's development, and to allow them to meet and socialize with other children. The municipality is responsible for ensuring that children are assigned a place in a preschool. Of all children aged 4–5 years, 95% were enrolled in preschool during autumn 2017 (Sveriges kommuner och landsting, 2018).

When children turn 6, they are entitled to attend *preschool class*, which is a voluntary preparation class for compulsory school (Skolverket, 2018a) The aim of this class is to stimulate students' development and learning and prepare them for compulsory school. Preschool activities comprise education and teaching. In the academic year 2016/17, 98% of six-year-olds were enrolled in preschool class. Since autumn 2018, preschool classes are compulsory, and thus mandatory schooling is now extended by 1 year to a mandatory 10-year period in Sweden.

All children attend *comprehensive school* from about the age of 7 (Skolverket, 2018b). Comprehensive school is compulsory, and all children attend it for 9 years. Most children begin Year 1 in the autumn of the year they turn 7 and complete compulsory school at age 16 (Year 9). There is no tracking; everyone follows the same path and the same curriculum from Year 1 to Year 9. National final grades use the average final grade of the best 16 subjects (i.e., the subjects with the highest grades) for each student. The grading system is a criterion reference system, designed to assess and grade skill and knowledge levels. School grades are awarded from Year 6. National tests are compulsory at the end of Years 3, 6, and 9 in Swedish, English as a second language, mathematics, and science. Students have access to school healthcare, study and career guidance, and a school library. There are also state-run *Sami schools* for the Sami population in the north of Sweden, with teaching in Swedish and Sami (Organisation for Economic Cooperation and Development, 2015a).

Upper secondary school in Sweden is voluntary, but almost all students, approximately 98%, go on to upper secondary school after comprehensive school (Statistics Sweden, 2017). Upper secondary programs are 3 years in most cases (Skolverket, 2018c). Many students begin immediately after comprehensive school, when they are 16 years of age. The limit for beginning upper secondary school is the year they turn 20. After the students turn 20, it is possible to attend upper secondary adult education. All students attending upper secondary school are entitled to study grants.

Children with intellectual disabilities are not always able to manage ordinary comprehensive school. In such a case, the child can instead attend a *special needs comprehensive school* (Skolverket, 2018d). This is a separate form of schooling, providing education that is adapted to each student's circumstances and needs. After special needs comprehensive school, students can go on to a 4-year *special needs upper secondary school*. Its aim is to teach the student to manage ordinary tasks in working life.

Comprehensive and upper secondary school are free of charge that means there is no payment required for tuition, textbooks, or other school material. School lunches are also free.

8 Socioeconomic Inequality and Student Outcomes … 135

There are also *international schools* that target children who temporarily reside in Sweden or who want to receive an education with an international dimension. These schools usually follow the curriculum of another country. Swedish children whose parents live abroad can be provided with nationwide boarding school education (Organisation for Economic Cooperation and Development, 2015a).

8.2 Governance and Financing

The municipalities are responsible for organizing and running primary, secondary, and adult education (Holmlund et al., 2014; SOU, 2014). An elected body, the Municipal Assembly, governs every municipality and appoints an education committee to govern its public education system. The municipalities and independent school providers are in charge of implementing educational activities, organizing and operating school services, allocating resources and ensuring that national goals for education are met (Organisation for Economic Cooperation and Development, 2015a). Since the municipalization reform in 1991, municipalities also received full employer responsibility for all school staff (SOU, 2014). The Ministry of Education and Research sets national educational goals and evaluates the results of the system, but decisions on how to achieve those goals are left to the municipal and school level. Both municipal and independent schools are funded through municipal grants from students' home municipalities and through state grants. Students are first allocated to a school based on geographical criteria. Families can then choose to stay in the school to which the student has been assigned or choose another public or independent school. A so-called school voucher, publicly funded can be transferred to the schools where students choose to be enrolled. School funding is shared between the state and municipalities. State funds are paid to municipalities through what is called the general state grant.

In 2016, the total cost for comprehensive school was 106 billion Swedish Crowns (Skolverket, 2018e) For municipal education providers it was 92 billion Swedish Crowns, which corresponds to 104,800 Swedish Crowns per student. For independent education providers, it was 14 billion Swedish Crowns, which corresponds to 96,000 Swedish Crowns per student. Compared to municipal schools, independent schools have on average higher costs per student for premises, school meals, and teaching materials. On the other hand, on average they have average lower costs for teaching, student health care, and other expenses.

8.3 Key Characteristics of the Swedish Student Population

Table 8.1 shows the number of students enrolled in the Swedish compulsory school system between 2008/09 and 2017/18. In 2017/18, around 1050 thousand students were enrolled, which was an increase of more than 25,000 students compared to the

Table 8.1 Total number of students in comprehensive school by school year and responsible authority, 2008–2018

	2008/09	2009/10	2010/11	2011/12	2012/13	2013/14	2014/15	2015/16	2016/17	2017/18
Comprehensive schools, total	906,189	891,727	886,487	888,658	899,185	920,997	949,460	985,613	1,023,944	1,049,476
Municipal education providers	816,606	795,648	781,210	776,356	779,327	794,869	815,361	839,981	870,246	887,837
Independent education providers	89,444	95,948	105,136	112,144	119,695	125,960	133,942	145,471	149,481	156,488
Sami schools	139	131	141	158	163	168	157	161	152	158
International schools									4065	4993

Source Skolverket (2018e)

8 Socioeconomic Inequality and Student Outcomes …

Table 8.2 Percent (%) of students in comprehensive school by parental education and migration background, by responsible authority, 2010–2018

	2010	2011	2012	2013	2014	2015	2016	2017	2018
Students with at least one parent with tertiary education									
Comprehensive school, total	50	51	53	54	55	56	56	57	58
Municipal education providers	48	50	51	52	53	54	55	55	56
Independent education providers	63	64	65	65	66	67	68	69	69
Students with migration background									
Comprehensive school, total	18	19	19	19	20	21	23	24	25
Municipal education providers	18	18	19	19	20	21	22	24	24
Independent education providers	21	22	22	22	22	23	24	23	25

Source Skolverket (2018f)

previous year (Skolverket, 2018e). The vast majority of students are enrolled in municipal schools, but the number of students enrolled in independent schools has increased considerably. In 2008/09, 90% of the students were enrolled in municipal schools and 10% in independent schools. In 2017/18, the corresponding figures were 85% and 15%, respectively. The number of students in Sami schools has been relatively stable for the whole period. International schools have only been reported as a separate category since 2016; previously, they were categorized as independent education providers.

Table 8.2 shows the percent of all students in comprehensive school during the Years one to nine, by parental education, migration background and school provider (Skolverket, 2018f). The percent of students with at least one parent with tertiary education increased from 50 to 58% between 2008/09 and 2017/18. For the whole period, the percent of students with at least one parent with tertiary education has been higher in independent schools, compared to municipal schools. The percent of students with migration backgrounds, defined as being born outside Sweden or born in Sweden but with both parents born outside Sweden, increased from 18% in 2009/10 to 25% in 2017/18. The percent has been slightly higher in independent schools compared to municipal schools.

The most striking change in the student population in comprehensive school, particularly after 2015, is the number of asylum seekers. In 2014/15, there were 6695 asylum seekers in Swedish compulsory schools; in 2015/16, it was 11,853 and in 2016/17 it was 22,095 (Swedish Migration Agency, 2018). Expressed as a percentage of the total school population, around 2% of the total school population were asylum seekers in 2016/17.

8.4 Educational Outcomes of Low SES Children

In Sweden, data sources to measure trends in educational outcomes and their association with socioeconomic background are international surveys such as the Programme for International Student Assessment (PISA) and Trends in International Mathematics and Science Study (TIMSS), as well as final national grades. Register data are records kept by government agencies or other organizations, where data can be traced to individuals. Different data sources have varying strengths and weaknesses. The international PISA study, for example, does not consider the participating countries' respective curriculum (Skolverket, 2016a). The questions are designed to measure skills that are considered particularly important for life which enables comparison over time and between countries. PISA also includes a lot of information on preferences of students, motivation of students, and parents. On the other hand, it is cross-sectional data which hampers causal inference.

In contrast, the final grades are census data and therefore encompass the entire student population for each cohort. A problem with the final grades, on the other hand, is that since the final grades are subject to different interpretation of grading criteria by different teachers, schools, and regions, the comparability of the final grades is questionable. The problem of grade inflation has also been discussed (Skolverket, 2016b). For example, Swedish students' final grades of Year nine gradually increased between 1998 and 2012, at the same time the performance in PISA and TIMSS declined (Skolverket, 2016a, 2016c). The discrepancy between survey and administrative data results could suggest a possible grade inflation (Skolverket, 2016b).

There are also differences in the accuracy of measuring socioeconomic background between the different data sources. The PISA study, for example, relies on self-reported data, which is prone to measurement errors due to i.e. recall-bias. Instead, register data, kept by government agencies or other organizations, makes it possible to link all students to their parents and data with detailed demographic information (e.g., completed education and annual earnings). Furthermore, student educational outcomes can be linked to later labor market outcomes opening opportunities to investigate the impact of schooling on future career. On the other hand, administrative data does not include information on motivation of students and teachers, which are important for examining school systems cross-nationally.

There are strengths and limitations with the different data sources. Therefore, when presenting educational outcomes and socioeconomic background, the following section uses different data sources, including data from the PISA surveys as well as national final grades.

8.4.1 Educational Outcomes in Sweden According to PISA and TIMSS

When PISA was conducted for the first time in 2000, Swedish 15-year-olds performed better than the standardized international mean of 500 points in mathematics and reading (Henrekson & Jävervall, 2016). After that, the performance fell continuously between 2000 and 2012, (see Fig. 8.1). The total decline was statistically significant in both subjects (Skolverket, 2016a). No other country participating in PISA experienced a steeper decline over the past decade than Sweden. In comparison, the average performance in mathematics across all Organisation for Economic Co-operation and Development (OECD) countries remained roughly stable between 2003 and 2012. According to PISA data from 2015, there was a statistically significant improvement in learning outcomes in mathematics as well as in reading comprehension, indicating that the downward trend has reversed though the results did not reach the same levels as in the early 2000s (Skolverket, 2016a). In science, there was a decrease in performance between 2006 and 2012, and an increase between 2012 and 2015, but none of these changes were statistically significant.

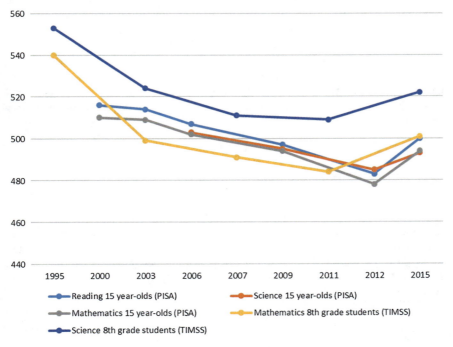

Fig. 8.1 Sweden's average scores in PISA and TIMSS by subject area, 2000–2015 *Sources* Organization for Economic Co-operation and Development (2016), Skolverket (2016c)

The results from the TIMSS assessment show similar trends (Fig. 8.1) (Skolverket, 2016c). Swedish 8th-grade students have participated in all of the TIMSS assessments since 1995. There was a significant fall in performance in both mathematics and science between 1995 and 2011. Like the PISA results, TIMSS 2015 results indicate significantly improved learning outcomes in mathematics and science between 2011 and 2015. (It is important to note that even though Fig. 8.1 provides the same scale for TIMSS and PISA, it is not directly comparable between both surveys due to different calculation methods.)

8.4.2 Performance Gap Among Low- and High-Achieving Students

A measure of student performance is the percent of students who attain at least proficiency Level 2 on the PISA assessment (Organisation for Economic Cooperation and Development, 2016). Proficiency Level 2 is considered a baseline that all students should be expected to reach by the time they leave compulsory education. Low-achieving students score below Level 2. On the other hand, top-performing students are those who perform at or above Level 5.

Between 2000 and 2012, the percent of low-achieving students increased in both reading and mathematics but decreased in 2015. In science, low-achieving students increased between 2006 and 2015 (Skolverket, 2016a). In reading and mathematics, top-performing students decreased between 2000 and 2012, and then increased in 2015. The percent of top-performing students in science decreased between 2006 and 2012 and increased in 2015. These results indicate that average lower performance in Swedish schools found in recent years was due to the entire educational achievement distribution being shifted instead of e.g. only an increase of low performing students.

8.4.3 Educational Outcomes by Gender

On average, girls and boys scored similarly in mathematics and science (Organisation for Economic Cooperation and Development, 2015b), but girls outperformed boys in reading. The Swedish gender gap was wider than the average across OECD countries. The gender gap in reading performance did not change since 2009. Twice as many boys (24%) than girls (12%) did not reach the baseline level of proficiency in reading in Sweden.

8.4.4 Educational Outcomes by Migration Background

Among the students in Sweden who participated in the PISA survey in 2015, 9.8% were born in Sweden with migration backgrounds, and 7.6% were born outside Sweden with migration backgrounds. Compared to 2006, the whole group of students with migration backgrounds increased by almost 7 percentage points (Skolverket, 2016a).

In 2015, approximately 10% of natives were top-performing students in science (Skolverket, 2016a). Among students born in Sweden with migration backgrounds it was 3%, and for students born outside Sweden with migration backgrounds it was around 2%. The percent of native students who were low-achieving students in science was 17%. For students born in Sweden with migration backgrounds it was 33%, and for students born outside Sweden with migration backgrounds it was 50%. The pattern is similar for reading and mathematics.

Students with migration backgrounds were more often from disadvantaged socioeconomic backgrounds, compared to native students. When socioeconomic status was taken into account using a regression design, the difference between native students and students with migration background was reduced, but did not disappear (Skolverket, 2016a). Approximately one-third of the difference in science between natives and migrants could be explained by differences in socioeconomic background. The pattern is robust for reading and mathematics.

8.4.5 Educational Outcomes by Students Socioeconomic Background

A student's socioeconomic status is estimated by the PISA index of economic, social, and cultural status (ESCS), which is derived from several variables related to students' family background: parents' education, parents' occupations, a number of home possessions that can be taken as proxies for material wealth, and the number of books and other educational resources available in the home (Organisation for Economic Cooperation and Development, 2016). Students are considered socioeconomically advantaged if they are at or above the 75th percentile of the ESCS index distribution in a respective country. Socioeconomically disadvantaged students are those placed at or below the 25th percentile and average socioeconomic status students are those in between both extremes of the distribution.

According to PISA 2015, in both reading and mathematics, socioeconomically advantaged students scored 41 points higher than disadvantaged students. This Swedish pattern is similar to the OECD average. Using a regression design, the share of the variation in student performance that can be attributed to students' socioeconomic background was 11% in reading and 14% in mathematics, which is similar to the OECD average (Skolverket, 2016a).

In science, socioeconomically advantaged students scored 37 points higher than disadvantaged students in 2006; the difference increased to 44 points in 2015 (Skolverket, 2016a). That means that the gap in science between advantaged and disadvantaged students in Sweden was wider than the average across OECD countries. On the other hand, the share of the variation in student performance that could be attributed to students' socioeconomic background was 12% in Sweden, which was similar to the OECD average and did not change significantly since PISA 2006. Countries where students' socioeconomic background was of great importance were France, Hungary, Czech republic, and Luxemburg, where socioeconomically advantaged students scored over 50 points higher than disadvantaged students and/or the share of the variation in student performance attributed to students' socioeconomic background was over 20%. Estonia and Iceland were those countries across the OECD where students' socioeconomic background was of least importance, but even in the other Nordic countries—Denmark, Finland and Norway, the importance of students' socioeconomic background was less compared to Sweden.

Up to now, PISA results on educational achievement by socioeconomic background were discussed. How do they compare to results from administrative data? The Swedish National Agency for Education has analyzed the effect of students' family background on learning outcomes in comprehensive school, using national final grades (Skolverket, 2006, 2012, 2018g). The latest report, published in 2018, described the trends between 1998 up to 2016.

The data sources used to measure students' performance were (a) final grades from all 16 mandatory subjects in comprehensive school to calculate merit rating values, and (b) final grades in English and mathematics. English and mathematics are subjects supported by national tests and are therefore assumed to be more resistant to grade inflation.

The data sources used to measure students' socioeconomic background were (a) level of parental education, (b) parental income, (c) proportion of parents receiving welfare, and (d) a socioeconomic index computed by the three previous variables. Students' migration background was classified as (a) the student and at least one parent were born in Sweden, (b) the student was born in Sweden but both parents were born outside Sweden, and (c) the student was born outside Sweden.

In 2000, approximately 18% of the variance of students' average merit value in grade 9 could be explained by the socioeconomic index. In 2015, it had increased to 23%. For grades in mathematics and English it increased from around 17 to 23%.

Between 2000 and 2015, the importance of the socioeconomic index for average merit value increased from 9% to over 22% for students born outside Sweden, and from 10 to 12% for students born in Sweden having parents both born outside Sweden. Also for students with a Swedish background, there was an increase in the importance of the socioeconomic index for average merit value, from almost 20 to 22%, but it was significantly less compared to students born outside Sweden.

8 Socioeconomic Inequality and Student Outcomes …   143

When analyzing the three variables included in the socioeconomic index separately, results showed that parental income was the main factor behind the increase for students with a Swedish background. The level of parental education was indeed the most important variable for the learning outcomes, but it has been relatively stable during the whole period. For students born in Sweden but with both parents born outside Sweden, there was no clear pattern. For students born outside Sweden, all three socioeconomic variables contributed to the importance of the socioeconomic background on learning outcomes, but it differed during different periods.

In sum, while administrative data and survey data results disagree on average achievement development in Sweden over time, both data sources indicate that the socioeconomic achievement gap has increased since 1995.

8.4.6 School Segregation

School segregation is presented in two ways. First, the focus is on the proportion of the total variation in socioeconomic background that can be explained by variation between schools. Secondly, school segregation is captured as the variation in student performance related to differences in the socioeconomic composition of the school's student population.

Using administrative data and analyzing school segregation separately for level of parental education, parental income, and the socioeconomic index, school segregation increased for all three socioeconomic variables (Skolverket, 2018g). During the 2000s, school segregation by parental education was relatively stable but started to increase during the 2010s. Between 2010 and 2016, it increased from 14 to 16%. School segregation by parental income, on the other hand, increased from 11% in 1998 to 20% in 2015. School segregation by the socioeconomic index increased by over 6 percentage points between 1998 and 2016, from approximately 15% to almost 22% (Skolverket, 2018g).

Segregation by migration background increased from 17 to 25% between 1998 and 2011, when students born in Sweden but both parents born outside Sweden and students born outside Sweden were combined. Segregation by migration for students born in Sweden but both parents born outside Sweden increased by almost 2 percentage points, from approximately 13 to 15%. For students born outside Sweden, school segregation increased from 1998 to the beginning of 2000s, but has remained at around 10% in recent years.

Once the focus is on survey data using PISA, school segregation in Sweden, according to PISA 2015, was over 13%, which is lower than the OECD average of over 23% (Skolverket, 2016a). Variation in student performance related to differences in the socioeconomic composition of the school's student population increased between 2003 and 2012, from 9 to 12% (Organisation for Economic

Cooperation and Development, 2015b). In PISA 2015, it was less than 16%. It is still lower than the OECD average of 30%, but still higher compared to the other Nordic countries. The lowest variation between schools was in Iceland, with less than 4% (Skolverket, 2016a).

Variation in student performance between schools, measured by final grades from comprehensive schools, increased from around 7% in 2000 to almost 14% in 2016, both for municipal and independent schools (Skolverket, 2018g). The importance of students' family background on learning outcomes increased for all students, especially from 2000 and onwards. The variation in student performance between schools almost doubled between 2000 and 2016.

Hence, results from both data sources confirm that school segregation has increased during the last decades. Still, according to PISA 2015, it is relatively low in Sweden, as well as in the other Nordic countries (Skolverket, 2016a). One reason why the Nordic countries have a relatively low level of segregation could be that the Nordic countries do not implement stratification policies, so-called *tracking*—the practice of sorting students into academic or vocational study programs. Instead everyone follows the same path and the same curriculum throughout compulsory school (Böhlmark, Holmlund, & Lindahl, 2015) (Skolverket, 2016a). Also for other countries, PISA results show that school systems with small between-school variations in performance tend to be those that are comprehensive, meaning that they do not sort students by programme or school based on ability (Organisation for Economic Cooperation and Development, 2016).

8.5 Major School Reforms in Sweden During the Last Decades

In the 1950s, the comprehensive school was introduced and formally decided upon in 1962 (Gustafsson & Yang Hansen, 2017). It meant that compulsory school was extended to comprise 9 years, and with a largely common and undifferentiated curriculum. The comprehensive school replaced a tracked school system in which the common elementary school in grade 6 was differentiated into a secondary grammar school with an academically oriented curriculum that prepared for further academic studies, while the remaining students finished school after 6 or 7 years or went into vocational education (Gustafsson & Yang Hansen, 2017; Husén, 1989). One main aim of the introduction of the comprehensive school was to provide equal educational opportunities for all children, irrespective of family background (Husén 1960).

In the 1990s, the Swedish society experienced several changes. The economic crisis had severe effects on employment and the state finances, while the Swedish school system needed to integrate a rising share of refugees (Holmlund et al., 2014). At the same time, income inequality increased.

After a series of parliamentary reforms in the early 1990s, a number of radical school reforms were launched. Until 1990, the Swedish education system had been largely centralized, and seen as a component of the social democratic welfare state (Organisation for Economic Cooperation and Development, 2015a). Many argued though that the centralized education system had become inefficient and too expensive. The 1990s series of reforms changed the education landscape in Sweden. The highly centralized Swedish school system was decentralized, giving the municipalities the responsibility for organizing and running the primary, secondary, and adult education (SOU, 2014). The intention of the new reforms was to make the school system more appropriate and effective and also to create an education system that increased cooperation between teachers and was better supported by citizens and school staff. A new curriculum for comprehensive and upper secondary school was implemented in 1994. It was designed as an adaptation to the new way of managing schools.

The development of independent schools was encouraged through a nationwide voucher system, which allowed private ("independent") schools to be run with public funding in a quasi-market system (Gustafsson, & Yang Hansen, 2017; Organisation for Economic Cooperation and Development, 2015a). Parents and students could choose which school to attend, depending on availability of places, and municipalities had to ensure that any student in their catchment area could attend one of the public schools in the municipality. The element of choice was motivated by the idea that choice and competition should increase efficiency and boost educational outcomes (Böhlmark, Holmlund, & Lindahl, 2016).

Through the municipalization reform, municipalities received full employer responsibility for all school staff as of 1991 (SOU, 2014). Municipalities were also given responsibility for: determining how resources should be allocated between different parts of the school system; following up and evaluating their own activities, and developing these activities and offering continuing professional development for staff.

As a response to the decline in students' performance, a new series of reforms were implemented in the 2000s. The aim was to give clearer learning goals, clearer performance requirements, more stringent qualification requirements, extensive initiatives for school improvement and continuing professional development, and stricter supervision (SOU, 2014).

In 2011, a new Education Act was implemented. The curricula from 1994 was redesigned, and a new grading system, with criterion-referenced grades in comprehensive school and criterion-referenced course grades in upper secondary school, was introduced.

Recent policy responses in form of "The Education Act" implemented in 2011, aim to provide all students with the opportunity to reach achievement targets and complete upper secondary school, with improved skills for both the labor market and further studies.

8.5.1 The Swedish School System Compensatory Assignment

The Swedish school system prioritizes equity which refers to equal access to high-quality education and aims to compensate for differences in students' capacity to benefit from education (Skolverket, 2018g). The school system shall also be compensatory, aiming at minimizing negative effects of student background on performance, and aims to provide all students with an equal opportunity to learn. All children and students should be provided with support and stimulation, so that they develop to the best of their abilities, regardless of their background or the school they attend (Skolverket, 2013).

8.5.2 Evaluations of the Reforms and Policy Response

The large school reforms of the 1990s resulted in the decentralization and municipalization of schools, the possibility to choose between schools (voucher system), and the establishment of independent schools. At the same time, according to international studies and administrative data, the socioeconomic achievement gap widened. Survey data indicate also a general decline in average achievement of Swedish 15-year-olds, which is not confirmed by administrative data.

Several studies and inquiries have been conducted in order to evaluate whether these extensive reforms have contributed to the decline in performances and weakening equity in Swedish schools, as well as offering proposals on how to improve learning outcomes and the quality of teaching and equity in Swedish schools.

8.5.3 The Effects of the Reforms on Learning Outcomes

The governmental inquiry *The Government Must not Abdicate*, initiated in 2012, aimed at analyzing the effects of the municipalization reforms on learning outcomes, the professional status of teachers and school heads' and teachers' working conditions, as well as equity in schools (SOU, 2014). The inquiry concluded that the reforms had a major impact on the declining results in Swedish schools. It declared that this was due to the transfer of power and responsibility for schools from the central government to municipalities, and the result-based and target-based management of schools. The municipalities were not prepared to take over the responsibility for the schools. Municipalization also resulted in poor salary growth for teachers for a long time, and the proportion of teachers lacking formal qualifications was high. In addition, teachers' working conditions deteriorated as a result of increased external management of schools and extensive documentation and other administrative requirements.

Also in 2012, the government assigned the Institute for Evaluation of Labour Market and Education Policy (IELMEP) the responsibility of evaluating the decentralization of the school system (Holmlund et al., 2014) The report *Decentralisation, school choice and independent schools: results and equivalence in the Swedish school system* focused on the period between the end of the 1980s and 2006. One of the most important conclusions of the report is that the decline in results in the Swedish school system seems to have started already before the reforms of the 1990s. The declining trend did continue throughout the entire reform period, however, and it cannot be excluded that the trend has been affected by changes in the school system due to the school reforms in the 1990s. The report concludes though that there is no evidence that the reforms and the changes at the municipal level would have driven the decline in school results.

In other words, the two investigations on the effects of the reforms on learning outcomes reached contradicting conclusions.

8.5.4 The Effects of the Reforms on Equity in Swedish Schools

Both the governmental inquiry *The Government Must not Abdicate* and the report *Decentralisation, school choice, and independent schools: results and equivalence in the Swedish school system* also analyzed the question of equity in Swedish schools. The governmental inquiry concludes that the municipalization reforms had an impact on equality in schools, as well as learning outcomes. The report *Decentralisation, school choice, and independent schools: results and equivalence in the Swedish school system* concluded that there was an increase in the differences between school results in comprehensive school since the end of the 1980s. This trend was partly explained by the fact that schools had become more segregated in relation to students' background characteristics, which was explained by increased housing segregation as well as school choice. The fact that the composition of students in the country as a whole had changed due to an increase in immigration, and strong increase in the income differences in society since the mid-1990s, were given as the main causes behind the housing segregation. The report concludes that the increased diversity in the results between schools can be related to the reforms.

The *Assessment of the Situation in the Swedish School System* reports published by the Swedish National Agency for Education focused on equity in Swedish schools (Skolverket, 2013, 2015). Even though only a proportion of the increased difference in results between schools can be explained by increased school segregation with regard to the socioeconomic composition of students, the schools seem to increasingly become different with respect to such qualities as students' motivation to study. Peer effects and teachers' expectations differ more and more between schools so that it has become increasingly important which school a student attends. The Agency states that the equity level has deteriorated, and that the school choice reform has most probably contributed to the increased differences between schools. Each student and their parents now have an increased possibility to choose the school they believe is the best for the child, and there are plenty of schools to choose from. At the same time, the choice of school implies an action that can negatively affect students whose parents do not make an active choice.

In April 2015, the Swedish government appointed the Swedish School Commission to submit proposals aimed at improving learning outcomes, quality of teaching, and equity in schools (Skolkommissionen, 2017). The Commission identifies deficient equity as a serious problem in the Swedish school system, which involves a lack of quality in the teaching in certain schools or school classes and shortcomings in the school systems' compensatory assignment, (which aims at minimizing negative effects of student background on performance). The problem seems to be increasing over time. The compensatory assignment is made more difficult in segregated environments. There is also a major risk that less is expected of students in these school environments, and it is also more difficult to recruit experienced teachers and school heads to work in schools in socioeconomically vulnerable areas.

When it comes to the importance of parental education for student academic achievements Holmlund et al (2014) found that it has been relatively stable during the last 20 years, but other studies using a more refined measurement of parental education show an increase also in the importance of parental education (Gustafsson & Yang Hansen, 2017; Skolverket, 2018g).

The evaluations of the effects of the reforms on equity in Swedish schools conclude that the equity level in Swedish schools has deteriorated (Böhlmark et al., 2016; Holmlund et al. 2014; Skolkommissionen, 2017; Skolverket, 2018g; SOU, 2014).

Jenkins, Micklewright, & Schnepf's (2006) study of social segregation in schools in England proposed three main determinants of school segregation: where parents of different social backgrounds live (residential segregation), how parents of different social backgrounds choose schools for their children (parental school choice), and whether school choice of students relates to their social background (schools' selection of students). When students are assigned to their neighborhood school through catchment areas, it is likely that parental choice is executed through the choice of neighborhood, leading to school segregation (Böhlmark et al., 2016; Jenkins et al., 2006). However, even in a fully choice-based school system, residential segregation may also lead to school segregation. Parents might prefer to let their children attend a local school, and factors such as mobility costs might hinder parents from choosing a school outside of their local neighborhood. School choice opportunities can also affect school segregation in other ways. For example, parents who are better informed and have the resources to act on their preferred choice of school for their children are likely to be found in schools of higher quality.

Immigrant families might lack the networks and language in order to make an informed choice. In a school system where schools can select their students, by family background, or by tuition fees, school segregation will also increase.

Böhlmark et al. (2016) examine the most important determinants of school segregation in Sweden. Their main findings show that school segregation has increased between students characterized by native/immigrant background and by high/low education background. The most important factor to explain this increase is neighborhood segregation. Still, in regions in Sweden where school choice has become more prevalent, the school segregation increase exceeded what should be expected given neighborhood segregation.

8.5.5 The Swedish School Commission

The shortcomings identified by the Commission have resulted in a weakened and partly fragmented school system in which there is a low degree of cooperation, collaboration, and collective effort to improve differences between schools and education providers. The same weaknesses have also been noted in the Organisation for Economic Co-operation and Development's (2015a) review of the Swedish school system.

One of the measures proposed to break the trend of increased school segregation and to create a more equitable school system concerns active school choice. The Commission states that mandatory school choice, combined with relevant and comprehensive information to students and their parents/guardians, should be considered. Like the Organisation for Economic Co-operation and Development (2015a), the Commission considers that there is a need to develop a model that enables school choice while counteracting segregation and reduced equity at the same time.

The Commission also proposed a central government grant of six billion Swedish crowns with the purpose of making high-quality teaching and compensatory initiatives for equitable education possible. The responsible authority, Statistics Sweden, should be tasked with drawing up an annual socioeconomic index on which the allocation of the central government grant should be based. The purpose of the index values would be to support education providers in order to assist in the allocation of resources with respect to pupils' varying requirements for compensatory initiatives (Skolkommissionen, 2017). The proposal was decided upon by the government in 2018, and will be implemented, stating 2019.

Other areas the Commission proposed for improvement included, for example, strengthening education providers through central government support and collaboration, skills supply to the school system, increased national responsibility for school funding, and curriculum development and evaluation systems.

8.6 Conclusion

During the last decades, survey results indicate a decline of performance in Swedish schools. For the same time period, survey and administrative data suggest that the importance of students' socioeconomic background for academic performance has increased, and school segregation has become more prevalent.

The last decades saw also an implementation of extensive school reforms. The comprehensive school that was decided upon in 1962, aimed at providing equal educational opportunities for all children, irrespective of family background (Husén, 1960). The reforms of the 1990s and the 2000s, aimed at making the school system more appropriate and effective, but did not explicitly focus on reducing the gaps between low- and high-achieving students.

There are no simple answers to how the reforms of the 1990s have affected the Swedish school system, especially on learning and equity. The school system is complex, making it hard to isolate the causal link between different possible explanatory factors and trends in students' results. However, several evaluations of the effects of the reforms on equity in Swedish schools conclude that equity levels in Swedish schools have deteriorated and that schools have become more segregated (Böhlmark et al., 2016; Holmlund et al., 2014; Skolkommissionen, 2017; Skolverket, 2018g; SOU, 2014).

The Swedish School Commission proposed a number of measures to break the trend of increasing school segregation and to create a more equitable school system thereby reducing the gaps between low- and high-achieving students. One of the measures proposed concerns active school choice. The Commission states that mandatory school choice, combined with relevant and comprehensive information to students and their parents/guardians, should be considered. Another proposed measure was to allocate money to responsible authorities according to a socioeconomic index. It would enable the allocation of resources with respect to pupils' varying requirements for compensatory initiatives (Skolkommissionen, 2017).

It remains to be seen whether the proposals suggested by the Commission will be implemented, and if so, if they will have an effect on school segregation.

References

Böhlmark, A., Holmlund, H., & Lindahl, M. (2015). *Skolsegregation och skolval Rapport 2015:5 (School segregation and school choice Report 2015:5)*. Uppsala, Sweden. Retrieved from https://www.ifau.se/globalassets/pdf/se/2015/r-2015-05-Skolsegregation-och-skolval.pdf.

Böhlmark, A., Holmlund, H., & Lindahl, M. (2016). Parental choice, neighbourhood segregation or cream skimming? An analysis of school segregation after a generalized choice reform. *Journal of Population Economics, 29*(4), 1155–1190.

Gustafsson, J.-E., & Yang, H. K. (2017). Changes in the impact of family education on student educational achievement in Sweden 1988–2014. *Scandinavian Journal of Educational Research, 2017*, 1–18.

8 Socioeconomic Inequality and Student Outcomes ...   151

Henrekson, M., & Jävervall, S. (2016). *Educational performance in Swedish schools is plummeting—What are the facts?* Stockholm, Sweden. Retrieved from https://www.iva.se/globalassets/info-trycksaker/iva/201611-iva-henrekson-javervall-english-e.pdf.

Holmlund, H., Häggblom, J., Lindahl, E., Martinson, S., Sjögren, A., Vikman, U., & Öckert, B. (2014). *Decentralisering, skolval och fristående skolor: resultat och likvärdighet i svensk skola RAPPORT 2014:25 (Decentralisation, school choice and independent schools: results and equivalence in the Swedish school system)*. Uppsala, Sweden. Retrieved from https://www.ifau.se/globalassets/pdf/se/2014/r-2014-25-decentralisering-skolval-och-friskolor.pdf.

Husén, T. (1960). Loss of talent in selective school systems: The case of Sweden. *Comparative Education Review, 4*(2), 70–74.

Husén, T. (1989). The Swedish school reform—Exemplary both ways. *Comparative Education Review, 25*(3), 345–355.

Jenkins, S. P., Micklewright, J., & Schnepf, S. V. (2006). Social segregation in secondary schools: How does England compare with other countries? In *IZA Discussion Paper No. 1959*, January 2006. Retrieved from https://pdfs.semanticscholar.org/6a24/a7d9917ff9f3d0e996e92e0f9fb25cc36834.pdf.

Organisation for Economic Cooperation and Development. (2015a). *Improving schools in Sweden: An OECD perspective*. Paris, France. Retrieved from http://www.oecd.org/education/school/Improving-Schools-in-Sweden.pdf.

Organisation for Economic Cooperation and Development. (2015b). *Sweden country note results from PISA 2015*. France, Paris. Retrieved from http://www.oecd.org/pisa/pisa-2015-Sweden.pdf.

Organisation for Economic Cooperation and Development. (2016). *PISA 2015 results (volume I): Excellence and equity in education*. Paris: France.

Skolkommissionen. (2017). *Samling för skolan. Nationell strategi för kunskap och likvärdighet (SOU 2017:35). (National strategy for improving learning outcomes and equality. Final report from the School Commission)*. Stockholm: 2017.

Skolverket. (2006). *Equity trends in the Swedish school system. A quantitative analysis of variation in student performance and equity from a time perspective*. Stockholm, Sweden: Fritzes.

Skolverket. (2012). *Likvärdig utbildning i svensk grundskola? En kvantitativ analys av likvärdighet över tid (Equity in Swedish comprehensive school? A quantitative analysis of equity trends)*. Stockholm, Sweden: Fritzes. Retrieved from https://www.skolverket.se/sitevision/proxy/publikationer/svid12_5dfee44715d35a5cdfa2899/55935574/wtpub/ws/skolbok/wpubext/trycksak/Blob/pdf2816.pdf?k=2816.

Skolverket. (2013). *An assessment of the situation in the Swedish school system 2013 by the Swedish National Agency for education*. Stockholm, Sweden: Fritzes.

Skolverket. (2015). *An assessment of the situation in the Swedish school system 2015*. Stockholm, Sweden. Retrieved from https://www.skolverket.se/sitevision/proxy/publikationer/svid12_5dfee44715d35a5cdfa2899/55935574/wtpub/ws/skolbok/wpubext/trycksak/Blob/pdf3551.pdf?k=3551.

Skolverket. (2016a). *PISA 2015 15-åringars kunskaper i naturvetenskap, läsförståelse och matematik (PISA 2015. 15-year-olds knowlege in science, reading and mathematics)* Stockholm, Sweden. Retrieved from https://www.skolverket.se/sitevision/proxy/publikationer/svid12_5dfee44715d35a5cdfa2899/55935574/wtpub/ws/skolbok/wpubext/trycksak/Blob/pdf3725.pdf?k=3725.

Skolverket. (2016b). *Utvärdering av den nya betygsskalan samt kunskapskravens utformning (En evaluation of the new grading system and curriculum)*. Stockholm, Sweden. Retrieved from https://mb.cision.com/Public/481/2000399/86ce713756a1eb2e.pdf.

152 P. Löfstedt

Skolverket. (2016c). *TIMSS 2015. Svenska grundskoleelevers kunskaper i matematik och naturvetenskap i ett internationellt perspektiv (TIMSS 2015 Swedish comprehensive school students' knowledge in mathematics and natural sciences in an international perspective).* Stockholm, Sweden. Retrieved from https://www.skolverket.se/sitevision/proxy/publikationer/svid12_5dfee44715d35a5cdfa2899/55935574/wtpub/ws/skolbok/wpubext/trycksak/Blob/pdf3707.pdf?k=3707.

Skolverket. (2018a). *For children aged 1–6 Preschool and preschool class.* Stockholm, Sweden. Retrieved from http://www.omsvenskaskolan.se/engelska/foerskolan-och-foerskoleklass/.

Skolverket. (2018b). *For children and young people aged 7–15. Comprehensive school and recreation centres.* Fritzes. Retrieved from http://www.omsvenskaskolan.se/engelska/grundskolan-och-fritidshem/.

Skolverket. (2018c). *For young people aged 16–20 Upper secondary school.* Stockholm, Sweden: Fritzes. Retrieved from http://www.omsvenskaskolan.se/engelska/gymnasieskolan/.

Skolverket. (2018d). *For children and young people aged 7–20. Special needs comprehensive and upper secondary school.* Stockholm, Sweden: Fritzes. Retrieved from http://www.omsvenskaskolan.se/engelska/grundsaerskolan/.

Skolverket. (2018e). *Beskrivande data 2017. Förskola, skola och vuxenutbildning. Rapport 468 (Descriptive Statistics 2017. Preschool, Coprehenseive school, and Adult Educaiton. Report 468).* Stockholm, Sweden. Retrieved from https://www.skolverket.se/sitevision/proxy/publikationer/svid12_5dfee44715d35a5cdfa2899/55935574/wtpub/ws/skolbok/wpubext/trycksak/Blob/pdf3953.pdf?k=3953.

Skolverket. (2018f). *Urval grundskolan - Elevstatistik.* Retrieved from https://siris.skolverket.se/siris/ris.elever_gr.rapport.

Skolverket. (2018g). *Analyser av familjebakgrundens betydelse för skolresultaten och skillnader mellan skolor. (Analysis of the importance of family background for school results, and differences between schools).* Stockholm, Sweden.

SOU. (2014). *Staten får inte abdikera. Om kommunaliseringen av den svenska skolan. Statens Offentliga Utredningar 2014:5 (The Government must not abdicate-about the municipalization of the school. SOU 2014:5).* Stockholm, Sweden. Fritzes.

Statistics Sweden. (2017). *Temarapport 2017:4. Unga utanför? Så har det gått på arbetsmarknaden för 90-talister utan fullföljd gymnasieutbildning. (Theme report 2017:4. Young people left behind? The situation on the labour market for those born in the 1990s without completed upper secondary education.).* Stockholm, Sweden.

Sveriges kommuner och landsting. (2018). *Fakta förskola. Barn och grupper* (Facts Preschool and groups). Retrieved from https://skl.se/skolakulturfritid/forskolagrundochgymnasieskola/forskolafritidshem/forskola/faktaforskola.3292.html.

Swedish Migration Agency. (2018). *Statistics.* Retrieved from https://www.migrationsverket.se/English/About-the-Migration-Agency/Facts-and-statistics-/Statistics.html.

Chapter 9
Socioeconomic Inequality and Student Outcomes in Finnish Schools

Katariina Salmela-Aro and Anna K. Chmielewski

Abstract Since the release of the results from PISA 2000, Finland has been lauded as a high-performing, high-equity country. This success has been attributed in part to an egalitarian 9-year comprehensive school created by dramatic de-tracking reforms in the late 1960s and early 1970s. However, recent international assessments show this picture may be changing. Not only has Finland's average performance fallen in recent cycles of PISA, but inequality in achievement appears to be increasing. In this chapter, we examine long-term trends in socioeconomic achievement gaps using data from 18 international assessments conducted between 1964 and 2015. We find that SES achievement gaps declined after de-tracking reforms but have increased more recently. These results are robust to two alternate methods of computing achievement gaps and do not appear to be an artifact of dramatic changes in Finland's SES distribution over the time period studied. We suggest possible explanations for this rising inequality.

Keywords Student achievement · Socioeconomic status · Inequality · Finland

9.1 Introduction

In the present chapter, we focus on socioeconomic inequality and student outcomes in Finland. Finnish students have been very successful in the Programme for International Student Assessment (PISA, see Fig. 9.1). In 2000, 2003, and 2006, Finland's academic performance in reading, mathematics, and science was ranked at or near number one among all participating Organisation for Economic

---

K. Salmela-Aro (✉)
University of Helsinki, Helsinki, Finland
e-mail: katariina.salmela-aro@helsinki.fi

ETH Zurich Collegium Helveticum, Zurich, Switzerland

A. K. Chmielewski
University of Toronto, Toronto, Canada

© Springer Nature Singapore Pte Ltd. 2019
L. Volante et al. (eds.), *Socioeconomic Inequality
and Student Outcomes*, Education Policy & Social Inequality 4,
https://doi.org/10.1007/978-981-13-9863-6_9

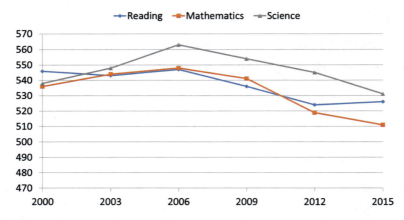

Fig. 9.1 Finnish scaled scores since the initial administration of PISA

Co-operation and Development (OECD) countries (Välijärvi et al., 2007). This exceptionally high attainment of Finnish students in PISA in 2000, 2003, and 2006 in all three literacy domains has led to continuous international interest towards the Finnish educational system (Välijärvi et al., 2007).[1] Finland was the top overall performing country among the OECD countries in 2000 and 2003 PISA studies. Finland was the only country that was able to improve performance (Välijärvi, Kupari, Linnakylä, Reinikainen, & Arffman, 2003). In the 2006 PISA survey, Finland maintained its high performance in all assessed areas of student achievement. In the context of science, the main focus of the PISA 2006 survey, Finnish students outperformed their peers in all 56 countries. Moreover, in the 2009 PISA study, Finland was again the best performing OECD country. According to the Organisation for Economic Co-operation and Development (2010), "Finland is one of the world's leaders in the academic performance of its secondary school students, a position it has held for the past decade. This top performance is also remarkably consistent across schools. Finnish schools seem to serve all students well, regardless of family background, socioeconomic status, or ability" (p. 117). Until the publication of the first PISA results in December 2001, education in Finland did not have a high international reputation. Finnish results on previous international assessments had been average, or even lower than average. Even the Finns themselves thought their education system was nothing special. Thus, this international interest was something new for Finnish education.

However, during recent years there has been a decline in the Finnish students' achievements in PISA. While Finnish students have continued to perform very well in PISA in recent years, there is a trend of decreasing scores. In 2009, 2012, and

---

[1]Finland has a new reform summer 2019 extending the compulsory education until age 18.

9 Socioeconomic Inequality and Student Outcomes … 155

2015, though still near the top, Finland's scores began to decrease slightly (see Fig. 9.1). What about the role of socioeconomic background for academic achievement? In this chapter, we will examine the trends in academic achievement and socioeconomic background. First, we introduce and present the structure of the Finnish compulsory school system, and its governance and administrative processes used to develop and refine educational policies. Second, we present key characteristics of the student population followed by the educational outcomes of low-SES children and educational policy in Finland. Finally, we discuss the most recent challenges in Finnish education.

9.2 Structure of the Finnish Education System

The Finnish educational system aims at achieving equal opportunity with high-quality performance. The main objective of Finnish education policy is to offer all citizens equal opportunities to receive education. The structure of the education system reflects this main principle.

Finland has two official languages, Finnish and Swedish. About 5% of students in basic and upper secondary education attend a school where Swedish is the language of instruction. Both language groups have their own institutions at all educational levels, also at the higher education level. Local authorities are also required to organize education in the Sami language in Sami-speaking areas of Lapland. During recent years, there has been an increase of migrants to Finland, particularly in the metropolitan area of Helsinki. Local authorities organize preparatory education for migrants to enable them to enter basic or upper secondary education.

Pre-primary education is compulsory for children of the age of 6. Pre-primary education is provided both in kindergartens and in schools. In pre-primary education, children acquire basic skills, but learning is primarily through play.

Compulsory basic education starts in the year when a child turns 7 and lasts 9 years. Basic education comprises elementary (grades 1–6) and lower secondary (7–9) level education. Upper secondary school comprises grades 10–12. In grades 1–6 the pupils are mainly taught by one classroom teacher and in grades 7–9 mostly by specialized teachers for each subject.

After completing compulsory basic education after grade 9, young Finns can choose their educational track for the first time—whether to opt for general upper secondary education (academic track, high school) or vocational upper secondary education (vocational track). Student selection is mainly based on their grades in their basic education certificate. This choice is usually split quite evenly, with half of the school population matriculating to general upper secondary school, and the other half attending vocational school. Upper secondary education takes 3–4 years. Completion of upper secondary education—either general or vocational—gives students eligibility to continue to higher education.

The Finnish educational system is highly permeable. There are no dead-ends preventing progression to higher levels of education. The focus in education is on learning rather than testing. There are no national tests for students in basic education in Finland. Instead, teachers are responsible for assessment in their respective subjects on the basis of the objectives included in the curriculum. In Finland, the main types of student assessments are continuous assessment during the course of studies and the final assessment. Also, the grades in the basic education certificate given at the end of year 9 are assigned by teachers. On the basis of this assessment, students are selected for further studies. The only national examination, the matriculation examination, is held at the end of general upper secondary education. Commonly, admission to higher education is based on students' results in the matriculation examination and/or entrance tests. At the moment, a new reform will give the matriculation examination more importance in the admission to higher education.[2]

The high level of equity in the Finnish educational system can be explained by the same 9-year comprehensive education for all, which was launched in 1972 in the whole country and previously in 1968 in some parts of Finland (Simola, 2005). The Finnish educational system was highly stratified before these great reforms in the 1970s (Sahlberg, 2011). There was a visible achievement gap among young adults at the start of comprehensive school in the early 1970s due to very different educational orientations associated with the old parallel system (Simola, 2005). Thus, the most important goal of comprehensive school reform was to strengthen educational and social equality. The old structure of education that served Finland's class-bound, rural society well for decades could no longer meet the new demands of a changing population and time. Finland really needed a system that could deliver an equally rigorous education whether a student came from the rural or an urban neighborhood. Every child thus deserved a good basic education regardless of socioeconomic background, family income, social status, or place of residence (Simola, 2005). When comprehensive school reform began in the early 1970s, its basic goal was to guarantee all children the equal opportunity to a 9-year basic education regardless of their parents' socioeconomic status (SES) and give up pupil tracking completely. Comprehensive school reform was very successful and it achieved all of its goals regarding the structure and accessibility of education before the end of the 1980s (Aho, Pitkanen, & Sahlberg, 2006).

Most education and training are publicly funded in Finland. There are few private schools, so the overwhelming majority of students attend common public comprehensive schools. Prior to the comprehensive education reform in 1972, about 30% of Finnish lower secondary school students attended private schools (authors' own calculations from First International Science Study—FISS—1970 data). During the reform, most of these schools changed into public schools. There are no tuition fees at any level of education. An exception is the tuition fees for non-EU and non-EEA students in higher education, effective from autumn 2016. Most higher education

---

[2]Finland has a new reform summer 2019 extending the compulsory education until age 18.

institutions introduced such tuition fees in 2017. In basic education, school materials, school meals, and transportation to school are also provided free of charge. In upper secondary education, students pay for their books and transport, but currently there is a reform in progress to provide them also free of charge. In addition, there is a well-developed system of study grants and loans.[3] Financial aid can be awarded for full-time study in upper secondary education and in higher education.

Governance has been based on the principle of decentralization since the early 1990s (Sahlberg, 2011). However, before the 1990s governance was very centralized. Broad core curricular guidelines are published for the basic and upper secondary school systems, but the local education providers (i.e., the municipalities) are typically responsible for the local design of the curriculum. Education providers are responsible for practical teaching arrangements as well as the effectiveness and quality of the education provided. Local authorities also determine how much autonomy is passed on to schools. For example, budget management, acquisitions, and recruitment are often the responsibility of the schools. Universities and universities of applied sciences (UAS) enjoy extensive autonomy. The operations of both UAS and universities are built on the freedom of education and research. They organize their own administration, decide on student admission, and design the contents of degree programs.

In the Finnish educational system, sociocultural factors—such as social capital, ethnic homogeneity, and the high professional status of teachers—play key roles when transferability of education policies is considered (Rinne, 2000). Teachers in Finland are well-respected, considered experts of their profession, and issues of classroom management and organization are less noticeable than in some other countries. Teachers have pedagogical autonomy. The Finnish educational system operates in collaboration with its Ministry of Education and Culture, municipalities, and schools. It calls upon all of these entities to be part of the process, with teachers having key roles. The national education administration is organized at two levels. Education policy is the responsibility of the Ministry of Education and Culture and the Finnish National Agency for Education is responsible for the implementation of policy aims. It works with the Ministry to develop educational objectives, content, and methods for education at all levels. Local administration is the responsibility of local authorities. Municipalities make the decisions of allocating of funding, local curricula, and they have autonomy to delegate decision-making power to the schools.

Finland as a country has suffered through major famines, unprecedented immigration, and foreign invasion (Sahlberg, 2011). As a consequence, Finland has had a difficult history and only achieved its independence about 100 years ago in 1917. Many leaders of the Finnish revolution were teachers and viewed as heroes. These early teacher leaders became identified with the importance of learning and its ability to allow for autonomous self-reflective choice. With limited natural resources, Finland's major resource is its population, its human capital which has

---

[3]Finland has a new reform (summer 2019) extending compulsory education until age 18.

survived these conditions, faced challenges with an inscrutable sense of "sisu"—determination and persistence that defines a national distinctive identity (Salmela-Aro, 2017).

9.3 Key Characteristics of the Student Population

According to the most recent data available, Finland had a relatively socioeconomically advantaged population, compared to other OECD countries. In PISA 2015 and the Trends in International Mathematics and Science Study (TIMSS) 2015 fourth grade, only about 2% of students met the definition of low-SES used in this volume (i.e., low-parental education; their most educated parent had ISCED 2 or less), while nearly 50% of students in TIMSS and 60% of students in PISA had high SES (parental education of ISCED 5A or more). Thus, as defined by parental education, Finland is among the highest-SES countries considered in this volume. As mentioned at the beginning of the chapter, the very high levels of educational attainment are a recent change in Finland, reflecting rapid industrialization of the country in the twentieth century. In the First International Mathematics Study (FIMS) 1964, over 90% of Finnish students reported that their most educated parent had ISCED 2 or less. Even as recently as TIMSS 1999 and PISA 2000, over 20% of Finnish students reported low-parental education.

Among low-SES students in Finland in PISA 2015, 22% were from immigrant backgrounds (13% first generation and 9% second generation). This is an over-representation of students from immigrant backgrounds in the low-SES group, in a country where immigrants constitute only about 4% of the student population overall. As mentioned at the beginning of the chapter, the traditionally low levels of immigration in Finland have increased markedly in recent years. In TIMSS 1999 and PISA 2000, less than 2% of students reported a first- or second-generation immigrant background. By 2015, the share of students with an immigrant background approximately doubled to nearly 4% of students in PISA 2015, and over 5% of students in the slightly younger 4th-grade cohort of TIMSS 2015. In addition to increasing levels of immigration, the immigrant student population in Finland has also become relatively more socioeconomically disadvantaged (Motti-Stefanidi & Salmela-Aro, 2018; Salmela-Aro, Read, & Rimpelä, 2018). In TIMSS 1999 and PISA 2000, students from immigrant backgrounds actually had slightly *more* educated parents than non-immigrant students. While over 20% of non-immigrant students had parents with less than ISCED 2, the share was a couple of percentage points lower for immigrant students. By 2015, both immigrant and non-immigrant parents had become more educated, but immigrant parents had not kept pace with the rapid educational upgrading of the native-born Finnish population. In PISA 2015 and TIMSS 2015 fourth grade, less than 2% of non-immigrant students had low-parental education compared to about 10% of immigrant students.

Among low-SES students in Finland in PISA 2012 (the most recent year available), 36% reported living in single-parent families. This is an overrepresentation of single-parent backgrounds among low-SES students, given that only about 16% of students overall come from single-parent families in Finland. The share of single-parent families in Finland is somewhat high by international standards. Although the rate of single-parent households did not change markedly in Finland between PISA 2000 and 2012, the overrepresentation of single-parent households among low-SES students increased substantially in this period, along with the dramatic decline in the share of low-SES students. By 2012, the degree of overrepresentation of single-parent households among low-SES students in Finland was among the highest of OECD countries.

9.4 Educational Outcomes of Low-SES Children

The main aim of the present chapter was to examine trends in socioeconomic inequality of student outcomes in Finland. In particular, we focus on SES achievement gaps, defined as disparities in academic achievement between students from low- and high-parental education backgrounds. In order to investigate long-term trends covering the period of comprehensive school reforms up to the present, we draw on data from 18 international large-scale assessments of math, science, and/or reading: the First and Second International Mathematics Studies (FIMS 1960 and SIMS 1980), the First and Second International Science Studies (FISS 1970 and SISS 1984), the first international reading comprehension study (FIRCS 1970), the Reading Literacy Study (RLS 1991), three cycles of TIMSS (1999, 2011, and 2015), one cycle of the Progress in Reading Literacy Study (PIRLS 2011), and six cycles of PISA (2000–2015). Although the different math, science, and reading assessments were not designed to be fully comparable, we standardize achievement by computing z-scores in each subject within the Finnish sample of each study, and then pool all subjects and studies into one analysis. We take this approach to maximize data coverage. In addition, as we have shown in previous research, trends in SES achievement gaps estimated from different studies (PISA, TIMSS, and PIRLS) tend to be similar to one another and to trends estimated from pooled data (Chmielewski, 2019).

We use parental education as our primary measure of family SES, taking the higher value when both parents' education is available. Parental education was generally reported in 6-8 categories, such as (1) None, (2) Primary/ISCED 1, (3) Lower secondary/ISCED 2, (4) Vocational upper secondary/ISCED 3B or C, (5) Academic upper secondary/ISCED 3A, (6) Postsecondary vocational certificate/ISCED 4, (7) Short or applied college degree/ISCED 5B, and (8) Bachelor's degree/ISCED 5A or more.

We impute missing parental education data in each study using multiple imputations by iterative chained equations and creating five imputed datasets for each study. We use two different methods to compute parental education achievement gaps. First, we follow the method of other chapters in this volume and compute gaps between students with low-parental education (ISCED 2 or less) and all other students. However, due to the rapid educational upgrading of the Finnish population during the twentieth century, any long-term trends in SES gaps in outcomes are likely to be confounded by changes in the distribution of the parental education variable used as a measure of SES. Therefore, our second (and preferred) method computes achievement gaps between the study-specific 90th and 10th percentiles of parental education (90/10 SES achievement gaps), following Reardon's (2011) method for income achievement gaps. We also compute gaps between the top and middle (90th and 50th percentiles) of the parental education distribution and between the middle and bottom (50th and 10th percentiles) of the parental education distribution. In order to compute 90/10, 90/50, and 50/10 achievement gaps, we retain the maximum available categories of parental education in each year and each study. For both types of SES achievement gaps, we adjust each gap for the estimated reliability of students' or parents' reports of parental education, as well as for each test. We compute bootstrap standard errors for each gap. (See Chmielewski (2019) for more methodological details.)

Figure 9.2 displays results from the first SES achievement gap method, the high–low-parental education category difference. Each data point represents this difference in the Finnish subsample of the international assessment indicated,

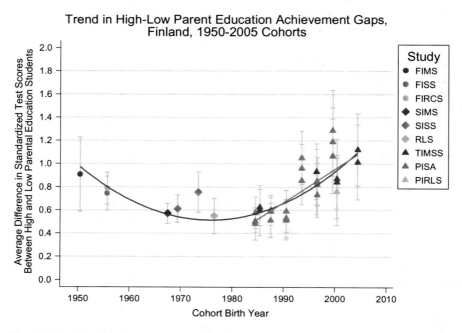

Fig. 9.2 Trend in high-low parent education achievement gaps, Finland, 1950–2005 cohorts

meaning that higher values correspond to greater socioeconomic inequality in achievement. The gaps are plotted against the birth year of sampled students, which ranges from approximately 1950, corresponding to 14-year-old students tested in FIMS 1964, to approximately 2005, corresponding to 10-year-old students tested in TIMSS 2015. The dark gray line is a quadratic fit line estimated from all data points in the figure, and the light gray line is a linear fit line estimated from only the cohorts born in or after 1984. Both fit lines are weighted by the estimated inverse sampling error variance of each gap. Figure 9.2 shows a pronounced U-shaped trend in SES achievement gaps across the Finnish 1950–2005 cohort birth years. SES achievement gaps declined to a low point in approximately the 1984 birth cohort (corresponding to the PISA 2000 sample) and then increased from 1984 to 2005 birth cohort.

However, the estimated trend in Fig. 9.2 is confounded by dramatic changes in the distribution of the parental education of children born over this 55-year period in Finland. Over time, as the high-parental education group expands, it becomes less positively selected and its achievement is expected to decline. Likewise, as the low-parental education group shrinks and becomes more negatively selected, its achievement is expected to decline as well. Thus, the achievement gaps in Fig. 9.2 may not capture well the overall level of socioeconomic inequality in achievement, as these selection effects drive high–low-parental education gaps higher in early and recent birth cohorts when the high- and low-parental education groups are very unequal in size and drive gaps lower in middle cohorts when the high and low groups are more evenly distributed.

The second method for computing SES achievement gaps avoids this issue by computing gaps between the cohort-specific 90th and 10th percentiles of the parental education distribution. This percentile-based approach relies on the assumption that SES is a positional good, and that having highly educated parents confers mainly relative rather than absolute advantages to children's academic achievement. In the FIMS 1964 Finnish sample, the 90th percentile of parental education falls at only 9 years of education, the 50th percentile at 6 years of education, and the 10th percentile at 4 years of education. In the TIMSS 2015 fourth-grade Finnish sample, the 90th percentile of parental education falls at graduate degree ("beyond ISCED 5A first degree"), the 50th percentile at ISCED 5B, and the 10th percentile at ISCED 3. In the PISA 2015 Finnish sample, the parental education gap is poorly estimated because both the 90th and 50th percentiles fall at ISCED 5A. Therefore, we also examine trends in SES achievement gaps for two other measures of SES—parental occupation and number of books in the household, which have more evenly distributed categories—to check the robustness of the parental education gap trend results.

Figure 9.3 displays the results of the 90/10 SES achievement gap analysis. Here each data point is the estimated gap between students at the 90th and 10th percentiles of parental education in a given study. Again, the two fit lines are derived from weighted least squares regressions with quadratic and linear cohort terms.

Figure 9.3 shows that the U-shaped trend in Fig. 9.2 is not entirely an artifact of the changing distribution of parental education. Using a method that captures

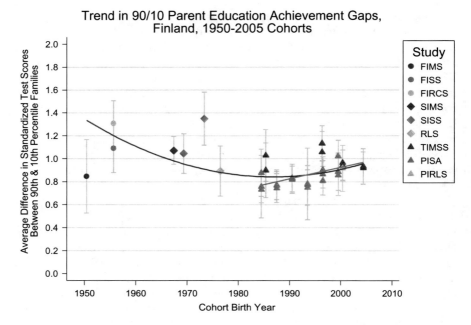

Fig. 9.3 Trend in 90/10 parent education achievement gaps, Finland, 1950–2005 cohorts

inequality in achievement across the entire SES distribution, we find that gaps in early birth cohorts do not decline as expected but in fact *increase*. This indicates that, at that time, there were large differences in achievement not only between the group whose parents had more than ISCED 2 and the rest but also among all the lower levels of parental education below ISCED 2. As expected, gaps in middle cohorts are larger in Fig. 9.3, reflecting that the more even distribution across the two SES groups in Fig. 9.2 does not fully capture inequality in achievement across the entire SES distribution. Also as expected, gaps in the most recent cohorts are smaller in Fig. 9.3, due to the extreme negative selection at work on the low-parental education group in these cohorts in Fig. 9.2. However, after all these changes, the quadratic trend seen in Fig. 9.2, though less extreme, is still visible in Fig. 9.3. A squared term for cohort birth year is significantly different from zero in the weighted least squares regression. As in Fig. 9.2, SES achievement gaps are smallest in the 1984 birth cohort, and the increase in gaps thereafter, though less extreme than in Fig. 9.2, is also still present. A linear term for cohort birth year is significantly different from zero in a weighted least squares regression for gaps from the 1984 cohort and later. Trends in 90/10 achievement gaps for two alternative measures of SES, parental occupation and books in the household, also displayed very similar U-shaped patterns, with a decline until the 1984 cohort and increase thereafter (results not shown).

9 Socioeconomic Inequality and Student Outcomes ...

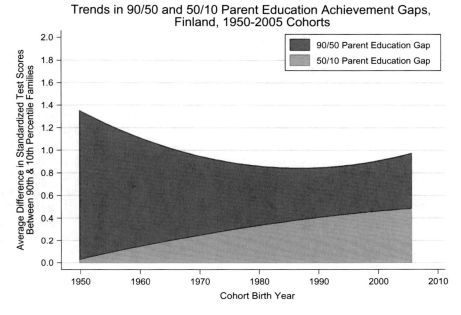

Fig. 9.4 Trends in 90/50 and 50/10 parent education achievement gaps, Finland, 1950–2005 cohorts

A further advantage of the percentile method is the ability to compute 90/50 and 50/10 parental education gaps. Figure 9.4 displays these results. The dark gray region represents the gap between the 90th and 50th percentiles of parental education, and the light gray region represents the gap between the 50th and 10th percentiles of parental education. It is apparent from Fig. 9.4 that there has been a marked change in 90/50 and 50/10 gaps across the 1950–2005 birth cohorts. In the 1950 cohort, the 90/10 gap was dominated by the gap between the top and middle of the parental education distribution; there was hardly any achievement difference between the 50th and 10th percentiles of parental education. By the 2005 cohort, the 90/10 gap was roughly evenly split between the top and bottom of the distribution. Therefore, the large decline in the 90/10 gap between the 1950 and 1984 birth cohorts seen in Fig. 9.3 was entirely due to an even more dramatic decline in the achievement gap between the top and middle of the parental education distribution. This decline was somewhat offset by a steady increase in the gap between the middle and bottom of the parental education distribution. Since the 1984 birth cohort, the 50/10 gap has continued to increase, while the decline in the 90/50 gap leveled off and even increased slightly in recent years. As mentioned above, the 90/50 gap may be underestimated in recent years of PISA due to the large number of observations in the ISCED 5A category. However, results are very similar when removing PISA 2009-2015 from the trend. 90/50 and 50/10 trend results for gaps based on parental occupation and household books are also similar (results not shown).

These results suggest that major Finnish educational reforms creating comprehensive lower secondary schools in the 1960s and 1970s may have reduced SES achievement gaps for subsequent cohorts, particularly gaps between the top and middle of the SES distribution. The timing of the reform would lead us to expect a decline in achievement gaps between the 1956 birth cohort (corresponding to FISS 1970) and the 1966 birth cohort (corresponding to SIMS 1980). That the declines continue for two more decades after these cohorts may indicate a prolonged implementation process and/or the effects of other equity-promoting reforms apart from de-tracking. That the reduction in gaps was concentrated between the top and middle of the distribution suggests that primarily only high-SES students benefitted from the old academic track schools, while middle- and low-SES students did not have access. The results for recent years suggest, however, that the equitable effects of the comprehensive school may not have been sustained in the long term, namely, that the Finnish educational environment has grown more unequal since the 1984 birth cohort (corresponding to PISA 2000). Increases in SES gaps have occurred primarily between the middle and bottom of the SES distribution. However, the gap between the top and middle of the distribution remains substantial, constituting about half of the total 90/10 SES gap.

9.5 Educational Policy

Finnish educational policies can be characterized by sustainable and stable rather than conflicting reforms and fundamental shifts in political directions. Rather than revolutions, the Finnish educational system has experienced a gradual evolution.

Providing equal opportunities for all citizens to high-quality education and training is a long-term objective of the Finnish education policy. The keywords in Finnish education policy are quality, efficiency, equity, and recently also internationalization (Lonka et al., 2015; Salmela-Aro & Trautwein, 2013; Wang, Chow, Hofkens, & Salmela-Aro, 2015). The basic right to education and culture is recorded in the constitution. The policy is built on the principles of lifelong learning and tuition-free education. Education is seen as a key to competitiveness and well-being of the society (Lonka et al., 2015).

There is a widespread consensus on the main pillars of education policy, and the policy is characterized by cooperation and continuity. Tripartite partnership among government, trade unions, and employer organizations is an integrated part of policymaking. Participation and consultation of a wide range of different stakeholders play a central role in educational reform. Teachers—with the Trade Union of Education as their representative—are key players in the development of education. The main objectives and broad lines of the policy are defined at the central level, but the implementation of these is the responsibility of the local level.

According to a recent international UN survey, Finnish people are the happiest population in the world (United Nations Sustainable Development Solutions Network, 2018), but they too are facing some of the same problems as other countries. The homogenous population in Finland is beginning to show some signs of the problems associated with integrating a diverse new immigrant population. And while the country as a whole holds its teachers in high regard and places a high degree of social trust in their expertise to provide all of their children with an excellent education, the teachers themselves are increasingly showing signs of burnout—which in Finland is shown by increased stress, absenteeism, and feelings of inability to work (Pietarinen, Pyhältö, Soini, & Salmela-Aro, 2013; Salmela-Aro, 2017).

9.6 Recent Challenges in the Finnish Education

Recently, in the interest of advancing technology, entrepreneurial activity, and environmental sustainability, the Finns began devising core aims and objectives for their elementary and lower secondary schools, and created the Finnish National Core Curriculum for Upper Secondary School, effective from 2010 onwards. The Finnish national core curriculum highlights the need for students to actively acquire and apply science knowledge and twenty-first century or generic competencies (attitudes, knowledge, and skills), with an emphasis on the use of technology in learning both in and out of school. The Finnish curriculum and models of learning and instruction emphasize the design and use of science and engineering practices in order to support students in learning science, prepare them for understanding the actual work of scientists, and make science careers more interesting to them. In Finland, decisions about which scientific practices and curriculum content should be enacted in classrooms are made with the deep involvement of professional teachers, who have subject area expertise and empirical science research experience.

Finnish students have traditionally performed very well in PISA, but in recent years there is a trend of decreasing scores. In 2000, 2003, and 2006, Finland's academic performance in reading, mathematics, and science was ranked at or near number one among all participating OECD countries. In 2009, 2012, and 2015, though still near the top, Finland's scores began to decrease slightly. A recent concern in Finland is that the country has the largest gap in PISA achievement between native-born and immigrant students (Motti-Stefanidi & Salmela-Aro, 2018; Salmela-Aro et al., 2018).

In Finnish comprehensive schools, there has historically been a rule of neighborhood school attendance (Söderström & Uusitalo, 2005). Thus, children enter the closest school in the area they live in. However, parental choice of schools outside of the assigned catchment area boundary was introduced in the Basic Education Act of 1998 (Seppänen, 2003) as a part of a larger school reform promoting freedom, decentralization, and choice in education (Seppänen, 2003). Studies in Finland show the influence of the distinctive school choices made by the upper social class (Kosunen & Seppänen, 2015). Since 1998, school choice has increased in popularity, as have schools with a special subject emphasis (e.g., science, arts, or sports) and selective admission by aptitude tests. Recent research shows that school enrollment in a major metropolitan area in Finland is more socioeconomically segregated than would be predicted based on assigned catchment areas, suggesting that school choice increases socioeconomic segregation (Bernelius & Vaattovaara, 2016; Kivirauma, Klemeä, & Rinne, 2006; Kosunen, Bernelius, Seppanen, & Porkka, 2016). The study paths of students from different socioeconomic backgrounds are now becoming diversified, meaning that students from different socioeconomic backgrounds tend to make different choices and end up in different study paths in relation to the selectiveness at comprehensive school (Kosunen, 2014; Seppänen, Kalalahti, Rinne, & Simola, 2015). In addition, peers seem to share a similar SES, educational aspirations, and educational pathways (Kiuru et al., 2012; see also Tynkkynen, Tolvanen, & Salmela-Aro, 2012; Tynkkynen, Vuori, & Salmela-Aro, 2012).

All of these recent policy developments, as well as our results in this chapter showing increasing SES achievement gaps in recent cohorts, indicate that Finland's international reputation as an extremely egalitarian system is in peril. Finnish education policymakers must take seriously this increasing inequality and seek to address it in future reform efforts.

References

Aho, E., Pitkanen, K., & Sahlberg, P. (2006). *Policy development and reform principles of basic and secondary education in Finland since 1969* (Education Working Paper Series No. 2). Washington, DC: The World Bank.

Bernelius, V., & Vaattovaara, M. (2016). Choice and segregation in the "most egalitarian" schools: Cumulative decline in urban schools and neighborhoods of Helsinki. *Finland. Urban Studies, 53*(15), 3155–3171. https://doi.org/10.1177/0042098015621441.

Chmielewski, A. K. (2019). The global increase in the socioeconomic achievement gap, 1964 to 2015. *American Sociological Review, 84*(3), 517–544. https://doi.org/10.1177/0003122419847165.

Finnish National Agency for Education. (n.d.). *Education system: Equal opportunities to high-quality education*. Retrieved from https://www.oph.fi/english/education_system.

Kiuru, N., Salmela-Aro, K., Nurmi, J.-E., Zettergren, P., Andersson, H., & Bergman, L. (2012). Best friends in adolescence show similar educational careers in early adulthood. *Journal of Applied Developmental Psychology, 33*(2), 102–111. https://doi.org/10.1016/j.appdev.2011.12.001.

Kivirauma, J., Klemelä, K., & Rinne, R. (2006). Segregation, integration, inclusion—The ideology and reality in Finland. *European Journal of Special Needs Education, 21*(2), 117–133. https://doi.org/10.1080/08856250600600729.

Kosunen, S. (2014). *Reputation and parental logics of action in local school choice in urban Finland*. Helsinki, Finland: Unigrafia.

Kosunen, S., Bernelius, V., Seppänen, P., & Porkka, M. (2016). School choice to lower secondary schools and mechanisms of segregation in urban Finland. *Urban Education*, 1–28. https://doi.org/10.1177/0042085916666933.

Kosunen, S., & Seppänen, P. (2015). The transmission of capital and a feel for the game: Upper-class school choice in Finland. *Acta Sociologica, 58*(4), 329–342. https://doi.org/10.1177/0001699315607968.

9 Socioeconomic Inequality and Student Outcomes …

Lonka, K., Hietajärvi, L., Moisala, M., Tuominen-Soini, H., Hakkarainen, K., & Salmela-Aro, K. (2015). *Schools and education in the digital era: EU overview and the Finnish case.* Presentation for the Committee on Culture and Education, European Parliament. Retrieved from http://www.europarl.europa.eu/cmsdata/84195/Presentation%20Kirsti%20Lonka.pdf.

Motti-Stefanidi, F., & Salmela-Aro, K. (2018). Challenges and resources for immigrant youth positive adaptation: What does scientific evidence show us? *European Psychologist, 23*(1), 1–5. https://doi.org/10.1027/1016-9040/a000315.

Organisation for Economic Co-operation and Development. (2010). *Strong performers and successful reformers in education: Lessons from PISA for the United States.* Paris, France: OECD Publishing.

Pietarinen, J., Pyhältö, K., Soini, T., & Salmela-Aro, K. (2013). Reducing teacher burnout: A socio-contextual approach. *Teaching and Teacher Education, 35,* 62–72. https://doi.org/10.1016/j.tate.2013.05.003.

Reardon, S. F. (2011). The widening academic achievement gap between the rich and the poor: New evidence and possible explanations. In G. J. Duncan & R. J. Murnane (Eds.), *Whither opportunity? Rising inequality, schools, and children's life chances* (pp. 91–115). New York, NY: Russell Sage Foundation.

Rinne, R. (2000). The globalisation of education: Finnish education on the doorstep of the new EU millennium. *Educational Review, 52*(2), 131–142. https://doi.org/10.1080/713664043.

Sahlberg, P. (2011). *Finnish lessons: What can the world learn from educational change in Finland?.* New York, NY: Teachers College Press.

Salmela-Aro, K. (2017). Dark and bright sides of thriving: School burnout and engagement in the Finnish context. *European Journal of Developmental Psychology, 14*(3), 337–349. https://doi.org/10.1080/17405629.2016.1207517.

Salmela-Aro, K., Read, S., & Rimpelä, A. (2018). Immigration status, gender and school burnout in Finnish lower secondary school students: A longitudinal study. *International Journal of Behavioral Development, 42*(2), 225–236. https://doi.org/10.1177/0165025417690264.

Salmela-Aro, K., & Trautwein, U. (2013). School success: Perspectives from Europe and beyond. *European Psychologist, 18*(2), 77–78. https://doi.org/10.1027/1016-9040/a000148.

Seppänen, P. (2003). Patterns of public-school markets in the Finnish comprehensive school from a comparative perspective. *Journal of Educational Policy, 18*(5), 513–531. https://doi.org/10.1080/0268093032000124875.

Seppänen, P., Kalalahti, M., Rinne, R., & Simola, H. (Eds.). (2015). *Loukoutuva peruskoulu—Perheiden kouluvalinnat, yhteiskuntaluokat ja koulutuspolitiikka* [Segmenting comprehensive school—Parental school choice, social classes and educational policies]. Research in Educational Sciences, 68, Jyväskylä, Finland: Finnish Educational Research Association.

Simola, H. (2005). The Finnish miracle of PISA: Historical and sociological remarks on teaching and teacher education. *Comparative Education, 41*(4), 455–470. https://doi.org/10.1080/03050060500317810.

Söderström, M., & Uusitalo, R. (2005). *School choice and segregation. Evidence from an admission reform* (IFAU Working Paper 2005:7). Retrieved from https://www.ifau.se/globalassets/pdf/se/2005/wp05-07.pdf.

Tynkkynen, L., Tolvanen, A., & Salmela-Aro, K. (2012a). Trajectories of educational expectations from adolescence to young adulthood in Finland. *Developmental Psychology, 48*(6), 1674–1685. https://doi.org/10.1037/a0027245.

Tynkkynen, L., Vuori, J., & Salmela-Aro, K. (2012b). The role of psychological control, socioeconomic status and academic achievement in parents' educational aspirations for their adolescent children. *European Journal of Developmental Psychology, 9*(6), 695–710. https://doi.org/10.1080/17405629.2012.671581.

United Nations Sustainable Development Solutions Network. (2018). *World happiness report.* Retrieved from http://worldhappiness.report/ed/2018/.

Välijärvi, J., Kupari, P., Linnakylä, P., Reinikainen, P., & Arffman, I. (2003). *The Finnish success in PISA—And some reasons behind it: PISA 2000.* Jyväskylä, Finland: Institute for Educational Research. Retrieved from https://eric.ed.gov/?id=ED478054.

Välijärvi, J., Kupari, P., Linnakylä, P., Reinikainen, P., Sulkunen, S., Törnroos, J., & Arffman, I. (2007). *The Finnish success in PISA—And some reasons behind it 2.* Jyväskylä, Finland: Institute for Educational Research. Retrieved from https://jyx.jyu.fi/bitstream/handle/123456789/37478/978-951-39-3038-7.pdf?sequence=1.

Wang, M.-T., Chow, A., Hofkens, K., & Salmela-Aro, K. (2015). The trajectories of student emotional engagement and school burnout with academic and psychological development: Findings from Finnish adolescents. *Learning and Instruction, 35,* 57–65. https://doi.org/10.1016/j.learninstruc.2014.11.004.

Chapter 10
Socioeconomic Inequality and Student Outcomes in Canadian Schools

Alana Butler

Abstract This chapter examines how income inequality in Canada has contributed to an "achievement gap" between students from lower and higher socioeconomic backgrounds in Canada. The impacts of socioeconomic inequality in the preschool and elementary years can lead to significant differences in academic achievement between children from affluent and lower income families. The chapter surveys existing research regarding low socioeconomic status and childhood academic outcomes and then explores structural and sociocultural factors associated with socioeconomic achievement gaps. Next, the chapter examines how cultural capital deficits directly affect access to postsecondary education. In conclusion, the chapter discusses some of the evidence-based interventions aimed at eliminating the socioeconomic achievement gap in Canadian schools.

Keywords Student achievement · Socioeconomic status · Inequality · Canada

10.1 Introduction

The 2015 PISA results continued to highlight Canada's high standing in terms of educational outcomes for its youths in comparison to other international jurisdictions. Since the inception of PISA in 2000, Canada has placed in the top 10 in each cycle across all three domains: Reading, Mathematics, and Science. The most recent results inspired the British Broadcasting Corporation (BBC) to call Canada an "education superpower" (Coughlan, 2017). These high levels of overall student performance have occurred in spite of Canada's relatively high level of immigration (Cheng & Yan, 2018; Klinger, Volante, & Bilgili, 2018; Volante, Klinger, Siegel, & Bilgili, 2017). PISA results and other international comparative measures of student achievement have each illustrated that between-school variation in student performance is very low in Canada, reflecting a high level of educational equity

---

A. Butler (✉)
Queen's University, Kingston, Canada
e-mail: alana.butler@queensu.ca

© Springer Nature Singapore Pte Ltd. 2019
L. Volante et al. (eds.), *Socioeconomic Inequality and Student Outcomes*, Education Policy & Social Inequality 4,
https://doi.org/10.1007/978-981-13-9863-6_10

(e.g., Coughlan, 2017; Organisation for Economic Co-operation and Development, 2016b). In spite of this overall relative success, the media and others have raised concerns about the lack of educational progress based on unchanging or decreasing PISA scores over time (e.g., Chu, 2017). Yet a review of PISA data demonstrates that very few high-performing countries have witnessed a growth in PISA scores over time (Organisation for Economic Co-operation and Development, 2018a). Overall, the ongoing high levels of relative performance coupled with the low between-school variation found across PISA cycles do indeed illustrate that children in Canada benefit from high levels of education.

In most industrialized developed countries, there exists an academic achievement gap between the wealthiest and poorest students (e.g., Organisation for Economic Co-operation and Development, 2017; Parker, Marsh, Jerrim, Guo, & Dicke, 2018; Schmidt, Burroughs, Zoido, & Houang, 2015; UNESCO, 2014). The Council of Education Ministers, Canada (2018) found that Canada has the second most equitable education system with respect to socioeconomic status (SES). As an example, evidence from the United States indicates that low SES has a significant effect on educational achievement among children and youths (Ainsworth, 2002; Evans, 2004; Fagan, 2017; Hoxby & Turner, 2013). Canadian studies show that the gap between low versus high SES families is not as wide as it is in the United States, where there are larger geographical areas with a concentration of low SES populations (Burton, Phipps, & Zhang, 2013; Ward & Belanger, 2010). Clearly, Canada has been able to ameliorate some of the educational impacts of socioeconomic inequity observed in other highly industrialized developed countries. One important consideration is that 6.0% of Canada's gross domestic product (GDP) is allocated to educational institutions, which is substantially higher than the Organisation for Economic Co-operation and Development (OECD) average of 5.2% (Statistics Canada, 2017c). As a result, teaching in Canada is considered to be a valued profession and teachers are well compensated.

While there may be much to celebrate in terms of educational equity in Canada relative to many other international jurisdictions, educational inequities do indeed exist in Canada and these are associated with economic disadvantages. PISA results, and other measures of achievement throughout the country do highlight a relatively high level of within-school variation in Canada (e.g., Organisation for Economic Co-operation and Development, 2016b). These findings demonstrate that in spite of the high level of overall equity in terms of schooling, substantial portions of the student population do not equally benefit from such educational opportunities.

These inequities can be found amongst the provinces, between communities, and within schools, and in each instance, a fundamental difference appears to be associated with socioeconomic factors. Achievement differences due to income inequality have been identified in preschool and elementary children and evidence strongly suggests these early "achievement gaps" either remain stable or increase throughout, which contributes to differences in academic achievement in later years (Burton et al., 2013; Caro, McDonald, & Willms, 2009; Cleveland & Krashinsky, 2003; Finnie, Childs, & Wismer, 2011).

10.2 Provincial Jurisdiction of Education and the National Achievement Gap

In Canada, education is regulated by each province and territory, which in turn each develops its own curricula. As a result, there are some structural differences amongst the provinces (e.g., Klinger & Saab, 2012). Children begin formal schooling in Kindergarten in the year they turn 5. Ontario offers Junior and Senior Kindergarten. Students enter Grade 1 and continue their schooling until Grade 12 in all of the provinces except Quebec, where Grade 12 is replaced by the first year of the CEGEP (*Collège d'enseignement général et professionnel*, and in English, *College of General and Vocational Education*). Schooling is typically divided into elementary and secondary components, although the grade at which the transition is made varies across provinces and many provinces further subdivide these two categories (e.g., primary and junior elementary, middle schools, junior and senior secondary). This transition typically occurs between Grades 7 and 9. The transition from primary to secondary is coupled with the shift from a single teacher to multiple subject area teachers. The vast majority of students attend publicly funded schools across Canada. These schools are non-sectarian, although Alberta, Saskatchewan, and Ontario provide full provincial funding for their religious-based Separate (most often Catholic) school systems. The secondary school graduation rate in Canada was 87% in 2015, slightly higher than the OECD average of 86% (Statistics Canada, 2017c).

While public schooling is free to all children, approximately 6% of children attend private schools in Canada, in which a portion or all of the student fees are paid for by the family (Frenette & Chan, 2015). These proportions vary by province, with the highest numbers attending private schools in Quebec, and much lower proportions in Alberta and Ontario, most likely due to the funding differences for Catholic education. While 94% of Canada's children receive free public education until the completion of secondary school, postsecondary education, while indirectly subsidized by provincial governments, is not free to attend. In spite of the presence of tuition fees, Canadians report a high level of postsecondary education. The proportion of adults in Canada between the ages of 25 and 64 with postsecondary education is 57%, with 28.5% having a Bachelor's degree or more, which is the highest among OECD countries (Statistics Canada, 2017c).

Nevertheless, these proportions vary by province, and these variations correlate with differences in educational measures. As an example, Table 10.1 illustrates the relationship between levels of education of adults and the PISA results of 15-year-olds for 2015. Acknowledging the error of measurement for the PISA 2015 scores varies by each province due to large differences in provincial sample sizes, and noting that the 2015 assessment had a primary focus on Science, these data illustrate positive correlations amongst the percentage of the provincial adult population (aged 25–64) where 0.55 was with Mathematics (1-tailed $p < 0.05$),

Table 10.1 Provincial-level PISA results and % of population with Bachelor's degree or more

Province	Pisa math 2015	Pisa reading 2015	PISA science 2015	% of adults with bachelor's degree or more	% of females with bachelor's degree or more
British Columbia	522	536	539	29.9	34.7
Alberta	511	533	541	28.2	30.7
Saskatchewan	484	496	496	22.5	25.9
Manitoba	489	498	499	25.2	28.4
Ontario	509	527	524	31.9	33.9
Quebec	544	532	537	25.5	28.0
New Brunswick	493	505	506	20.2	23.1
Nova Scotia	497	517	517	25.5	28.9
Prince Edward Is.	499	515	515	23.7	27.9
Newfoundland	486	505	506	18.3	20.9
Canada	516	527	528	28.5	30.9

Note Census data obtained from Statistics Canada (2017a, 2017b, 2017c, 2017d); Canadian PISA data obtained from O'Grady et al. (2016)

0.72 with Reading ($p < 0.01$), and 0.67 with Science ($p < 0.05$). The correlations were found to be slightly smaller for the percentage of the female adult population at 0.52 with Mathematics ($p < 0.05$), 0.71 with Reading ($p < 0.01$), and 0.65 with Science ($p < 0.05$). In contrast, correlations with other measures of provincial wealth such as median income and per capita GDP have insignificant correlations below 0.30 with PISA results.

As noted previously, Canada has shown a relatively high level of educational equity. How does this compare to measures of economic inequity? The Gini coefficient is a measure of inequality of income distribution or inequality of wealth distribution. It is defined as a ratio with values between 0 and 1, in which 0 equates to every individual in a society having the same income, and 1 representing complete inequality (Organisation for Economic Co-operation and Development, 2006). Based on most recently available statistics, Canada has an after-tax Gini Coefficient of 0.306 (Statistics Canada, 2018a). Canada ranks 7 out of 17 peer countries for income equality (Organisation for Economic Co-operation and Development, 2018b). Breau (2015) found that income inequality between Canadian provinces was highly variable because of differing policy contexts, labor regulations, and taxation policies. Across all Canadian provinces, the highest income inequality was found in Newfoundland and Labrador, Alberta, Ontario, and British Columbia (Breau, 2015). Interestingly, the correlations amongst the Gini coefficient and the PISA results were lower and insignificant in comparison to the associations found for education levels of adults in each province. This may be partially explained by the relatively similar Gini coefficients found across the provinces, varying between 0.27 and 0.32. Thus, it appears that in Canada, broad measures of inequality are less predictive of children's educational outcomes than measures related to adults (parents) and families and that measures related to education levels are the most predictive of educational outcomes. Who are these parents and families? And what are the barriers they face or the decisions they are making that may lead to the relatively high levels of observed within school variability in educational outcomes?

10.3 Between- and Within-School Variation

One of the challenges of large data sets is that they can often mask small but systematic differences. As an example, the Canadian PISA results have noted that the between-school variation in PISA results is small in Canada. Nevertheless, these same data have shown that 15-year-old students attending private schools attain higher PISA scores than their peers attending publicly funded schools, scoring 8–9% higher (Frenette & Chan, 2015). These are substantial differences (over 40 points) but the small proportion of children in private schools, and in the PISA sample, masks this substantial between-school effect. Interestingly, this observed inequity occurs along with a similar socioeconomic predictor. Specifically, the families of children in private schools have higher average incomes and are much more likely to have completed university education.

These same private school data provide an insight into the higher levels of observed within-school variation in educational outcomes found in Canada. Private schools tend to reflect relatively homogeneous populations in terms of social capital. In contrast, Canada's public schools are much more heterogeneous given that 94% of children attend public schools. Thus, public schools across the country largely reflect the population of the country. Overall, the Canadian population is varied, certainly in terms of culture, as expected given the high rates of immigration in Canada, but also, and of relevance to our work here, in the dispersion of social and economic capital.

Which brings us back to the question of who are the parents and families who face economic disadvantages that may impact their children's educational achievement and school engagement? According to the most recent Canadian census, 4.8 million Canadians live in poverty and 1.2 million Canadians under the age of 18 live in low-income households (Statistics Canada, 2017a). While Canada has no official definition of poverty, Statistics Canada defines low-income cut-offs (LICO) as income thresholds below which a family will likely devote 20 percentage points more of its income on the necessities of shelter, food, and clothing than the average family (Lightman & Gingrich, 2013; Satzewich & Liodakis, 2013). Hence Statistics Canada's LICO figures serve as a proxy for poverty in Canada.

Three subgroups of the Canadian population appear to represent the greatest proportions of those falling below LICO thresholds. As found in other international jurisdictions, single-parental households are a strong predictor of socioeconomic inequality in Canada. The 19% of Canadian children living in a lone parent household are more than three times as likely to live in a low income household as children living in a two parent household (Statistics Canada, 2017a). In what has been termed the "feminization of poverty," scholars have further noted that women face greater risks of poverty because of the male–female wage gap (Kwok & Wallis, 2008). Currently, there remains a gender pay gap between males and females in the Canadian labor market. Recent estimates are that women earn 74 cents for every dollar earned by a male (Statistics Canada, 2017c). Most of the variance in wages can be attributed to occupational sex segregation, since women tend to occupy lower paying, part-time, temporary positions more often than do males (Kwok & Wallis, 2008). In 2015, 18.9% of Canadian women were working part-time versus 5.5% of Canadian men (Statistics Canada, 2018b).

Approximately 21% of the Canadian population was born outside Canada (Statistics Canada, 2017b) and the visible minority population constitutes 22.3% of the total Canadian population. The majority of immigrants arrive as skilled immigrants through the federally regulated points system for immigration which allocates "points" for education, skills, language ability, and training. Despite this, many recent immigrants face barriers as they endeavor to enter the labor market due to official language fluency, foreign credential devaluation, and discrimination (Esses & Bhardwaj, 2006; Galabuzi, 2006; Lightman & Gingrich, 2013; Oreopoulos, 2011; Reitz, 2016). As a result, recent immigrants to Canada are also more likely to experience low SES (Picot & Hou, 2014).

Lastly, the Statistics Canada (2017b) census report indicated that the Indigenous population was 1,673,785 or 4.9% of the total Canadian population. Indigenous families living on reserves have the lowest standard of living in Canada (Statistics Canada, 2011, 2013). Current reserves in Canada have poor living conditions and many Indigenous families have low SES (Statistics Canada, 2013). Forty percent of off-reserve Indigenous persons live in poverty. A substantial proportion of Canada's Indigenous population resides in "at-risk" communities. According to the 2011 National Household survey, only 9.8% of Indigenous persons held a university degree in contrast to the Canadian average of 27% and 36% had not completed high school (Statistics Canada, 2013). Statistics indicate that there is a large gap between Indigenous and non-Indigenous persons for all levels of education. The 2016 Canadian census indicated that 28.5% of Canadians between the ages of 25 and 64 had a Bachelor's degree or higher, while only 10.9% of Indigenous persons between the ages of 25 and 64 had a Bachelor's degree or higher (Statistics Canada, 2017d). Indigenous persons living on reserves have lower educational attainment than those living off-reserves (Statistics Canada, 2017d).

Added to these three predominant groups facing economic disadvantages, other sub-populations, while smaller in number, have also been shown to face economic challenges at a much greater rate than the "average" Canadian family. As an example, and consistent with U.S. findings, Black Canadians, especially those from low-income communities, have lower rates of high school completion and university degree attainment (Abada, Hou, & Ram, 2009; Caldas, Bernier, & Marceau, 2009; Dei, 2008; James & Turner, 2017; Livingstone & Weinfeld, 2017). Similar disadvantages are found for adults with disabilities.

10.4 Low SES and Childhood Educational Outcomes

Evidence shows that Canadian children from lower socioeconomic backgrounds tend to have higher secondary school drop-out rates, lower academic achievement at all levels of schooling, and more emotional and behavioral problems in school (Belley, Frenette, & Lochner, 2014; Evans, 2004; Ferguson, Bovaird, & Mueller, 2007; Portnow & Hussain, 2016; Shaker, 2014). In Canada, some of the evidence to support these claims comes from longitudinal studies. An analysis of the most recent cycle from Statistics Canada's *National Longitudinal Study of Children and Youth (1994–2008)* showed that children from affluent socioeconomic backgrounds score better academically on the CAT/2 standardized math test than children from economically disadvantaged backgrounds (Burton et al., 2013). The researchers noted that over 50% of children from low-income Canadian households had below-average math scores whereas 33% of children from high-income households scored below-average (Burton et al., 2013). Caro et al. (2009) used the same national data set to show that the academic achievement gap between low and high SES students was stable from ages 7 through 11, but widened between the ages of 11–15. They concluded that the advantages of high SES constitute a cumulative advantage that widens the gap over time (Caro et al., 2009).

As further evidence, Roos et al. (2006) conducted a longitudinal study using data from the *Population Health Research Data Repository* located in the province of Manitoba. The researchers studied all children born in the province in 1984 using 18 years of data that included standardized test results. They found that the standard examination pass rates of those students living in the poorest neighborhoods were less than half that of those living in the wealthiest neighborhoods (Roos et al., 2006). Similar results have been found across provincial testing programs in British Columbia and Ontario, in which associated demographic data are available. As one example, in Ontario, students from families earning less than $30,000 per year score 20–30% lower on the Grade 3 math and literacy tests than families who earn more than $100,000 per year (Education Quality and Accountability Office, 2017).

The previously discussed sub-populations of single parent, immigrant, and Indigenous families provide further insights into these relationships and some of the ongoing challenges and opportunities to address the impact of these inequities. In a cross-national study of PISA scores among 17 countries, Garriga and Martínez-Lucena (2018) found that growing up in a single-parent household had a negative effect on academic achievement in most developed countries. Research findings indicated that Canadian children who grow up in single-parent households are more likely to have academic, behavioral, and psychological problems (Ward & Belanger, 2010). The proportions of single-parent families vary across provinces and perhaps surprisingly, these proportions are moderately correlated with provincial PISA results, -0.58 with mathematics ($p < 0.05$), -0.65 with science ($p < 0.05$), and -0.70 with reading. These values are comparable to the correlations found between PISA results and the proportion of adults with a Bachelor's degree or more. The 0.68 correlation between single-parent households and adult education levels (0.65 for education levels of females) suggest a substantial level of shared variance.

While PISA results are not subdivided based on indigeneity, data from provincial assessment systems highlight the association of these socioeconomic and educational data with Indigenous children's educational achievement. For example, 2016–2017 data from the Foundation Skills Assessment (FSA) in British Columbia indicated that 35% of Aboriginal students failed to meet provincial standards for fourth-grade reading comprehension. For non-Aboriginals the percentage was 18% (British Columbia Ministry of Education, 2017). For numeracy, the percentage of Aboriginal test takers not meeting provincial standards was 45% compared to 23% for non-Aboriginal students (British Columbia Ministry of Education, 2017). While not all provinces obtain Aboriginal/Indigenous status from students in relation to their provincial testing programs, those that do highlight similar achievement gaps (e.g., Ontario, Quebec).

Educational achievement gaps between Indigenous and non-Indigenous peoples are recognized as a critical issue and a policy challenge in the Canadian context. Indigenous children and their families continue to face barriers to achievement at all levels, including access to postsecondary education. While measures highlighting economic disadvantages may be associated with the observed achievement gaps, they also hide much deeper issues that need to be addressed to resolve ongoing inequities and societal challenges. For example, funding for federally run schools for Indigenous communities is less than provincially funded schools, even when factoring in higher Northern or remote operating costs (Blatchford, 2016; Statistics Canada, 2013). Historical oppressions arising from colonialism have contributed to intergenerational poverty among Canada's Indigenous peoples. The reserve system in the 1800s, followed by the system of forced residential schooling that separated children from their families—the "Sixties Scoop" of forced adoptions—and other injustices have resulted in intergenerational trauma. This history of intergenerational trauma related to residential schooling has contributed to perceptions of "not fitting in" within schools (Blue & Pinto, 2017; Cassidy, 2015; Guinan, 2016). These findings suggest that children from Indigenous families may experience a double disadvantage, due to economic inequity and historical injustices that continue to reverberate. Given this, efforts to reduce ongoing inequities and support Indigenous learning will require substantial effort. As an example, some scholars have argued for a curriculum that embeds content based on Indigenous cultures, perspectives, and histories. This would better serve Indigenous students and foster respect for cultural diversity among non-Indigenous students (Milne, 2016). Timmons (2013) and Restoule et al. (2013) suggest that Indigenous students require comprehensive cultural supports in order to succeed in non-Indigenous postsecondary institutions.

In contrast to the aforementioned findings for single parent and Indigenous families, the academic achievement of the children of Canadian immigrants is higher than would be predicted by SES, although it varies greatly by ethnicity (Abada et al., 2009; Clandfield et al., 2014; Glick & Hohmann-Marriott, 2007). Klinger et al. (2018) noted that internationally, "with rare exceptions, immigrant students have lower levels of academic achievement than their non-immigrant peers" (p. 199). An examination of Canada's PISA results indicates that both first- and second-generation students in Canada have similar results as their Canadian-born counterparts, but there are provincial variations (Klinger et al., 2018). Abada et al. (2009) found that most Asian immigrant children performed as well or better than their Canadian counterparts on measures of academic achievement. The children of Filipino and Black immigrants performed less well, as did some European immigrant groups such as the Portuguese (Abada et al., 2009).

Given the large intake of immigrants to Canada, the federal government has implemented a series of policy initiatives to support immigrant families. The point system used to attract highly skilled workers has attracted immigrants with high levels of education. While these families may not be able to attain economic parity based on their training, it is not surprising that immigrant children have high postsecondary participation given the strength of parental education as a predictor of children's educational attainment (Childs, Finnie, & Martinello, 2017). The majority of skilled immigrants to Canada in the past decade have come from Asian and South Asian countries. Hence the point system may also serve to attract skilled immigrants who value further education for their children.

Educational policies in Canada have also been implemented to support immigrant children. As Volante et al. (2017) assert, educational policies in Canada facilitate the integration of immigrant students by focusing on language, cultural development, and inclusion, which provides additional supports to ameliorate potential educational disadvantages, at least for a sector of the immigrant families who come to Canada. Similar policies are now being implemented to support the children of refugees, along with targeted resources to address the trauma refugee families and children often face.

10.5 Cultural Capital, SES, and Access to Postsecondary Education

In Canada, recent provincial policy initiatives have focused on the provision of financial support for low-income students to access postsecondary education (Policy Horizons Canada, 2017). This includes specific efforts (e.g., scholarships) to attract "first-generation" students who come from families with no history of postsecondary education. Nevertheless, postsecondary participation rates for low-income youths from "at-risk" communities have not risen significantly in spite of these increased financial aid options (Cassidy, 2015; Higher Education Quality Council of Ontario, 2017; Oreopoulos, Brown, & Lavecchia, 2017).

The Canadian research on barriers to postsecondary access for students from low-income families has focused primarily on financial barriers (Belley et al., 2014; Frempong, Ma, & Mensah, 2012; Imbeau, 2017; Jones, 2014; King, Warren, King, Brook, & Kocher, 2009). For low-income Canadian students, community college and apprenticeship programs appear to be promising and lower cost, but data from the most recently available Youth in Transition Survey (YITS) in 2009 showed that 25% of low-income students dropped out of community college and roughly 40% of students failed to complete vocational apprenticeship training programs (Shaker, 2014). Davies, Maldonado, and Zarifa (2014) reported that in spite of the fact that Canadian postsecondary participation rates are rising, the percentage of students who attend from low SES backgrounds has not risen. Berger, Motte, and Parkin (2009) found that only one-quarter of low-income 19-year-old Canadians enrolled in university while 46% of high-income 19-year-olds enrolled in university. Davies et al. (2014) also found that affluent youths sought to maintain their social class status through postsecondary selection, favoring more prestigious institutions.

Ability grouping or what is more commonly known as academic streaming is another barrier for certain low-income populations deemed "at-risk." Most secondary school systems in Canadian provinces offer high school credit courses that are streamed into "general" (or "applied") and "advanced" levels. The advanced level credit courses are required in order to gain entry to most 4-year university programs that offer Bachelor's degrees or higher. Students from low SES are twice as likely to be streamed into "general" or "applied level" courses (Clandfield et al., 2014; James & Turner, 2017; King et al., 2009; Lyon, Frohard-Dourlent, Fripp, & Guppy, 2014). Educational sociologists argue that teachers may have lower academic expectations for students enrolled in applied or general academic streams and that students form peer relationships within their academic streams (Parekh, Killoran, & Crawford, 2011).

Curricular differentiation through tracking creates unequal learning experiences in similar topic areas. In some instances, the content is designed for the vocational workplace context. Theoretical content is not included that would adequately prepare students for postsecondary content. Schmidt et al. (2015) studied tracking internationally, and although tracking and curricular differentiation vary between contexts, they found that tracking perpetuates socioeconomic inequality. Similar findings were published by Chmielewski (2014), who studied the effects of course-by-course tracking and SES by examining PISA scores. The author concluded that this had the effect of segregating students by SES and recommended that more empirical research be conducted in the area of international course-by-course tracking (Chmielewski, 2014).

The most recently available provincial data tables on streaming were published by Krahn and Taylor (2007) who used information from cycle 1 of Statistics Canada's YITS. They compared streaming by ability in Ontario, Saskatchewan, Alberta, and British Columbia. The results showed a strong parental education effect. Fifteen-year-old youths who were enrolled in courses that would leave their postsecondary options open were two and half times more likely to do so if they had at least one university-educated parent. The existing research shows a strong effect of parental transmission. One explanation provided by researchers is that parents are able to transmit cultural capital to their children. Cultural capital theory refers to the accumulation of cultural knowledge that confers privilege and facilitates social mobility in a particular society (Bourdieu, 1976, 1984; Bourdieu & Passeron,

1977). Recent Canadian research has begun to examine cultural barriers (Cassidy, 2015; Childs et al., 2017; Childs, Finnie, & Mueller, 2018; Finnie, 2012; Finnie et al., 2011; Guinan, 2016).

Perna (2006) found that parents transmit cultural capital to their children that strongly influences their postsecondary decision-making. Utilizing quantitative YITS data, recent Canadian studies have identified parental educational attainment as the most important predictor of postsecondary participation for youths (Childs et al., 2017, 2018; Finnie et al., 2011). Certain forms of cultural capital such as books, attending cultural events, and other educational resources facilitated postsecondary participation among youths. Indirect benefits were high parental expectations to pursue postsecondary education and its related socialization. Finnie (2012) has argued that youths must develop a "culture of postsecondary education" that begins in early adolescence in order to increase the probability that they will attend later on. The results of the YITS showed that 40% of students who attended university reported that they had "always known" they would attend (Childs et al., 2018; Finnie, 2012). The high postsecondary participation rates of certain Canadian immigrant groups like the Chinese, Japanese, and South Asians have been attributed to parental cultural expectations that place high value on postsecondary participation (Abada et al., 2009; Cox & Strange, 2016; Klinger et al., 2018).

10.6 Evidence-Based Solutions to Reduce the Socioeconomic Achievement Gap in the Canadian Context

Decades of studies have explored the academic achievement gap between different social classes. SES differences in educational achievement remain persistent. Systemic efforts to improve outcomes for children from low SES backgrounds must be comprehensive and sustainable. Researchers have attributed some of these disparities to a combination of structural and social factors which have a cumulative effect on child academic and life outcomes. These factors include a multiplicity of overlapping socioeconomic factors such as nutrition, housing, parenting styles, household stress, the environment, and family structure (Fagan, 2017; Keeley, 2015; Thomson, Guhn, Richardson, Ark, & Shoveller, 2017). As an example, PISA scores show that 15-year-old students whose parents often read books with them during their first year of primary school show markedly higher PISA scores than students whose parents read with them infrequently or not at all (Organisation for Economic Co-operation and Development, 2017). The challenge for low SES parents is that they may have irregular working hours and lack the time to devote to such tasks or may lack basic literacy skills themselves. This is one of the reasons why effective interventions must include the family.

Successful evidence-based interventions focus on addressing the structural and individual level challenges faced by low-income students and their families. Many evidence-based interventions emphasize the importance of the early years to support school readiness. Early years intervention programs are offered in most OECD countries (Fillis, Dunne, & McConnell, 2018; van Huizen & Plantenga, 2018). Canada is one of 36 member countries in the OECD. Unlike many European countries such as Sweden, Denmark, Iceland, Norway, or Finland, Canada does not have universal access to high-quality preschool programs in all provinces (Organisation for Economic Co-operation and Development, 2016a). As a result, many families cannot afford to access early childhood education and care during critical periods of child development. Some researchers have linked international performance on the PISA and TIMSS to countries that have made the largest investments in early learning relative to their GDP (Merry, 2013; White, Prentice, & Perlman, 2015).

Fillis et al. (2018) conducted a systematic review of early intervention programs in Canada and the United States for 2- to 3-year olds. The intervention programs studied provided a combination of family support, cognitive and emotional development, and holistic development. The researchers failed to provide empirical evidence to support the idea that there are effective interventions for young children aged 24–36 months. Similarly, a meta-analysis of 30 studies published by van Huizen and Plantenga (2018) found mixed results for early childhood intervention programs, although they suggested that intensive, high-quality programs offered the strongest evidence for long-term positive effects.

According to Canadian economists Cleveland and Krashinsky (2003) in their report entitled *Fact and Fantasy: Eight Myths About Early Childhood Education and Care*, early childhood education is a key factor in reducing overall poverty rates. The researchers have determined in many studies that the social and economic benefits of a publicly financed system for early childhood education and care (ECEC) for children between the ages of 2 and 5 exceed the costs by a margin of 2:1 (Cleveland & Krashinsky, 2005). One early intervention program that has gained global prominence is Head Start, which was introduced in the United States in 1965 to target low-income, urban children. The design of the program includes cognitive, nutritional, medical, and parental support (Deming, 2009; Koehler, 2012). The United States evidence indicated that the gains for disadvantaged groups are short-term and diminish upon entering adolescence (Koehler, 2012). Nevertheless, the program has proven to have long-term effectiveness in other contexts. In Canada, the federal government invested over $170 million to introduce Aboriginal Head Start programs in Canada in 1995 and the program still exists (Health Canada & Public Health Agency of Canada, 2017).

A recent systematic program evaluation of 2000 3- to 5-year-old Aboriginal Head Start participants found statistically significant improvements in language, motor skills, and academic skills (Health Canada & Public Health Agency of Canada, 2017). A longitudinal study by Laurin et al. (2015) found that children from low socioeconomic backgrounds who received high-intensity early learning at a daycare center had significantly higher reading and mathematics scores by age 12 than those children who did not receive high-intensity early learning and care. The researchers defined high-intensity as 35 or more hours per week at a quality child care center. While the research evidence for the effectiveness of early childhood education is mixed, the research does support the fact that early interventions may be of most benefit to those with a low SES.

National and provincial educational policies are needed to ensure that students succeed regardless of their SES. According to the Organisation for Economic Co-operation and Development (2017), "A student is classified as resilient if he or she is in the bottom quarter of the PISA index of economic, social and cultural status (ESCS) in the country or economy of assessment and performs in the top quarter of students among all countries and economies, after accounting for socio-economic status" (p. 47). In Canada, about one-third of 2015 PISA test takers from low SES backgrounds were considered resilient (Organisation for Economic Co-operation and Development, 2017). In many countries, resilient students account for about 40% of the low-income student population. The factors that support resilience in schooling have been found to correlate with teacher quality, opportunities for extra/tutorial support for both subject matter and language, disciplined learning environments, parenting support, and the provision of resource support—such as food, clothing, or financial aid (Organisation for Economic Co-operation and Development, 2017).

Teacher quality is another factor that has been shown to improve outcomes for low-income children. Many OECD countries with high rankings on international assessments have very selective criteria for the admission of teacher candidates and offer decent compensation (Tuovinen, 2008). Campbell (2017) has argued that teacher development in Canada has contributed to relatively high PISA scores and that teacher quality and professional learning will be critical for supporting low SES children in the future. Liebenberg et al. (2016) studied 1068 Canadian youths living in marginalized communities and found that a positive student–teacher relationship had a direct moderating effect on risk factors. The authors noted that for many low socioeconomic youths, school may be the only source of formal social support. Similarly, Ingvarson and Rowley (2017) compared the processes for teacher recruitment and selection in 17 countries and concluded that those countries with policies that ensured teacher quality had students with higher scores on international tests of mathematics achievement.

Many of the most successful intervention programs aimed at increasing the participation of low-income students in postsecondary education provide extensive cultural supports in addition to financial aid (Hoxby & Turner, 2013; Oreopoulos et al., 2017; Pathways to Education, 2017). Dei (2008) and Ladson-Billings (2014) argue that educational institutions should strive to affirm the cultural identities of all students. Latif's (2017) Canadian study of educational mobility found that public spending on education helped to foster intergenerational social mobility. Strong public financing of education at all levels from preschool to postsecondary with comprehensive supports for low-income children and youths will help to reduce the probability that SES in Canada determines one's academic achievement.

Overall, the Canadian achievement results and research suggest that access to postsecondary education may be a defining predictor and issue to address ongoing educational challenges associated with economic disparity. Admittedly, the broader Indigenous issues and challenges described previously, coupled with the lack of success of many of the current initiatives to increase participation rates do suggest caution against adopting simplistic efforts to increase access to postsecondary education. The previous policy options and interventions discussed suggest that Canada is attempting to address the structural and sociocultural factors that contribute to socioeconomic achievement gaps. Admittedly, the progress is less than stellar and will require the ongoing commitment of the national and provincial governments.

References

Abada, T., Hou, F., & Ram, B. (2009). Ethnic differences in educational attainment among the children of Canadian immigrants. *Canadian Journal of Sociology, 34*(1), 1–28. Retrieved from https://journals.library.ualberta.ca/cjs/index.php/CJS/article/view/1651.

Ainsworth, J. (2002). Why does it take a village? The mediation of neighborhood effects on educational achievement. *Social Forces, 81*(1), 117–152. https://doi.org/10.1353/sof.2002.0038.

Belley, P., Frenette, M., & Lochner, L. (2014). Post-secondary attendance by parental income in the U.S. and Canada: Do financial aid policies explain the differences? *Canadian Journal of Economics/Revue canadienne d'économique, 47*(2), 664–696. https://doi.org/10.1111/caje.12088.

Berger, J., Motte, A., & Parkin, A. (2009). *The price of knowledge: Access and student finance in Canada* (4th ed.). Montreal, QC: Canada Millennium Scholarship Foundation.

Blatchford, A. (2016, December 6). Report by Parliament's budget office finds on-reserve schools underfunded by thousands of dollars per student. *CBC News.* Retrieved from https://www.cbc.ca/news/politics/budget-watchdog-pbo-first-nations-education-schools-1.3883301.

Blue, L. E., & Pinto, L. E. (2017). Other ways of being: Challenging dominant financial literacy discourses in Aboriginal context. *Australian Educational Researcher, 44*(1), 55–70. https://doi.org/10.1007/s13384-017-0226-y.

Bourdieu, P. (1976). Systems of education and systems of thought. In R. Dale, G. Esland, & M. MacDonald (Eds.), *Schooling and capitalism: A sociological reader* (pp. 192–200). London, UK: Routledge.

Bourdieu, P. (1984). *Distinction: A social critique of the judgement of taste* (R. Nice, Trans.). Cambridge, MA: Harvard University Press.

Bourdieu, P., & Passeron, J. (1977). *Reproduction in education, society and culture.* London, UK: Sage.

Breau, S. (2015). Rising inequality in Canada: A regional perspective. *Applied Geography, 61,* 58–69. https://doi.org/10.1016/j.apgeog.2014.11.010.

British Columbia Ministry of Education. (2017). *Aboriginal report 2012/13–2016/17: How are we doing?* Retrieved from https://www2.gov.bc.ca/assets/gov/education/administration/kindergarten-to-grade-12/reports/ab-hawd/2016-ab-hawd-school-district-public.pdf.

Burton, P., Phipps, S., & Zhang, L. (2013). From parent to child: Emerging inequality in outcomes for children in Canada and the U.S. *Child Indicators Research, 6*(2), 363–400. https://doi.org/10.1007/s12187-012-9175-1.

Caldas, S. J., Bernier, S., & Marceau, R. (2009). Explanatory factors of the Black achievement gap in Montréal's public and private schools: A multivariate analysis. *Education and Urban Society, 41*(2), 197–215. https://doi.org/10.1177/0013124508325547.

Campbell, C. (2017). Developing teachers' professional learning: Canadian evidence and experiences in a world of educational improvement. *Canadian Journal of Education, 40*(2), 1–33. Retrieved from http://journals.sfu.ca/cje/index.php/cje-rce/article/view/2446/2411.

Caro, D. H., McDonald, J. T., & Willms, J. D. (2009). Socio-economic status and academic achievement trajectories from childhood to adolescence. *Canadian Journal of Education/Revue canadienne de l'éducation, 32*(3), 558–590.

Cassidy, K. (2015). *Barriers to post-secondary education: Perspectives from Niagara* (NCO Policy Brief #22). St. Catharines, ON: Brock University. Retrieved from https://brocku.ca/brock-news/wp-content/uploads/2015/03/marchfinalniagara-community-observatory-policy-paper-201412-8pp-print-march.pdf.

Cheng, L., & Yan, W. (2018). Immigrant student achievement and education policy in Canada. In L. Volante, D. Klinger, & Ö. Bilgili (Eds.), *Immigrant student achievement and education policy: Cross-cultural approaches* (pp. 137–153). Dordrecht, Netherlands: Springer.

Childs, S. E., Finnie, R., & Martinello, F. (2017). Postsecondary student persistence and pathways: Evidence from the YITS-A in Canada. *Research in Higher Education, 58*(3), 270–294. https://doi.org/10.1007/s11162-016-9424-0.

Childs, S., Finnie, R., & Mueller, R. E. (2018). Assessing the importance of cultural capital on post-secondary education attendance in Canada. *Journal of Further and Higher Education, 42*(1), 35–57. https://doi.org/10.1080/0309877X.2016.1206853.

Chmielewski, A. K. (2014). An international comparison of achievement inequality in within- and between-school tracking systems. *American Journal of Education, 120*(3), 293–324. https://doi.org/10.1086/675529.

Chu, M. (2017, September 11). Why Canada fails to be an education superpower. *The Conversation.* Retrieved from https://theconversation.com/why-canada-fails-to-be-an-education-superpower-82558.

Clandfield, D., Curtis, B., Galabuzi, G.-E., San Vicente, A. G., Livingstone, D. W., & Smaller, H. (2014, Winter). Restacking the deck: Streaming by class, race and gender in Ontario schools [Special issue]. *Our Schools/Our Selves.* Retrieved from https://crpstem.files.wordpress.com/2017/04/restacking-the-deck.pdf.

Cleveland, G., & Krashinsky, M. (2003). *Fact and fantasy: Eight myths about early childhood education and care.* Toronto, ON: Childcare Resource and Research Unit.

Cleveland, G., & Krashinsky, M. (2005). *Financing early learning and care in Canada.* Ottawa, ON: Canadian Council for Social Development. Retrieved from http://www.childcarepolicy.net/wp-content/uploads/2013/04/WinnipegPaper.pdf.

Coughlan, S. (2017, August 2). How Canada became an education superpower. *BBC News.* Retrieved from https://www.bbc.com/news/business-40708421.

Council of Ministers of Education, Canada. (2018). *Quality education for all: Canadian report for the UNESCO Ninth Consultation of Member States on the Implementation of the Convention and Recommendation Against Discrimination in Education.* Retrieved from https://www.cmec.ca/Publications/Lists/Publications/Attachments/382/Canadian-report-on-anti-discrimination-in-education-EN.pdf.

Cox, D. G. H., & Strange, C. C. (2016). *Serving diverse students in Canadian higher education.* Kingston, ON: McGill-Queen's University Press.

Davies, S., Maldonado, V., & Zarifa, D. (2014). Effectively maintaining inequality in Toronto: Predicting student destinations in Ontario universities. *Canadian Review of Sociology/Revue canadienne de sociologie, 51*(1), 22–53. https://doi.org/10.1111/cars.12032.

Dei, G. S. (2008). Schooling as community: Race, schooling, and the education of African youth. *Journal of Black Studies, 38*(3), 346–366. https://doi.org/10.1177/0021934707306570.

Deming, D. (2009). Early childhood intervention and life-cycle skill development: Evidence from Head Start. *American Economic Journal: Applied Economics, 1*(3), 111–134. Retrieved from http://www.people.fas.harvard.edu/~deming/papers/Deming_HeadStart.pdf.

Education Quality and Accountability Office. (2017). *Provincial assessment results.* Retrieved from http://www.eqao.com/en/assessments/results.

Esses, V., & Bhardwaj, A. (2006). The role of prejudice in the discounting of immigrant skills. In R. Mahalingam (Ed.), *Cultural psychology of immigrants* (pp. 114–127). Mahwah, NJ: Lawrence Erlbaum Associates.

Evans, G. W. (2004). The environment of childhood poverty. *American Psychologist, 59*(2), 77–92. https://doi.org/10.1037/0003-066X.59.2.77.

Fagan, J. (2017). Income and cognitive stimulation as moderators of the association between family structure and preschoolers' emerging literacy and math. *Journal of Family Issues, 38* (17), 2400–2424. https://doi.org/10.1177/0192513X16640018.

Ferguson, H., Bovaird, S., & Mueller, M. (2007). The impact of poverty on educational outcomes for children. *Paediatrics & Child Health, 12*(8), 701–706.

Fillis, S., Dunne, L., & McConnell, B. (2018). Empirical studies on early intervention services for toddlers aged 24–36 months: A systematic review. *International Journal of Educational Research, 89,* 119–138. https://doi.org/10.1016/j.ijer.2017.10.008.

Finnie, R. (2012). Access to post-secondary education: The importance of culture. *Children and Youth Services Review, 34*(6), 1161–1170. https://doi.org/10.1016/j.childyouth.2012.01.035.

Finnie, R., Childs, S., & Wismer, A. (2011). *Access to post-secondary education among under-represented and minority groups: Measuring the gaps, assessing the causes* (Working Paper No. 2011-2001). Ottawa, ON: Education Policy Research Initiative.

Frempong, G., Ma, X., & Mensah, J. (2012). Access to postsecondary education: Can schools compensate for socioeconomic disadvantage? *Higher Education, 63*(1), 19–32. https://doi.org/10.1007/s10734-011-9422-2.

Frenette, M., & Chan, P. C. W. (2015, March 31). Why are academic prospects brighter for private high school students? *Economic Insights* (Statistics Canada catalogue no. 11-626-X-No. 044). Retrieved from https://www150.statcan.gc.ca/n1/en/catalogue/11-626-X2015044.

Galabuzi, G. (2006). *Canada's economic apartheid: The social exclusion of racialized groups in the new century.* Toronto, ON: Canadian Scholars' Press.

Garriga, A., & Martínez-Lucena, J. (2018). Growing up in a single mother family and student's tardiness: A cross-national study exploring the moderating role of family resources. *Journal of Divorce & Remarriage, 59*(1), 1–24. https://doi.org/10.1080/10502556.2017.1343564.

Glick, J., & Hohmann-Marriott, B. (2007). Academic performance of young children in immigrant families: The significance of race, ethnicity, and national origins. *The International Migration Review, 41*(2), 371–402. https://doi.org/10.1111/j.1747-7379.2007.00072.x.

Guinan, D. (2016). *The social environment and Indigenous student success in a Canadian post-secondary institution* (Doctoral dissertation). Royal Roads University, Victoria, British Columbia. Retrieved from https://viurrspace.ca/handle/10170/1039.

Health Canada & Public Health Agency of Canada. (2017). *Evaluation of the aboriginal head start in urban and northern communities program 2011–2012 to 2015–2016.* Ottawa, ON: Author.

Higher Education Quality Council of Ontario. (2017). *Quick stats.* Retrieved from http://www.heqco.ca/en-ca/Research/quickstats/Pages/default.aspx.

Hoxby, C., & Turner, S. (2013, Fall). Expanding college opportunities. *Education Next, 13*(4). Retrieved from https://www.educationnext.org/expanding-college-opportunities/.

Imbeau, E. (2017). *Saving for post-secondary education: Findings from the Canadian financial capability survey: Technical study prepared for the Canada education savings program summative evaluation.* Gatineau, QC: Employment and Social Development Canada. Retrieved from http://publications.gc.ca/site/eng/9.834539/publication.html.

Ingvarson, L., & Rowley, G. (2017). Quality assurance in teacher education and outcomes: A study of 17 countries. *Educational Researcher, 46*(4), 177–193. https://doi.org/10.3102/0013189X17711900.

James, C. E., & Turner, T. (2017). *Towards race equity education: The schooling of Black students in the Greater Toronto Area.* Toronto, ON: York University. Retrieved from http://edu.yorku.ca/files/2017/04/Towards-Race-Equity-in-Education-April-2017.pdf.

Jones, G. A. (2014). Building and strengthening policy research capacity: Key issues in Canadian higher education. *Studies in Higher Education, 39*(8), 1332–1342. https://doi.org/10.1080/03075079.2014.949543.

Keeley, B. (2015). *Income inequality: The gap between rich and poor Paris*. France: OECD Publishing. https://doi.org/10.1787/9789264246010-en.

King, A. J. C., Warren, W. K., King, M. A., Brook, J. E., & Kocher, P. R. (2009). *Who doesn't go to post-secondary education? Final report of findings for Colleges Ontario Collaborative Research Project*. Toronto, ON: Colleges Ontario. Retrieved from https://www.collegesontario.org/research/who-doesnt-go-to-pse.pdf.

Klinger, D. A., & Saab, H. (2012). Educational leadership in the context of low-stakes accountability: The Canadian perspective. In L. Volante (Ed.), *School leadership in the context of standards-based reform: International perspectives* (pp. 73–96). Dordrecht, Netherlands: Springer.

Klinger, D. A., Volante, L., & Bilgili, Ö. (2018). Cross-cultural approaches to mitigating the immigrant student performance disadvantage. In L. Volante, D. A. Klinger, & O. Bilgili (Eds.), *Immigrant student achievement and education policy: Cross-cultural approaches* (pp. 197–206). Dordrecht, Netherlands: Springer.

Koehler, C. (2012). Effects of the Head Start program in the USA as indicators of ethnic inequalities. In Z. Bekerman & T. Geisen (Eds.), *International handbook of migration, minorities and education* (pp. 383–401). Dordrecht, Netherlands: Springer.

Krahn, H., & Taylor, A. (2007). "Streaming" in the 10th grade in four Canadian provinces in 2000. *Education Matters, 4*(2), 16–26. Retrieved from https://www150.statcan.gc.ca/n1/pub/81-004-x/81-004-x2007002-eng.htm.

Kwok, S., & Wallis, M. A. (2008). *Daily struggles: The deepening racialization and feminization of poverty in Canada*. Toronto, ON: Canadian Scholars' Press.

Ladson-Billings, G. (2014). Culturally relevant pedagogy 2.0: a.k.a. the Remix. *Harvard Educational Review, 84*(1), 74–84. https://doi.org/10.17763/haer.84.1.p2rj1314854875 l.

Latif, E. (2017). The relationship between intergenerational educational mobility and public spending: Evidence from Canada. *Economic Papers, 36*(3), 335–350. https://doi.org/10.1111/1759-3441.12177.

Laurin, J. C., Geoffroy, M., Boivin, M., Japel, C., Raynault, M., Tremblay, R. E., et al. (2015). Child care services, socioeconomic inequalities, and academic performance. *Pediatrics, 136*(6), 1112–1124. https://doi.org/10.1542/peds.2015-0419.

Liberal Party of Canada in Alberta. (2011, March 11). *The Canadian learning strategy*. Retrieved from http://alberta.liberal.ca/canadian-learning-strategy/.

Liebenberg, L., Theron, L., Sanders, J., Munford, R., van Rensburg, A., Rothmann, S., et al. (2016). Bolstering resilience through teacher-student interaction: Lessons for school psychologists. *School Psychology International, 37*(2), 140–154. https://doi.org/10.1177/0143034315614689.

Lightman, N., & Gingrich, L. G. (2013). The intersecting dynamics of social exclusion: Age, gender, race and immigrant status in Canada's labour market. *Canadian Ethnic Studies, 44*(3), 121–145. https://doi.org/10.1353/ces.2013.0010.

Livingstone, A., & Weinfeld, M. (2017). Black students and high school completion in Quebec and Ontario: A multivariate analysis. *Canadian Review of Sociology/Revue canadienne de sociologie, 54*(2), 174–197. https://doi.org/10.1111/cars.12144.

Lyon, K., Frohard-Dourlent, H., Fripp, P., & Guppy, N. (2014). Canada. In P. A. Stevens & A. G. Dworkin (Eds.), *The Palgrave handbook of race and ethnic inequalities in education* (pp. 170–204). Singapore: Springer.

Merry, J. J. (2013). Tracing the U.S. deficit in PISA reading skills to early childhood: Evidence from the United States and Canada. *Sociology of Education, 86*(3), 234–252. https://doi.org/10.1177/0038040712472913.

Milne, E. (2016). Educational issues and inequalities: Experiences of Indigenous Canadian students. In Y. Besen-Cassino (Ed.), *Education and youth today* (Sociological studies of children and youth, Vol. 20, pp. 65–89). Bingley, UK: Emerald Group.

O'Grady, K., Deussing, M.-A., Scerbina, T., Fung, K., & Muhe, N. (2016). *Measuring up: Canadian results of the OECD PISA study* (Statistics Canada catalogue no. 81-590-X). https://www150.statcan.gc.ca/n1/pub/81-590-x/81-590-x2010001-eng.htm.

Oreopoulos, P. (2011). Why do skilled immigrants struggle in the labor market? A field experiment with thirteen thousand resumes. *American Economic Journal: Economic Policy, 3* (4), 148–171. https://doi.org/10.1257/pol.3.4.148.

Oreopoulos, P., Brown, R. S., & Lavecchia, A. M. (2017). Pathways to education: An integrated approach to helping at-risk high school students. *Journal of Political Economy, 125*(4), 947–984. https://doi.org/10.1086/692713.

Organisation for Economic Co-operation and Development. (2006). *Glossary of statistical terms.* Retrieved from https://stats.oecd.org/glossary/detail.asp?ID=4842.

Organisation for Economic Co-operation and Development. (2016a). *PF3.1: Public spending on childcare and early education.* Retrieved from https://www.oecd.org/els/soc/PF3_1_Public_spending_on_childcare_and_early_education.pdf.

Organisation for Economic Co-operation and Development. (2016b). *PISA 2015 results (Volume I): Excellence and equity in education, PISA.* Paris, France: OECD Publishing. https://doi.org/10.1787/9789264266490-en.

Organisation for Economic Co-operation and Development. (2017). *Educational opportunity for all: Overcoming inequality through the life course.* Paris, France: OECD Publishing. Retrieved from http://www.oecd.org/education/educational-opportunity-for-all-9789264287457-en.htm.

Organisation for Economic Co-operation and Development. (2018a). *Education GPS.* Retrieved from http://gpseducation.oecd.org/.

Organisation for Economic Co-operation and Development. (2018b). *OECD social and welfare statistics: Income distribution.* https://doi.org/10.1787/data-00654-en.

Parekh, G., Killoran, I., & Crawford, C. (2011). The Toronto connection: Poverty, perceived ability, and access to education equity. *Canadian Journal of Education, 34*(3), 249–279.

Parker, P. D., Marsh, H. W., Jerrim, J. P., Guo, J., & Dicke, T. (2018). Inequity and excellence in academic performance: Evidence from 27 countries. *American Educational Research Journal, 55*(4), 836–858. https://doi.org/10.3102/0002831218760213.

Pathways to Education. (2017). *Community mapping tool: Mapping at-risk communities in Canada.* Retrieved from https://www.pathwaystoeducation.ca/community-mapping-tool-mapping-risk-communities-canada.

Perna, L. W. (2006). Studying college choice: A proposed conceptual model. In J. C. Smart (Ed.), *Higher education: Handbook of theory and research* (Vol. 21, pp. 99–157). Boston, MA: Kluwer Academic.

Picot, G., & Hou, F. (2014). *Immigration, low income and income inequality in Canada: What's new in the 2000s?* (Statistics Canada catalogue no. 11F0019M). Ottawa, ON: Statistics Canada. Retrieved from https://www150.statcan.gc.ca/n1/pub/11f0019m/11f0019m2014364-eng.htm.

Policy Horizons Canada. (2017). *Unlocking the potential of marginalized youth.* Ottawa, ON: Government of Canada. Retrieved from http://horizons.gc.ca/en/content/unlocking-potential-marginalized-youth.

Portnow, S., & Hussain, S. (2016). Income and cognitive stimulation: A reanalysis of the Minnesota family investment program. *Prevention Science, 17*(5), 565–571. https://doi.org/10.1007/s11121-016-0650-7.

Reitz, J. G. (2016). Towards empirical comparison of immigrant integration across nations. *Ethnic and Racial Studies, 39*(13), 2338–2345. https://doi.org/10.1080/01419870.2016.1203448.

Restoule, J., Mashford-Pringle, A., Chacaby, M., Smillie, C., Brunette, C., & Russel, G. (2013). Supporting successful transitions to post-secondary education for Indigenous students: Lessons from an institutional ethnography in Ontario, Canada. *The International Indigenous Policy Journal, 4*(4), Art. 4. Retrieved from https://ir.lib.uwo.ca/iipj/vol4/iss4/4/.

Roos, N., Brownell, M., Guevremont, R., Levin, B., MacWilliam, L., & Roos, L. (2006). The complete story: A population-based perspective on school performance and educational testing. *Canadian Journal of Education, 29*(3), 684–705.

Satzewich, V., & Liodakis, N. (2013). The concepts of ethnicity and "race". In V. Satzewich & N. Liodakis (Eds.), *Race and ethnicity in Canada: A critical introduction* (pp. 9–28). Toronto, ON: Oxford University Press.

Schmidt, W. H., Burroughs, N. A., Zoido, P., & Houang, R. T. (2015). The role of schooling in perpetuating educational inequality: An international perspective. *Educational Researcher, 44* (7), 371–386. https://doi.org/10.3102/0013189X15603982.

Shaker, E. (2014). *Our schools/our selves: Poverty, polarization, and the educational achievement gap.* Ottawa, ON: Canadian Centre for Policy Alternatives.

Statistics Canada. (2011, December 16). *Postsecondary education participation among underrepresented and minority groups.* Retrieved from https://www150.statcan.gc.ca/n1/pub/81-004-x/2011004/article/11595-eng.htm.

Statistics Canada. (2013, November 25). The education and employment experiences of first nations people living off reserve, Inuit, and Métis: Selected findings from the 2012 Aboriginal Peoples survey. *The Daily* (Statistics Canada catalogue no. 99-012-X201100311849). Retrieved from https://www150.statcan.gc.ca/n1/daily-quotidien/131125/dq131125b-eng.pdf.

Statistics Canada. (2017a, September 13). *Children living in low-income households.* Retrieved from http://www12.statcan.gc.ca/census-recensement/2016/as-sa/98-200-x/2016012/98-200-x2016012-eng.cfm.

Statistics Canada. (2017b, October 25). *Ethnic and cultural origins of Canadians: Portrait of a rich heritage.* Retrieved from http://www12.statcan.gc.ca/census-recensement/2016/as-sa/98-200-x/2016016/98-200-x2016016-eng.cfm.

Statistics Canada. (2017c, November 29). *Does education pay? A comparison of earnings by level of education in Canada and its provinces and territories.* Retrieved from http://www12.statcan.gc.ca/census-recensement/2016/as-sa/98-200-x/2016024/98-200-x2016024-eng.cfm.

Statistics Canada. (2017d, November 29). *Education in Canada: Key results from the 2016 census.* Retrieved from https://www150.statcan.gc.ca/n1/daily-quotidien/171129/dq171129a-eng.htm.

Statistics Canada. (2018a, March 13). *Gini coefficients of adjusted market, total and after-tax income.* Retrieved from https://www150.statcan.gc.ca/t1/tbl1/en/tv.action?pid=1110013401.

Statistics Canada. (2018b, July 30). *Women in Canada: A gender-based statistical report.* Retrieved from https://www150.statcan.gc.ca/n1/pub/89-503-x/89-503-x2015001-eng.htm.

Thomson, K., Guhn, M., Richardson, C. G., Ark, T. K., & Shoveller, J. (2017). Profiles of children's social–emotional health at school entry and associated income, gender and language inequalities: A cross-sectional population-based study in British Columbia, Canada. *BMJ Open, 7*(7). https://doi.org/10.1136/bmjopen-2016-015353.

Timmons, V. (2013). Aboriginal students' perceptions of post-secondary success initiatives. *Canadian Journal of Native Studies, 33*(1), 231–236.

Tuovinen, J. (2008). Learning the craft of teaching and learning from world's best practice: The case of Finland. In D. McInerney & A. Liem (Eds.), *Teaching and learning: International best practice* (pp. 51–77). Charlotte, NC: Information Age.

UNESCO. (2014). *The diversification of post-secondary education.* Retrieved from http://unesdoc.unesco.org/images/0022/002269/226981e.pdf.

van Huizen, T., & Plantenga, J. (2018). Do children benefit from universal early childhood education and care? A meta-analysis of evidence from natural experiments. *Economics of Education Review, 66,* 206–222. https://doi.org/10.1016/j.econedurev.2018.08.001.

Volante, L., Klinger, D. A., Siegel, M., & Bilgili, Ö. (2017). Making sense of the performance (dis)advantage for immigrant students across Canada. *Canadian Journal of Education, 40*(3), 330–361.

Ward, M., & Belanger, M. (2010). *The family dynamic: A Canadian perspective* (5th ed.). Toronto, ON: Nelson.

White, L. A., Prentice, S., & Perlman, M. (2015). The evidence base for early childhood education and care programme investment: What we know, what we don't know. *Evidence & Policy, 11* (4), 529–546. https://doi.org/10.1332/174426415X14210818992588.

Chapter 11
Socioeconomic Inequality and Student Outcomes in Australia

Philip Parker, Jiesi Guo and Taren Sanders

Abstract This chapter provides an overview of (a) the Australian education system (including a historical overview from 1970 to today); (b) an exploration of socioeconomic inequality in IQ, academic achievement in high-stakes tests, and critical non-cognitive factors from the start of school to near the end of middle school; (c) an exploration of socioeconomic inequality in achievement in adolescent birth cohorts from the 1960s to 2000; and (d) a reflection on how education policy has influenced inequality and what may need to be done to redress it in the future. We find that inequalities present at the beginning of school tend to get larger as children age and that historical inequalities have also tended to increase over time. While Australia has had a large number of private schools since the 1970s, we argue that recent cultural changes have resulted in schools being seen as a market and that this has driven up ability stratification between schools and may account for increased inequality over time.

Keywords Student achievement · Socioeconomic status · Inequality · Australia

11.1 Introduction

The development of [school choice] arrangements such as those outlined above would make capital more widely available and would thereby do much to make equality of opportunity a reality, to diminish inequalities of income and wealth, and to promote the full use of our human resources. And it would do so not by impeding competition, destroying

---

P. Parker (✉) · J. Guo · T. Sanders
Institute for Positive Psychology and Education, Australian Catholic University,
North Sydney, Australia
e-mail: Philip.parker@acu.edu.au

© Springer Nature Singapore Pte Ltd. 2019
L. Volante et al. (eds.), *Socioeconomic Inequality
and Student Outcomes*, Education Policy & Social Inequality 4,
https://doi.org/10.1007/978-981-13-9863-6_11

> incentive, and dealing with symptoms, as would result from the outright redistribution of income, but by strengthening competition, making incentives effective, and eliminating the causes of inequality. (Friedman, 2009, p. 107)

This stirring passage extolling the virtues of school choice was present in the 1982 edition of Friedman's *Capitalism and Freedom*. Reagan was President of the United States and Margaret Thatcher the Prime Minister of the United Kingdom. Yet it was Australia and not the UK or the US, "that has gone the furthest in creating school markets" and has done so under near bi-partisanship agreement between conservative and liberal governments (Campbell, Proctor, & Sherington, 2009, p. 6). As the debate rages about the role of school markets in socioeconomic disadvantages in education, Australia's embrace of school markets provides a laboratory to investigate its effect on educational inequality. In this chapter, we summarise the Australian school system, provide a descriptive analysis of academic disadvantage in Australian schools, and investigate the effectiveness of Australia's endorsement of neo-liberal education policy.

11.2 The Australian Education System

There is no single "Australian" education system. Rather, the various states and territories of Australia are primarily responsible for the delivery of education (Gonski et al., 2011; Ledgar, 1996). Thus, education policy differs across Australia. This includes the presence or absence of academically selective schools, the degree of centralization, and school starting age policy. There are also notable differences between the public, Catholic, and independent school systems (Campbell & Proctor, 2014). There is always then some inexactitude in discussing the Australian education experience. Nevertheless, it is true that the variation within the country is smaller than the variation between Australia and other countries, and to this degree it makes sense to discuss the Australian system as a whole.

Australia has a nominally comprehensive school system that runs in most states for 13 years. Starting at age 5, students in most states undertake six years of primary school, four years of secondary school, and two years of senior secondary school. Most states include a single year of kindergarten within primary school and most students need not change schools when transitioning from secondary school to senior high-school. In 2017, 65% of students attended a government school, 20% attended Catholic schools, and 15% attended independent schools (Australian Bureau of Statistics [ABS], 2018; Cat. No. 4221.0). By international standards, this appears to be a remarkable number of students being educated in schools that are not directly controlled by the government. Yet school funding complicates this picture. All government schools are funded by the states, with parents required to make minimal additional contributions. Private schools have considerable autonomy, yet both Catholic and independent school receive extensive federal government funding and in return are subject to government regulations. Most Catholic schools are also overseen by a Catholic Education office which oversees large districts of schools (Campbell & Proctor, 2014).

In Australia, there is little explicit school tracking. The two largest states have academic selective schools—but even here there are few. Nevertheless, implicit tracking via private schooling, social stratification between school catchment areas, and other factors mean that Australia has a moderate stratified education system (Parker, Jerrim, Schoon, & Marsh, 2016; Parker, Marsh, Jerrim, Guo, & Dicke, 2018b). Within-school tracking—mostly via subject-by-subject tracking—is common across all school types.

The first decade of the 2000s saw notable changes to the Australian education system. Many of the changes led to greater alignment between the various systems of the states and territories. These changes included an increase in mandatory school attendance rules. Previously, children were required to stay in school till the age of 15. This has now been raised to age 17 and includes a requirement to complete at least secondary school. This has led to an associated increase in secondary school to senior high-school retention rates in most states. As such, Australia now has effectively no age of first selection (i.e., tracking into vocational vs university pathway school systems) with 83 percent of children remaining in school from Year 10 to Year 12.

The alignment of states in relation to mandatory schooling is part of a wider trend toward consistency across the country. All states now undertake the same standardized tests in literacy and numeracy for Grades 3, 5, 7, and 9 called the National Assessment Program – Literacy and Numeracy (NAPLAN). While not designed to rank schools, the Australian government provides a website where the average NAPLAN scores for every school can be accessed (www.myschool.edu.au). All but one state, and all states by 2020, provide senior high-school graduating students wishing to attend university an *Australian Tertiary Admissions Rank*. This score, along with student preferences, is used by a central agency to assigns students to university places at the end of Year 12. This is the most used pathway to higher education.

Australia has seen an increase, if not centralization, in alignment of educational policy among states. Yet, differentiation between states has occurred alongside this alignment. Several states—including the largest two—have introduced "local schools local decisions" or similar named frameworks. In direct contrast to other changes within the education system toward more central control, these frameworks have aimed to decentralize school processes from government control and have provided greater autonomy to principals and/or school boards (Campbell & Proctor, 2014).

Despite the various nuances, the Australia system is consistent in structure to that of other Anglophone educational systems (Jerrim, Parker, Katyn Chmielewski,

& Anders, 2015; Parker et al., 2016, 2018a, b). Australia's most notable deviation from this group of countries is the significant amount of school choice parents have due to a varied and large private school sector that is supported by the government (Campbell & Proctor, 2014; Campbell et al., 2009). Associated with this is a growing mindset that a major parenting responsibility, and one that causes parents considerable stress, is choosing the right school for their child (Campbell et al., 2009).

11.3 Low Socioeconomic Status Numbers

Throughout this chapter, we use a coding system for educational attainment based on Jerrim et al. (Chap. 1 this book). Thus, the term *high SES* refers to children where at least one parent attained a university level of education; *moderate SES* to refer to children with at least one parent who has completed upper high-school (Grade 12) or have completed an equivalent vocational level of education; and *low SES* to refers to children whose parents did not complete high-school or vocational education. We also provide statistics, and as a separate group in all analyses, those with missing information on educational attainment.

Australia is an educated population. And thus many children are classified as high SES. We cannot provide population-level information on the average education level of parents of school-age children in Australia. However, census 2016 data on the educational attainment of individuals aged between 25 and 50—typical age of parents—suggests 32.6% of this population had a high level of education, 53.4% had a moderate education level, 2.7% had a low level of education, and 11.6% did not provide sufficient information to determine a level of education.

This chapter explores both early youth development with a single longitudinal cohort of children; and historical change in multiple cohorts of adolescent aged children. Against the census information above our databases are representative of the Australian population. In the developmental data, we used to explore changes in educational inequality from childhood to adolescence, 32.6% of parents had a high level of education, 45.9% had a moderate level of education, 6.2% had a low level of education, and 15.8% did not report education information. The historical databases we used to show changes in educational inequality from the 1970s to the 2000s showed considerable change in the proportion of young people with parents of different levels of education. Figure 11.1 shows the dramatic expansion of education, and particularly higher education that began in the 1970s.

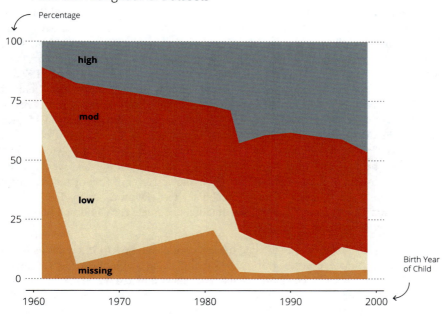

Fig. 11.1 SES levels in the historical databases we use in this chapter. Based on parents' education level

11.4 Educational Outcomes

This section comprises two parts driven by the high-quality childhood and adolescence datasets available in Australia. In Part 1, we will explore cognitive and non-cognitive outcomes by SES from the ages of 4 through to 15. We will consider differences in and trajectories of cognitive constructs: IQ and achievement in numeracy, writing, and reading. We will also consider non-cognitive constructs that have received increasing attention outside of their normal home in psychology since Heckman (2006). In Part 2, we will focus on a restricted age range (with most of each sample aged 14–16) years of age. Here we focus on historical trends rather than developmental trends. The historical period we will consider was restricted by data availability but covers most of the period from the 1970s to today which reflect what can broadly be referred to as the neo-liberal era of education in Australia (Campbell & Proctor, 2014).

11.5 The Datasets

Developmental Trend Data For the first part, we used the Longitudinal Study of Australian Children (LSAC; Sanson et al., 2002). LSAC is a representative sample of two cohorts. Cohort B is a sample of children who were 0/1 years old in 2003. Cohort K is a sample of children who were aged 4/5 in 2003—and were thus eligible to start kindergarten. As our focus was on the development of SES differences across schooling, we used the older Cohort K in this chapter (the B cohort contains fewer time waves but these show similar patterns to those we report here). Thus, we provide estimates over the developmental period from 4/5 to 14/15 year of age. The Australia wide NAPLAN tests were used as a measure of cognitive ability. These tests were given to all children in years 3, 5, 7, and 9. More information can be found at https://goo.gl/MuaS7L. Supplementing this, we included teachers' estimates of literacy and numeracy in the first year of school and measures of IQ including the Peabody Picture Vocabulary test (Dunn & Dunn, 1997) and a matrix reasoning test from the Wechsler Intelligence Scale for Children (WISC-IV; Petermann & Petermann, 2011).

For non-cognitive factors, we included overall conduct and peer difficulties as given by a single estimate derived from the Strengths and Difficulties Questionnaire (SDQ; Goodman, 1997). The participants' teachers completed the SDQ. Finally, we included parent reported persistence, reactivity, and introversion as measured by the Short Temperament Scale for Children (Paterson & Sanson, 1999).

Historical Trend Data To explore historical trends in SES discrepancies in education we combined a series of education databases targeting adolescence, first collected in the 1970s. These included:

(a) The Australian Youth in Transition survey (YIT; Research, 2018) which was a representative sample of youth born in 1961 who had taken part in the 1975 National Testing Program in math and literacy. We have also included the second cohort (born in 1965) of this study but achievement scores for this group were collected at age 10 rather than 14 and were the youngest group represented in our historical data.
(b) The 1995 and 1998 cohorts of the Longitudinal Study of Australian Youth (LSAY; Marks & Rothman, 2003). This was a two-stage probability samples of year 9 students who completed achievement tests in literacy and numeracy.
(c) The final studies are the 2000–2015 Programme for International Student Assessment (PISA; Ray & Margaret, 2003).

In Australia, most of the PISA samples are followed for 10 years. Collectively the LSAY, PISA, and YIT studies have been brought together under the umbrella name of LSAY (Marks & Rothman, 2003). The databases included in this chapter have the school or postcode as the primary sampling unit and include standardized test scores of achievement in mathematics and English—PISA databases also include science. We accounted for the complex sampling procedures in all reported results.

Before reporting on the data, we want to make a few preliminary points about our approach. First, we decided to preference data availability over data comparability. In our developmental trends, we include teacher subjective assessment of ability at the beginning of school along with high-quality national standardized testing. Likewise, when exploring historical trends each standardized test is different and, apart from the PISA databases, has not been designed to be comparable with each other. Thus, our focus is on comparing relative magnitudes of difference at each time wave and not on comparing absolute change in performance over development or historical period. Where comparability is a particular concern, we alert the reader. Second, we do not aim in this chapter to provide an empirical assessment of the data. Our focus is purely descriptive.

11.6 Developmental Trends in Socioeconomic Disparity

Before looking at historical trends we consider how much socioeconomic disparity is present at the beginning of schooling and how it progresses over elementary and middle school. We consider achievement, IQ, and non-cognitive factors. All variables were within wave standardized for ease of comparison.

Achievement Changes Figure 11.2 displays the changes in achievement disparities. Consistent with similar findings in the United States (Heckman, 2006), differences in achievement by socioeconomic status is large even at the beginning of school at about half a standard deviation. This difference increased over time—particularly if we assume that those with missing SES are most likely to be members of the "low" SES group.

It is possible that the initial smaller educational inequalities are due to the fact that teachers assess ability on a graded curve. Australian schools are implicitly stratified by socioeconomic status. Low SES students are more likely to go to poorer performing schools while high SES students are more likely to go to higher performing schools. For students of equal ability, those in better performing schools are treated more harshly by grading on curve effects than students in poorer performing schools (Murphy & Weinhardt, 2018). As such, low SES students may have a positive bias in their teacher ratings, while high SES students may have a negative bias (Parker et al., 2018a). Thus the differences in kindergarten may be bigger than they appear. To account for this, we also consider differences in IQ as measured by the Peabody Picture Vocabulary test, given at ages 4, 6, and 8; and a matrix reasoning test given at ages 6, 8, and 10. No IQ test was given at age 14. Figure 11.3 shows the presence of large disparities that grow over time. What causes this growing discrepancy and the degree to which differences in schooling can account for it is not clear. There is an interesting contrast between the achievement scores and IQ in relation to the medium SES group. This group sit between the low and high group for achievement but is not distinguishable from the low SES group in IQ. Taken together it may not be that there is a social gradient to

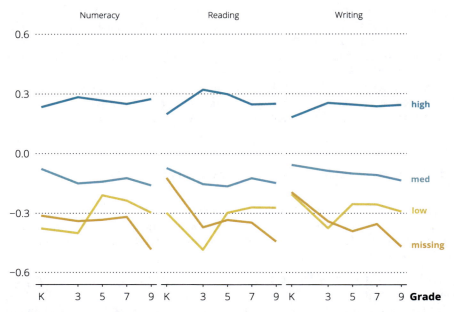

Fig. 11.2 SES differences in achievement as measured by parents' educational attainment. *Notes* Achievement in Kindergarten (K) taken from teacher assessments. Grades 3–9 takes from NAPLAN scores. Units are in grade specific standard deviations

achievement and IQ in Australia as there is a qualitative shift between children whose parents have a university level of education and those that do not (Hancock, Mitrou, Povey, Campbell, & Zubrick, 2018).

NAPLAN differences were large in year 3 and only grew larger as children aged. Like IQ there appears to be a qualitative gap between students whose parents have a university level of education and everyone else. Recent evidence on inequality in education has suggested that the primary stratification point in Australia is between children of parents with a postgraduate degree and everyone else (Hancock et al., 2018; Hetherington, 2018). Stratification among children whose parents do not have a university degree is thus small. Our evidence is consistent with this view.

Differences in Non-cognitive Factors Since Heckman's (2006) influential article on educational inequality, fields across the social sciences have devoted more attention to the influence of non-cognitive factors. This is due to the role these variables play in later life educational and occupational success. There is a general

SES Differences on IQ

Differences by parental education levels:

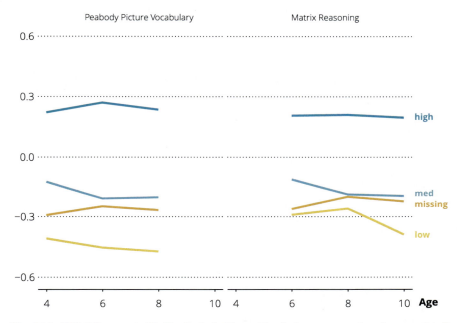

Fig. 11.3 SES differences in IQ. The Peabody Picture Vocabulary test was given from age 4 to 8. *Notes* The Matrix Reasoning test from the WISC-IV was given from age 6 to 10

belief, stemming from Heckman and colleagues' work that non-cognitive factors are a prime target for intervention and have a positive cost-benefit trade-off that intervention on cognitive skills do not (Heckman, 2006; Heckman & Rubinstein, 2001; Kautz, Heckman, Diris, Ter Weel, & Borghans, 2014). Here we look at parents' perspectives on a child's overall difficulties via the strengths and difficulties questionnaire (high scores equal more difficulties) and parents' perceptions of their child's persistence (high scores equal more persistence), reactivity (lower scores equal less reactivity), and introversion (higher scores equal more introversion). Figure 11.4 shows that there are positive signs. In particular, differences between introversion and reactivity are negligible—particularly by age 14. However, there are also signs of concern. First, differences in persistence are moderate at age 4 but grow across development. Second, differences in overall SDQ difficulties are large at age 4. There is evidence that children of parents with low levels of education improve over time, but by age 14 the low and high SES groups still differ by about a quarter of a standard deviation.

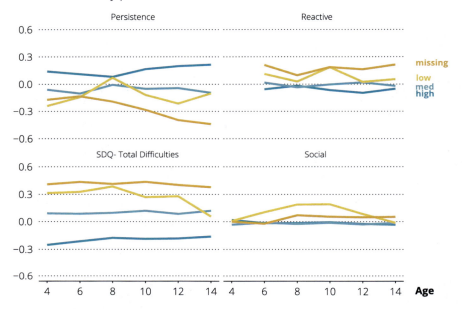

Fig. 11.4 SES differences in non-cognitive factors

Taken together, the cognitive and non-cognitive results suggest that differences by SES group appear to reflect differences between children who have a parent with a university degree and everyone else (Hancock et al., 2018; Hetherington, 2018).

11.7 Historical Trends in Socioeconomic Status

Finally, we consider historical trends in differences in math, reading, and science for cohorts of adolescents born between 1961 and 1999. We combine Australia's YIT, LSAY, and PISA databases (see above). Only the PISA databases include a measure of science. These studies use a variety of different tests that have different designs. For example, the LSAY studies used a representative sample of Grade 9 students. Yet PISA and the Youth in Transition is a representative sample of particular age cohorts. Nevertheless, each uses a standardized test given to a representative sample of Australian youth. Post-1965, discrepancies in achievement increased over time, although the gaps have appeared to be closing in the last few cycles of PISA (see Fig. 11.5). However, the gaps are still very large.

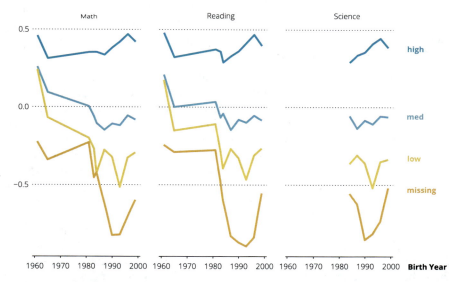

Fig. 11.5 SES differences in achievement for age cohorts born between 1961 and 1999

11.8 Educational Policy

Australia appears to have two reasons for concern. The first concern is the SES gap in achievement present at age 4–5 appears to grow as children age. The second concern is that the historical SES discrepancy in academic performance for similar aged adolescents has grown over the past four decades—though with some evidence that this trend has leveled off in recent times. We explore each of these and what they mean for policy.

Child Development and Socioeconomic Gaps We show that there is a gap in both achievement and IQ at age 4–5 in a representative sample of Australian children. While the gap in IQ appears to be smaller and more stable—even closing slightly for some comparisons—the gap in achievement shows a steady increase when comparing children whose parents have a university education with everyone else. This gap is not surprising. In his famous paper, Heckman (2006) shows a very similar trend in the US for ages 6–12. The evidence presented by Heckman has sobering policy implications. He argues that interventions to address this gap declines in cost-benefit as children age—meaning interventions after school provide little return on investment. He has also argued that, while non-cognitive skills are also socially graded, interventions targeting them may provide better returns on investment (Heckman, 2006; Heckman & Rubinstein, 2001). In comparison to academic achievement and IQ developmental trends in non-cognitive skills gaps presented both reasons for optimism and pessimism. Yes, there were gaps in many of the non-cognitive factors at age 4 but these gaps were smaller than for achievement—sometimes negligible—and they mostly did not show an increasing pattern over development. Yet gaps were still large for the teacher reported total difficulties score and the amount of persistence parents observed in their children. The gap in persistence widened as children aged.

What is the Australian government doing about socioeconomic gaps in non-cognitive skills? Since 2008 there has been renewed a focus on educational inequality. In particular, the Melbourne Declaration (Barr et al., 2008) focused on inequality and promoting non-cognitive skills. Much of the focus, however, has been on self-concept and self-worth, which we have shown elsewhere may be the wrong non-cognitive construct to focus on. This is because academic self-concept is an area that, all else being equal, low SES students do well in. They have significantly higher academic self-concepts than their equally able high SES peers (Parker et al., 2018a). Rather, it is self-regulatory processes like persistence that are more important (see Steinberg, 2014).

A more convincing intervention approach has been Australia's adaptation of the *Positive Behavioral Interventions and Supports* called *Positive Behaviour for Learning* (PBL; Mooney et al., 2008). This is a structured approach to identifying the right interventions for the right students with a focus on self-regulation skills. For example, our results noted that self-regulatory processes like persistence, differ by socioeconomic status. With government and industry funding, we are implementing a program in poor schools in Australia called *Check and Connect* (Anderson, Christenson, Sinclair, & Lehr, 2004). This program is focused on Tier 2 children (moderate at-risk status) under the PBL framework. This program uses a metrics-based mentoring program—using metrics such as class attendance, grades, and completed homework percentage—to help students clarify goals and use feedback to persist in meeting those goals. This program has been successfully implemented overseas and is listed on the *What Works Clearing House* (https://goo.gl/1zuYZM). Whether this program works in Australia or if the effect suffices to justify the large per student cost, is yet to be seen.

Historical Trends in Socioeconomic Gaps Above, we focused on interventions implemented in standard school structures, aimed at a minority of students with identifiable risks. Evaluation of historical trends, however, suggests that we must also consider the role of the education system as a whole. In several studies (Parker et al., 2016, 2018a, b) we have focused on the amount of achievement stratification a country has—that is the degree to which students of similar levels of academic achievement are schooled together. On this measure, Australia has both high stratification and has seen this stratification grow in recent times (see Fig. 11.6).

Given the general increase of inequality over time, built on already large socioeconomic disparities, it is tempting to suggest neo-liberal education policies in

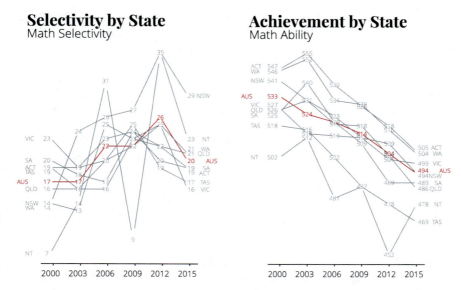

Fig. 11.6 Changes in achievement and stratification in Australia. *Notes* PISA estimates from 2000–2015 in math achievement

Australia have been a failure. And because Australia has gone further than most countries with policies related to school choice, then this failure has implications for neo-liberal polices everywhere. Yet, this is a simplistic view. First, early PISA and the Trends in International Mathematics and Science Study (TIMMS) results reveal that Australia was one of the best-performing countries in the world, with only moderate stratification.

Australians have had considerable school choice since the 1970s. But it has only been in the last 10–20 years that between-school stratification in achievement has soared. We have argued elsewhere that the between-school intra-class correlation of achievement—that is the expected correlation in achievement between two randomly chosen students in the same school—provides a useful summary measure of the amount of stratification by ability (Parker et al., 2016, 2018a, b). Further, we have argued that higher stratification is the most likely outcome of increased school choice (Parker et al., 2018b). Figure 11.6 shows that stratification in Australia (as measured by the intra-class correlation in math achievement in PISA tests) has grown at an alarming rate in Australia and has doubled in the most populous state.

The increase in stratification has co-occurred with almost exact inverse declines in Australia's academic performance on these tests (see Parker et al., 2018b and Fig. 11.6). The cause of stratification growth since 2000 is not clear. If what we have argued elsewhere is true—that increased school choice means increased stratification—then the only conclusion is that Australia has seen a vast increase in school choice. An initial analysis of the history of Australian schools suggests this does not appear to be the case. Private schooling in Australia has been a central feature of the education system since the 1970s. Yet this simple view lacks nuance. While school choice has been a persistent feature of the Australian system, the nature of and importance applied to school choice has changed in the last two decades starting with the conservative Howard government (1996–2007). The Howard government introduced measures that effectively treated government schools as part of the school market place and directed most funding from the federal sources to private schools—funding these schools at a much greater level than even its own formulas suggested was appropriate (Campbell, Proctor, & Sherington, 2009; Forsey, Proctor, & Stacey, 2017). This raised the stakes for parents in choosing the right school and thus may be the driving force behind increased stratification.

Campbell et al. (2009) have claimed that Howard era policies led to the transformation of Australian private schools from religious institutions to a high-stakes school marketplace. This change has meant that choosing the right school has become central to the Australian conception of what being a good parent means. The increasing between-school stratification observed in the last few decades may drive strategic choice by parents at a level that has not been present in the past. Campbell and colleagues have noted that, in past generations, children entered Catholic or public schools only if their parents had done so where school choice was a function of sociocultural factors like religion. This is now less the case. So changed are the school selection practices of Australian parents that some Catholic educators are complaining about the decentering of religion from Catholic schools that is being driven by the increasingly non-religious school community. This appears to result from parents choosing Catholic schools not out of religious conviction but perceptions of school quality.

While school choice has become a central parenting concern in Australia in the last decade, it is also clear that there are class divides in the degree school choice behaviors are activated. Deliberate and sustained attention and angst applied to school choice have become a defining feature of white middle-class parenting (Campbell et al., 2009). This is partly because schools tend to actively court children from such backgrounds but also because parents from this group tend to engage in more strategic planning—including deciding where to live and buy property in order to qualify for prestigious government schools—than do other groups of parents. Middle-class parents also have access to and actively gathered information from a network of formal and informal networks on what schools could be considered "good" (Campbell et al., 2009). Though it remains unclear whether such parents receive sufficient information on which to judge what a good school is; or are merely choosing schools with children that have the same sociodemographic characteristics as their own (Rowe & Lubienski, 2017). This is not dissimilar to other countries where school choice is increasingly a strategy of the middle-class as well as a leading driving force behind the reproduction of social class positions (Ball, 1993; Holme, 2002) and increased income inequality (Owens, 2016).

Educational inequality in Australia is large and, for much of our recent history, on the rise. Recent trends hint that this trend may be leveling off and this may be due to considerable bi-partisan government attention devoted to the issues

(Barr et al., 2008; Bradley, Noonan, Nugent, & Scales, 2008; Gonski et al., 2011). Behind this silver lining is a large and dark cloud. Educational inequality for both cognitive and non-cognitive skills remains persistent over time and across children's development. Indeed, our developmental data suggest that children whose parents have not attended university trail behind children whose parents did in IQ, academic achievement, overall conduct, and peer difficulties, and persistence. These gaps mostly grow during children's educational careers. These gaps may very well be driven by an increasingly stratified educational system in Australia and a growing eagerness of middle-class parents to embrace school choice. While the increased focus on school choice by middle-class parents has been in response to government policy, policy alone cannot explain it. School choice is also a function of demographic and geographic change in Australia (Campbell et al., 2009). These latter issues will not be resolved by educational policy alone and suggest the need for a wider social debate about what sort of society Australians wish to live in.

References

Anderson, A. R., Christenson, S. L., Sinclair, M. F., & Lehr, C. A. (2004). Check & connect: The importance of relationships for promoting engagement with school. *Journal of School Psychology, 42*(2), 95–113.

Ball, S. J. (1993). Education markets, choice and social class: The market as a class stratergy in the UK and the USA. *British Journal of Sociology of Education, 14,* 3–19.

Barr, A., Gillard, J., Firth, V., Scrymgour, M., Welford, R., Lomax-Smith, J., … Constable, E. (2008). *Melbourne declaration on educational goals for Young Australians.* USA: ERIC.

Bradley, D., Noonan, P., Nugent, H., & Scales, B. (2008). *Review of higher education in Australia: Final report.* Canberra: Australian Government.

Campbell, C., & Proctor, H. (2014). *A history of Australian schooling.* Crows Nest: Allen & Unwin.

Campbell, C., Proctor, H., & Sherington, G. (2009). *School choice: How parents negotiate the new school market in Australia.* Crows Nest: Allen & Unwin.

Dunn, L. M., & Dunn, L. M. (1997). *PPVT-III: Peabody picture vocabulary test.* American Guidance Service.

Forsey, M., Proctor, H., & Stacey, M. (2017). A most poisonous debate: Legitimizing support for Australian private schools. In T. Koinzer, R. Nikolai, & F. Waldow (Eds.), *Private schools and school choice in compulsory education* (pp. 49–66). Wiesbaden: Springer.

Friedman, M. (2009). *Capitalism and freedom.* Chicago: University of Chicago Press.

Gonski, D., Boston, K., Greiner, K., Lawrence, C., Scales, B., & Tannock, P. (2011). *Review of funding for schooling: Final report.* Canberra: Department of Education, Employment and Workplace Relations.

Goodman, R. (1997). The strengths and difficulties questionnaire: A research note. *Journal of Child Psychology and Psychiatry, 38*(5), 581–586.

Hancock, K. J., Mitrou, F., Povey, J., Campbell, A., & Zubrick, S. R. (2018). Educational inequality across three generations in Australia. *Australian Journal of Social Issues, 53*(1), 34–55.

Heckman, J. J. (2006). Skill formation and the economics of investing in disadvantaged children. *Science, 312*(5782), 1900–1902.

Heckman, J. J., & Rubinstein, Y. (2001). The importance of noncognitive skills: Lessons from the GED testing program. *American Economic Review, 91*(2), 145–149.

Hetherington, D. (2018). *What price the gap? Education and inequality in Australia*. Retrieved from https://publiceducationfoundation.org.au/what-price-the-gap-education-and-inequality-in-australia/.

Holme, J. J. (2002). Buying homes, buying schools: School choice and the social construction of school quality. *Harvard Educational Review, 72*, 177–205.

Jerrim, J., Parker, P. D., Katyn Chmielewski, A., & Anders, J. (2015). Private schooling, educational transitions, and early labour market outcomes: Evidence from three anglophone countries. *European Sociological Review, 32*(2), 280–294.

Kautz, T., Heckman, J. J., Diris, R., Ter Weel, B., & Borghans, L. (2014). *Fostering and measuring skills: Improving cognitive and non-cognitive skills to promote lifetime success*. National Bureau of Economic Research.

Ledgar, J. (1996). Overview of the Australian education system. *Higher Education in Europe, 21*(4), 102–115.

Marks, G. N., & Rothman, S. (2003). Longitudinal studies of Australian youth. *Australian Economic Review, 36*(4), 428–434.

Mooney, M., Dobia, B., Yeung, A. S., Barker, K. L., Power, A., & Watson, K. (2008). *Positive behaviour for learning: Investigating the transfer of a United States system into the New South Wales Department of Education and Training Western Sydney Region Schools: Report*.

Murphy, R., & Weinhardt, F. (2018). *Top of the class: The importance of ordinal rank* (No. w24958). National Bureau of Economic Research.

Owens, A. (2016). Inequality in children's contexts: Income segregation of households with and without children. *American Sociological Review, 81*(3), 549–574.

Parker, P. D., Jerrim, J., Schoon, I., & Marsh, H. W. (2016). A multination study of socioeconomic inequality in expectations for progression to higher education: The role of between-school tracking and ability stratification. *American Educational Research Journal, 53*(1), 6–32.

Parker, P. D., Marsh, H. W., Guo, J., Anders, J., Shure, N., & Dicke, T. (2018a). An information distortion model of social class differences in math self-concept, intrinsic value, and utility value. *Journal of Educational Psychology, 110*, 445–463.

Parker, P. D., Marsh, H. W., Jerrim, J. P., Guo, J., & Dicke, T. (2018b). Inequity and excellence in academic performance: Evidence from 27 countries. *American Educational Research Journal, 55*, 836–858.

Paterson, G., & Sanson, A. (1999). The association of behavioural adjustment to temperament, parenting and family characteristics among 5-year-old children. *Social Development, 8*(3), 293–309.

Petermann, F., & Petermann, U. (2011). *Wechsler intelligence scale for children®* (4th ed.).

Ray, A., & Margaret, W. (2003). *PISA Programme for International Student Assessment (PISA) PISA 2000 technical report: PISA 2000 technical report*. Paris, France: OECD Publishing.

Research, A. C. O. E. (2018). Youth in transition, 1961 Cohort (Publication no. doi/https://doi.org/10.4225/87/gb0kc4) from ADA Dataverse http://dx.doi.org/10.4225/87/GB0KC4.

Rowe, E. E., & Lubienski, C. (2017). Shopping for schools or shopping for peers: Public schools and catchment area segregation. *Journal of Education Policy, 32*(3), 340–356.

Sanson, A., Nicholson, J., Ungerer, J., Zubrick, S., Wilson, K., Ainley, J., … Harrison, L. (2002). *Longitudinal study of Australian children* (Discussion Paper 1). Melbourne, Australia: Australian Institute of Family Studies.

Steinberg, L. (2014). *Age of opportunity: Lessons from the new science of adolescence*. Boston: Houghton Mifflin Harcourt.

Part III
Cross-Cultural Trends

Chapter 12
Cross-National Trends in Addressing Socioeconomic Inequality in Education

Sylke V. Schnepf, Don A. Klinger, Louis Volante and John Jerrim

Abstract This chapter takes the results of all previous chapters into account and provides a cross-national evaluation of educational policies designed to reduce socioeconomic inequalities among pupils. By stocktaking on this Volume's choices for examining socioeconomic inequality and student outcomes, the chapter first reviews the most recent trends of socioeconomic inequality in the nine countries covered. Second, the chapter assesses which national policies appear to have been successful for reducing disadvantaged students' outcomes, by relating these trends with recent and preceding education policies. In order to cover most of the education policies featured in the single country chapters, this discussion of policies is structured along three dimensions: (a) school autonomy versus centralization; (b) tracking versus comprehensive schooling; and (c) instruction time and curricula. Third, the chapter concludes by addressing existing research caveats and future research directions from a cross-national perspective.

Keywords Student achievement · Socioeconomic status · Inequality · Comparative analysis · Education policies

---

S. V. Schnepf (✉)
European Commission's Joint Research Centre, Ispra, Italy
e-mail: sylke.schnepf@ec.europa.eu; viola.schnepf@gmx.de

D. A. Klinger
University of Waikato, Hamilton, New Zealand

L. Volante
Brock University, Hamilton, ON, Canada

J. Jerrim
Institute of Education, University College London, London, UK

© European Union, under exclusive licence to Springer Nature, part of Springer Nature 2019
L. Volante et al. (eds.), *Socioeconomic Inequality*
and Student Outcomes, Education Policy & Social Inequality 4,
https://doi.org/10.1007/978-981-13-9863-6_12

12.1 Introduction

Over the last decade, no topic has attracted as much attention among social and educational academia and policymakers than inequality. Rising income inequality (Alvaredo, Chancel, Piketty, Saez, & Zucman, 2017; Organisation for Economic Co-operation and Development, 2012), globalization, and the financial crisis have led to people being left behind. The recent developments of inequality are precarious since the combination of poverty and lack of opportunities of people living in declining regions drives the populism (Rodriguez-Pose, 2018) that is building the political landscape of more and more countries in Europe and beyond. Education is often discussed as a major factor leading to overall income inequality (see Jerrim, Volante, Klinger, & Schnepf, in this Volume; De Gregorio & Lee, 2003). As such, education serves as a central determinant as well as a remedy for current political and social trends in our societies that result in increased inequity. This recognition can be observed in a key European Policy Cooperation in Education and Training (ET 2020) benchmark: less than 15% of European 15-year-olds should have low educational achievement in reading, math, and science by 2020 (European Union, 2009). Equitable opportunities for our children to achieve high educational attainment are in the interest of our societies to realize social justice as well as economic efficiency. Efforts to enhance such opportunities and thereby narrow the education gaps decrease societies' risks resulting from poverty and improves their resilience to cope with economic crises.

How can we decrease the persistence of educational inequalities? Educational achievement surveys have shown large cross-country variability in educational inequalities even among countries with similar average achievement levels. As a consequence, a key question is how country-specific institutions and policies impact on educational inequalities. One way to answer this question is to investigate the impacts of education reforms across countries or regions (e.g., Kerr, Pekkarinen, & Uusitalo, 2013; Meghir & Palme, 2005). Another possibility is to examine cross-country institutional variability with respect to similarly focused policies (e.g., Chmielewski & Reardon, 2016; Hanushek & Woessmann, 2006). Even though very valuable, both of these quantitative approaches first need to summarize existing and often complex education policies into a small number of variables that are unable to account for between-country variation in implementation strategies of different policies.

The policy conclusions that can be drawn from such quantitative cross-national research can therefore never go beyond the very broad aggregation level of the variables used. In contrast to the pure quantitative cross-country research, this edited volume goes beyond by contributing to the discussion and reflection on effective policies for closing the education gap by describing and investigating in great detail different national policy implementations and subsequent inequality changes across nine Western industrialized countries.

At the same time, much of the research in the field of socioeconomic inequality and student outcomes that has traditionally utilized large-scale assessment measures such as PISA, has focused on countries within the global north. This book is no exception. Thus, we recommend caution when trying to extrapolate findings, and indeed policy lessons, from richer countries in the global north to poorer countries in the global south. Drawing comparisons between such different educational contexts has limited utility and may lead to inappropriate policy development. Despite this limitation, collectively the countries covered in this Volume possess a range of achievement results and successes with respect to addressing achievement gaps for lower socioeconomic background student populations. In addition, the authors of the chapters in this Volume have provided important summaries and insights that now enable us to draw conclusions about those policies that are likely to work for reducing persistent educational inequalities. While causal inferences are difficult to achieve with this comparative approach, the in-depth cross-national comparisons allow a detailed investigation of the association of education policies and inequalities. The different facets of policies and their implementation demonstrate that it is the unique combination of policies and institutional features that is likely to mitigate or aggravate educational inequalities, yet the similarities across countries are apparent and therefore make it possible to disentangle possible effects of a number of educational policies.

12.2 The Context

This Volume frames the in-depth focus on country-specific education policies and inequality patterns around a specific context which is important for the messages to be drawn from the different chapters.

First, the countries within this Volume have reduced heterogeneity in terms of basic economic factors like income inequality, economic growth, and poverty incidence. All these factors are indirectly affected by but difficult to control with educational policies. Nevertheless, the different choices of educational policies and school system factors vary considerably across these countries. It is the focus on these different country choices in addressing socioeconomic inequalities that provides the main contributions and cautions of our Volume. A country's policymakers might contemplate to implement structural education policy reforms that were successful in another country experiencing similar demographic shifts. Finland is often regarded as such a so-called high achieving "global reference society" and other countries might seek to borrow from its relevant policies and practices. The comparison of strategies across countries with similar settings makes it possible to not only learn from successful and unsuccessful cross-national policies, but also repeat those shown to be most effective. However, we note the need for caution in the search for the general applicability resulting from policy comparisons across countries. Even though we focus on similar countries, we cannot exclude that inequality patterns based on specific policies are moderated by specific national contexts. Furthermore, countries' policies (like autonomization and centralization of schools) differ in their design, which makes them more difficult to compare. In addition, it can be challenging to isolate the effects of policy changes that occur in a country if different policies are implemented at the same time and the legislative power on education policies is held by sub-regions (like for example in Germany, Spain, Australia, and Canada).

Second, our Volume's examination of countries' educational disadvantage goes beyond examining educational achievement data deriving from surveys like PISA or other sources (as TIMSS or PIRLS). Where possible, national longitudinal administrative data covering the pupil population of a country were employed. This robustness check is of importance in a research environment where the majority of analyses are based on cross-sectional survey data. Indeed, as illustrated by Anders and Henderson for the English chapter and by Löfstedt for the Swedish chapter, different national data sources do not always yield the same results, perhaps due to different measures of "skills". In addition, different data sources likely vary in their power to reflect the influences of recent policy changes. Anders and Henderson conclude that national GCSE scores have improved most likely due to an introduction of modular education into the curriculum, while a similar "effect" cannot be found with PISA data in England.

Third, the comparison of administrative and survey data sources comes with the cost of a limited choice of socioeconomic background measures. In order to focus on a comparable definition of the disadvantaged across countries and data sources, we used the categorical variable of parental education as a measure of socioeconomic background. As a consequence, the share of the disadvantaged differs across countries as discussed in detail in Chap. 1, comprising around 20% of children in Italy, Germany, and Spain while only around 5% of children in Canada, Finland, England, and Sweden. Disadvantaged individuals (defined as having parents with low educational attainment) in a society where most others are advantaged are likely to have a more disadvantaged composition than disadvantaged in a society with less privileged people. The less likely you are to be disadvantaged in a society, the more likely it is you are highly disadvantaged if you fall into this group. Economists referred to this problem as "selection". However, it is not only cross-national differences in the composition of the pupils with low educated parents that likely is challenging for cross-country comparisons of educational inequality changes. Socioeconomic backgrounds changed rapidly in some countries also over time. For example, Finland, as reported by Salmela-Aro and Chmielewski, witnessed a rapid and substantial shift in terms of parental education with over 90% of children having low educated parents (ISCED 2 or less) in 1964, but only 20% in 2000 and just 2% of non-immigrant students in 2015. The pattern is similar in the Netherlands, where this problem of increasing selection with decreasing number of disadvantaged students could explain why the chances of being tracked in higher school tracks recently decreased for students with low socioeconomic background. The extent of inequalities between countries and over time can therefore not be detached from the problem of cross-nationally varying composition of students with low educated parents. Nevertheless, in contrast to levels of inequalities, the changes in inequalities described in Chap. 1 are robust to different choices of socioeconomic background measures. Similar to results presented in Chap. 1, but based on a continuous socioeconomic background measure, Finland, the Netherlands, and Sweden witnessed increased inequalities, while inequalities declined in Germany over the last decade (Organisation for Economic Co-operation and Development, 2016a). Since this chapter isolates patterns of policy change and subsequent trends in educational inequality, the main focus of this chapter is on changes in inequality in contrast to its absolute level.

12.3 Cross-National Socioeconomic Inequality in Education

A worrying result from Chap. 1 is that the educational achievement of pupils whose parents completed at most ISCED Level 2 has decreased or stayed similar in most of the nine countries covered in this Volume since 2003. In the Netherlands, Finland, Canada, Sweden, and Australia achievement of those students declined by at least one grade of schooling (equal to 30 PISA points). Only in Germany (and very slightly in Italy and Spain) the disadvantaged could increase their educational achievement over time. Germany introduced a number of education reforms after having faced the "PISA shock" in 2000, when results revealed that Germany was an Organisation for Economic Co-operation and Development (OECD) country with much lower than expected achievement along with very large educational inequalities. A first conclusion is that if this Volume were to feature any "global reference society" as having successfully decreased educational inequality recently, Germany would come closest to it. Certainly, as discussed above, the decline in achievement of the disadvantaged over time is probably related to selection, which makes it likely that the disadvantaged of today are more disadvantaged than those in 2003 for most of the countries. Among our country groups, Germany has, together with Spain and Italy, one of the largest proportions (around 20%) of pupils with parents not having attained education levels higher than ISCED 2. Nevertheless, the 2015 cohort of German 15-year-olds have PISA scores approximately one grade ahead of their similarly disadvantaged peers of 2003. In contrast, the comparable Finnish students' scores have dropped two grades behind their similarly disadvantaged peers of 2003 (assuming that 30–40 PISA points are equivalent to one grade). (For more detail, see Table 1.3 in Chap. 1 of this Volume.) It is quite unlikely that selection in terms of educational attainment shifts of pupils' parents over time alone is the only explanation for the inequality changes found.

Given that the achievement of economically disadvantaged children has become worse over time (with the exception of Germany, Italy, and Spain), it is not surprising that the education gap between the advantaged and disadvantaged has increased (as long as the advantaged do not deteriorate as well). The biggest increase in the achievement gap appeared in Sweden, Finland, and the Netherlands. Where the gap between the advantaged and disadvantaged decreased, it appears to be due to the improvement of the disadvantaged in Spain and Italy, and a combination of improvement for the disadvantaged population coupled with a decline in achievement of the advantaged in Germany (see Table 1.3, Chap. 1). The remaining three English speaking countries—Canada, Australia, and England—mingle in between, with no clear direction of change of educational inequality over time, but a decline of achievement of low socioeconomic background students (Australia and Canada). In sum, these differing jurisdictional results indicate that changes in achievement gaps found can clearly not be explained by changes in the composition of the disadvantaged between countries and over time alone, and there are likely policies that either ameliorate or exacerbate these gaps.

12.4 National Choices of Education Policies and Lessons to Draw

This Volume's chapters present a vast range of policy efforts to enhance student achievement, and the varied unintended and intended consequences of these policies. These education policies also differ in the extent of their more radical or moderate execution in specific country settings. While Strietholt, Gustafsson, Hogrebe, Rolfe, Rosén, Steinmann, and Hansen (Chap. 2 of this Volume) comprehensively describe the impact of policies on educational inequalities using a systematic literature review, single country chapters highlight policy choices during the last decades with the greatest emphasis on currently most pressing strategies on nations' agendas to tackle inequalities. Summarizing these different policies and their possible influence on educational inequalities must necessarily to some degree be exclusive.

Three education policy continua seem most important across the majority of the chapters. First, in line with a recent Western tendency of public management regimes, the continua of policy choices along *school autonomy versus centralization* are touched on in most chapters. This dimension covers *where* power on education implementation and decision making is placed within a country. Second, the educational policy choices of *"tracking" versus comprehensive schooling* are the most important educational policy generally discussed to tackle inequalities, as was concluded in Chap. 2 of this Volume. This *institutional* dimension impacts student distribution across schools. Third, the dimension of *curriculum and instruction* describes those strategies related to *content and teaching* that successfully support students with different backgrounds and needs.

12.4.1 School Autonomy Versus Centralization

School autonomy is intended to give local actors more freedom in how they manage and lead schools to best support their students' achievement of educational outcomes. Proponents of school autonomy associate it with an improvement in public administration, a rationalization of public spending, and possibly higher

12 Cross-National Trends in Addressing …

cooperation between teachers and citizens. In its most extreme implementation, school autonomy can increase competition between schools creating a market of education providers. Current literature generally agrees that school autonomy leads to an increase in average achievement, at least in developed countries (Clark, 2005; Hanushek, Link, & Woessmann, 2013). However, its impact on socioeconomic inequalities is more contested, with Hanushek et al. (2013) not finding a heterogeneous effect. In contrast, Han (2018) and Horn (2009) demonstrated that greater school autonomy seems to be associated with higher socioeconomic disadvantages in educational outcomes (see also Chap. 2). Opponents of greater school autonomy denote that it leads to a lack of coherence, clear planning frameworks, and limited evaluability of the way schools move forward.

Results derived from the country chapters indicate that countries' most recent introductions of decentralization without balancing with other centralization policies might not have served the socioeconomic disadvantaged. As an example, the formerly highly centralized Swedish school system has allocated more responsibility to schools for organizing and running the primary, secondary, and adult education since the 1990s. Municipalities held responsibilities on staffing and budgeting. Decentralization was partly mitigated by policies on clearer performance and more stringent qualification requirements but only since the early 2000s, when educational inequalities started to increase. The 1990s were also the time in which greater decentralization occurred across the education system in Finland, followed much later (after 2010) by the establishment of greater core aims and objectives for primary and secondary schooling.

The Dutch school system is shaped by a high degree of autonomy. The government only sets the legislation and determines the structure and funding for the education system. As outlined in Chap. 7, the country currently lacks clearer central targets on explicitly planned programs, stricter accountabilities, and better program evaluation. Without an intermediate level of education administration, schools enjoy great freedom leading to reforms being "bottom up" and reinvented at the lowest levels over time. As a final example of strong school autonomy, Australia (see Chap. 11) can be considered a market-driven school choice model in which decentralization has led to student segregation between schools. Sweden, Finland, the Netherlands, and Australia represent jurisdictions in which student inequality increased or stayed at relatively high levels during the last two decades. And each of these countries have a high level of decentralization, leading to a reasonable hypothesis that this decentralization may be a factor that results in greater inequality.

Greater school autonomy was also introduced in those countries where educational inequalities improved recently. For example, Italian schools (see Chap. 5) received more liberties regarding the organization of the curriculum and extracurricular projects at the end of the 1990s. Yet this autonomy still remains rather limited compared to countries such as Sweden and Finland that extend autonomy to include other practices such as teacher recruitment. Of potential importance, Italy's decentralization policies are paired with policies on centralization that create more *accountability of schools* and hold them responsible for their performance. This is usually done with the introduction or continued use of central exams and some form of school inspections or accreditation. Italy has a long history of standardized national testing of pupils, but the release of these test results only began in 2017. This public release of national test results is a common practice in Australia, England, and Sweden. As a consequence, competition between Italian schools may increase in the future as some parents begin to use this public exam information to select the "best" schools for their children to attend. As a further public account-ability effort, policies were introduced in 2014 requiring Italian schools to go through a quality assessment as well. It does appear that this school accountability is limited since there are no consequences for schools not reaching centrally set standards.

Similar balances of centralized expectations and monitoring coupled with decentralized school autonomy can be observed throughout Canada (Chap. 10; see also Klinger, DeLuca, & Miller, 2008). Provincial examination results are often a required measure for schools to use to monitor the effectiveness of self-directed school improvement efforts or internally driven accreditation. In Canada, there are few if any explicit policy-driven consequences associated with these examinations or school improvement goals. Nevertheless, the public release of examination results has led to an unofficial ranking of schools within several provinces by the media or special interest groups. This ranking has been associated with increased mobility of students to schools outside of neighborhood boundaries, a sign of augmenting competition.

This combination of centralization and decentralization may have some merit to address the challenges of inequality of educational outcomes. The observed decrease in the achievement gap observed in Germany has occurred in a policy climate in which decentralization in the form of school autonomy was implemented alongside centralization policies covering standardization, monitoring, and centralization of exams. According to Davoli and Entorf (Chap. 4), school autonomy in itself was not seen as a component leading to efficiency, but rather as a feature necessary to equip schools with the needed freedom for successfully implementing new education policies. Before the German PISA shock in 2000, responsibility for school education was attributed to the Länder. The introduction of clear national education standards for different age groups, the creation of the new Institute for Educational and Quality Improvement to monitor education outcomes, and the centralization of exams led to a greater alignment of educational policies among Länder. Jürges, Schneider, and Büchel (2010) argue that the introduction of standardized tests together with clear education standards to be met at different ages were important determinants leading to the unusual consistent decrease in educational disadvantages.

Definitive links between centralized exams, increased achievement, and achievement gaps related to socioeconomics have yet to be established. Nevertheless, Woessmann (2018) argues that central exams improve student out-comes. This potential achievement "effect" of national (or jurisdictional) external tests needs to be separated from the "effect" of the explicitly required use and public release of these test results. Parental access to school-level results are found in Sweden, the U.K., Australia, and most recently also in Italy among the countries highlighted in this Volume. Where these results are publicly available, this information would mostly be considered by higher educated parents. In countries in which parental choice of schools is given, it is not at all unreasonable to expect that many of these parents would use this information to select schools, thus leading to increased school segregation. A potentially important caveat to this option of choice and selection is the unequal access to choice. Families in urban and suburban settings have much greater access to relatively nearby schools than those families in rural communities. Instances of this lack of school choice have also been found in inner-city communities due to transportation issues. This caveat highlights that even across national jurisdictions, school choice and competition among schools may vary widely. This variability may also help to partially explain the high levels of within-country variations observed for the achievement of disadvantaged students.

A final remark needs to be made about education expenditure. Higher expenditure is associated with lower inequalities, although the relationship is not linear. In a number of countries, policymakers currently discuss the implementation of pupil premiums, a compensatory policy that provides higher funding for those schools with more disadvantaged students. Nevertheless, previous literature suggests little if any success resulting from pupil premiums on dispersion of education (De Witte, Smet, & Van Assche, 2017; Rochex, 2012). In addition, there is no evidence yet that autonomous schools allocate these premiums effectively to disadvantaged students.

12.4.2 Tracking Versus Comprehensive Schooling

The recent UNICEF Innocenti Report Card stipulates that decreasing segregation of children with different family backgrounds into different schools is one key to combat educational inequalities (Chzhen, Gromada, Rees, Cuesta, & Bruckauf, 2018). School segregation by socioeconomic background can be the result of many institutionalized education policies. An overt form of student segregation is that of "tracking". In the presence of tracking, children are taught in different school types or programs that follow curricula that vary in their learning targets and prestige. Proponents of tracking stress that teaching of homogenous ability groups is more efficient for learning and higher levels of systematic achievement and improved educational outcomes. Opponents emphasize that lower ability students, often those with lower socioeconomic background, will be left behind in slower learning environments. While tracking is not explicitly intended to separate children based on socioeconomic backgrounds, the evidence presented by the authors in this Volume certainly highlight this as an unintended consequence. The tracking system, therefore, leads to socioeconomic selectivity which then translates into socioeconomic inequality of education outcomes. Strietholt et al. (Chap. 2) conclude that the most compelling evidence for a policy to foster socioeconomic achievement inequality was found for early tracking of children between schools. Contini and Scagni (2011) found that the earlier tracking takes place, the greater the resulting educational inequalities. The inequality associated with early tracking is consistent with the findings reported by Löfstedt for Sweden (Chap. 8) and by Salmela-Aro and Chmielewski for Finland (Chap. 9). In Sweden, tracking was replaced by comprehensive schooling in the 1950s and in Finland in the 1970s. Thereafter, socioeconomic inequalities of education outcomes declined in both countries. The Finnish chapter states that the reduction in the gap took place mainly between the top and middle distribution, which would suggest that mainly top students benefited from tracking. Unfortunately, these decreases in the socioeconomic achievement gap that occurred with the shift away from tracking do not help to explain the increases in the gaps that have been observed over the last two decades in these countries. However, on average early tracking has been associated with a reduction in mean performance (Hanushek & Woessmann, 2006). While several countries in this Volume do not engage in early tracking, countries such as Germany, Italy, and the Netherlands continue to use early tracking. Of these, Germany has the earliest tracking, occurring between the ages of 10 and 12 as compared to age 12 in the Netherlands and age 14 in Italy.

Tracking also has consequences for future career opportunities. In Italy, university attendance is possible with whatever school track was attended, conditional on passing a university entry exam. In contrast, in the Netherlands and Germany pupils with lower school track certificates cannot attend higher education. The tracking decision is generally taken by the teacher, which is however only binding in the Netherlands and some German Länder. Teachers' recommendations are not only guided by pupils' abilities but also by socioeconomic and migration background. Certainly, this use of social and migration backgrounds is not an explicit practice; as shown for other countries before (e.g., Jackson, 2013; Schnepf, 2002), Scheerens, Timmermans, and van der Werf (Chap. 7) highlight that even conditional on ability, low socioeconomic background students are more likely to be recommended to lower tracks.

While absolute levels of social segregation can be explained to some degree by tracking (Jenkins, Micklewright, & Schnepf, 2008), tracking is not the key for understanding most recent country trends in inequalities discussed in this Volume. Sweden, Finland, and Spain do not use tracking. The same is generally true for English speaking countries, although many provinces in Canada provide program options in the secondary school, typically intended to give students educational pathways towards the workplace or further tertiary education. Nevertheless, these are the countries (with the exception of Spain) in which educational inequalities increased or stagnated during the last two decades. In contrast, the decreasing inequality observed in both Germany and Italy in the presence of tracking underscores that the definitive link between early tracking and inequality has to be established taking into account other mitigating national education policies.

What are the links between tracking and inequality? How can other educational policies mitigate the often reported inequalities associated with tracking (e.g., Chzhen et al., 2018)? Davoli and Entorf explore this policy link within the German context (Chap. 4). As they note, some Länder introduced policies to reduce the potentially negative effects of early tracking by expanding comprehensive education until Grade 6. Second, in many Länder, the two lowest tiers, Hauptschule and Realschule, were merged into one school type: the Regionalschule. School segregation due to tracking was thereby mitigated by admitting pupils with greater heterogeneity of abilities to the same schools. In addition, ability grouping between schools was partly replaced by ability grouping within schools, the latter having no clear effect on socioeconomic educational inequalities as argued by Strietholt et al. (Chap. 2). The effect of these policy choices can be observed by PISA score variation increasing within German schools while decreasing between schools between 2006 and 2015.

While the introduction of tracking at an older age and the reduction of lower tiers seem to have contributed to reduced social selection in schools within schools across Germany, countries with comprehensive schooling have policies and practices that appear to have resulted in the higher social stratification of pupils. England provides one such example (Chap. 3). The combination of school league tables, and competing private, Catholic, and government have resulted in the institutionalization of parental choice of schools and fee-based private schools. The result is social segregation and school selection "by house price": only the rich can afford houses in the catchment areas of best schools. Highly educated parents are more likely and have more means to channel their children into schools that score high on the annually published school performance league tables. In such an environment, it is not at all surprising that increased social segregation and educational inequalities arise.

Similarly, Salmela-Aro, Chmielewski, and Löfstedt argue that the new policy of parental choice introduced in Finland and Sweden in the 1990s likely increased school segregation during the 2000s (Chaps. 8 and 9). The availability of school performance league tables is also assumed to have shaped decisions and choices differently for higher and lower educated parents in Sweden. In contrast, Parker, Guo and Sanders discuss that school choice has been a long-standing feature in the Australian education system and is therefore unlikely to have impacted on the recent increase in between school segregation (Chap. 11). They consider unequal government funding and the school system being similar to a marketplace to be the culprit for higher educational inequalities. School choice is much more complex in Canada due to the provincial control of education and the resulting provincial differences with respect to access to private schools, Catholic schools, and student access to schools outside of neighborhood catchment areas. Yet even within Canada, differential school selection is observed through specialty programs such as French Immersion or specialty programs in middle and secondary schools (e.g., International Bacclaureate, Fine Arts Programs, Challenge Programs). These programs are intended to meet the diverse learning needs of children in a community; however, the location of these schools creates barriers to access that are more pronounced for disadvantaged and rural families.

Social segregation in education is a result of differential access. Also, the Spanish school system is divided into public, private but publicly funded, and private independent schools that are socially segregated. However, Choi and Calero (Chap. 6) state that the main achievement gap found between schools can be entirely explained by different socioeconomic composition of children in schools indicating that children's streaming into different school types does not further increase educational inequalities in Spain.

A considerable number of this Volume's chapters highlight the importance of social segregation into schools by immigrant background. Countries such as Italy, Spain, Germany, and Sweden have witnessed substantial increases in migration during the last two decades. Given that immigrants generally have a lower socioeconomic background, they constitute almost half of pupils with low parental education in the Netherlands, which explains why Scheerens et al. discuss inequalities of migrants separately throughout their Dutch chapter.

As a consequence, recent changes in educational inequality indicate that early tracking and comprehensive schooling cannot be viewed in isolation in order to explain educational inequalities. A variety of different policies can mitigate segregation deriving from tracking as well as aggravate segregation even if comprehensive schooling is in place. The combination of different policies and the educational context within a country shape the trajectories of socioeconomic inequalities in educational outcomes. The "effect" of these educational policies alone and in combination cannot be measured in any systematic quantiative cross-country model since the number of countries is usually too small (Contini & Cugnata, 2018).

12.4.3 Instruction Time and Curricula

While the dimensions of school segregation and comprehensive schooling focus on the institutional components for distributing students into school, this last dimension of *instruction time and curricula* describes how policies on *content and teaching* can reduce educational inequalities by being inclusive and meeting children's differing needs *within* schools. Strietholt et al. (Chap. 2) conclude that any kind of increase in instruction time of children decreases the socioeconomic gap in educational achievement. Three main different policies for increasing instruction time were regularly discussed through this Volume's chapters: expanding the coverage of pre-schooling, longer instruction time in schools, and expansion of compulsory school age.

Children with different socioeconomic background differ already in basic cognitive and non-cognitive skills before school starts (Bradbury, Corak, Waldfogel, & Washbrook, 2015), showing that these inequalities are generated at home whereby genetics and varying parental interaction, stimulus, and time investment into children's development play important roles. Existing research shows that high-quality universal preschool programs can intervene to lessen social inequalities (e.g., Blossfeld, Kulic, Skopek, & Triventi, 2017; Bradbury et al., 2015). Certainly, it is most efficient to combat inequality early, and the countries covered in this Volume provide publicly funded preschools in order to lessen educational inequalities (see also Heckman, 2006). With the exception of Australia and Canada, these countries have more than 90% of 3- to 5-year-olds enrolled into preschool (Organisation for Economic Co-operation and Development, 2016b). In Denmark, the Netherlands, Sweden, and Portugal, even 50% of 0- to 2-year-olds attend formal child care (Chzhen et al., 2018). There is variation in the responsibilities and expectations of such childcare. As an example, Sweden and Finland provide universal public childcare compared to less formalized childcare programs in Germany, Italy, and the U.K. Recently, Germany and England have started to explore policies that expand access to public preschool to children below age 3, with the intent to decrease existing inequalities before entering school. While preschool has different impact on inequality trajectories in different countries (Blossfeld et al., 2017), it remains to be seen how further expansions implemented will help to reduce socioeconomic inequalities.

If earlier access to education results in reduced inequalities, it would seem reasonable that increased instructional time would similarly combat inequalities. Two policy practices to achieve this are increasing the number of years of compulsory schooling and expanding instructional time in schools. During the last two decades, countries such as Australia and Italy have raised their compulsory school age, a policy acknowledged to decrease school dropout rates (De Witte et al., 2017) and consequently also inequality in educational attainment. By comparison, Germany—where especially younger pupils attended school only in the morning—has introduced the "Ganztagsschule", a school that extends teaching time also to afternoon hours.

Lastly, we cannot underestimate the power of more inclusive school curricula to reduce educational inequalities, even though the effect of curricula changes is difficult to measure as Strietholt et al. discuss in Chap. 2. A reduction of the curricula to basic and factual content has the potential to provide teachers with more freedom to adapt their teaching to pupils' needs. While the intentions of such curricula reform may enable teachers to better meet their students' needs, there currently is a lack of research and policy recommendations related to curricula content and educational inequalities. Some scholars have argued that narrowed curricula have only served to exacerbate social inequalities, enabling high achieving pupils and those in advantaged communities' greater access to varied curricula, while narrowing the curricula presented to pupils in disadvantaged communities. Approximately half of the country chapters in this Volume describe recently introduced curricula change. For example, the English curricula was slimmed down alongside a greater focus on scientific knowledge. Germany introduced more Anglo-American literacy content, while Sweden integrated clearer learning goals and performance and qualification requirements into the definition of its educational content. Most recently, Australia launched a metrics-based mentoring program that aims to help students clarify their learning goals. Pensiero, Giancola and Barone explain that the recent exclusion of the previously compulsory subjects Latin and Philosophy from the Italian higher-track curriculum is probably a main reason for socioeconomic disadvantaged pupils' increasing access to higher academic tracks. These curricula changes highlight national efforts to provide more universal access or more effectively engage learners, independent of their background.

Nevertheless, the variety in the approaches described serves to further illustrate the current lack of research to inform such policy decisions. We suspect the collective set of authors within this Volume would agree that this is a critical area of research moving forward.

12.5 Conclusions and Future Directions

Efforts to reduce the socioeconomic inequality that result in unequal educational outcomes for our children are central to policy reforms across national jurisdictions. The authors of this Volume have highlighted the challenges and opportunities associated with the implementation of such policies, along with some of the broader observations of their impact on student outcomes. Missing from our Volume is an in-depth review and analysis of teachers, and the efforts needed to best support their practices. The enactment of policy requires teachers who have the skills to translate curricula into successful teaching practices and materials that meet the varied needs of children with diverse socioeconomic backgrounds. This is a considerably difficult task which is not equally valued across countries. The recognition of the teaching profession is rather low in Spain while Finnish teachers enjoy high respect within their society. Other countries lie in between. With this limitation acknowledged, this edited Volume examined the association of education policies with recent developments of socioeconomic inequalities across a selection of Western countries similar in their macroeconomic conditions: England, Finland, Germany, Italy, the Netherlands, Spain, Sweden, Canada, and Australia.

The different contributions in this Volume discussed each country's education system and linked recently implemented education policies with subsequent trends in socioeconomic differences in education outcomes, thereby employing not only survey but also national administrative data sources where available. Chap. 1 provided a comparison of trends in educational inequalities among the nine countries covered and Chap. 2 gave an in-depth review and supplied the framework for reading the country chapters. Based on the summary of this material, this chapter demonstrates that it is possible to identify similarities across countries and therefore disentangle possible effects of educational policies on inequalities focusing on the three dimensions of *school autonomy versus centralization*, *"tracking" versus comprehensive schooling*, and *curriculum and instruction*. Where possible, the collection of this Volume's contributions makes it also clear that it is the unique combination of national policies and institutional features that are likely to mitigate or aggravate educational inequalities. Only in this light can we understand the most recent trend of declining educational inequalities in Germany, a country with early tracking, and the increasing inequalities in Finland, a country embracing comprehensive schooling and access to free early years preschool.

The landscape of implemented policies seems to have become more complex recently. There is not one clear policy package that could be measured with a single set of variables in a cross-national data set quantitatively. Policies on autonomy are merged with policies on centralization. Tracking policies go together with elements of comprehensive schooling, often within the same country. This raises the hurdle of policy evaluation even higher than previously perceived. However, as Scheerens et al. state (Chap. 7), the *evaluation of policy effectiveness* is key to tackle future educational inequalities. Our future success of answering the question on which policies work to decrease educational inequalities will depend on the availability of *data*, the *evaluation spirit* of policymakers, and the *methodological tools* of researchers.

The three most extensive and budget intensive cross-national educational achievement surveys (PISA, TIMSS, and PIRLS) have created immense opportunities to investigate educational inequalities cross-nationally. Unfortunately, these surveys do not enable subsequent access to the cohort of students to explore inequality trajectories of these students. Recently, methodological work has been done on how to overcome these problems and estimate such trajectories of educational inequalities (Contini & Cugnata, 2018; Cordero, Cristóbal, & Santin, 2017). However, such models still rely on data assumptions, and if given the choice, researchers would certainly prefer a cross-national longitudinal survey that follows students over time rather than three that do not.

A second data challenge is related to the presence of national data. Longitudinal national data are of a huge advantage for analyzing effects of education policies, since they tend to cover the entire population of students. However, administrative data are generally limited since their access to researchers is not always granted due to disclosure control and a restricted coverage of research variables. Where possible, the authors used these national administrative data to inform their review of social inequality and student outcomes. Yet even with national efforts to obtain data beyond administrative data, the ability to combine these data with cross-national surveys also remains limited due to protocols that prevent data linkages. These linkages are needed to enable the use of more sophisticated and trustworthy modeling.

Our comments here highlight the importance of an *evaluation spirit* required of policymakers, stakeholders, and researchers. The design of any policy should have its evaluation already in focus. This requires a clear planning of the kinds of data to be collected and the collection methods to be used during the policy implementation phase. National administrative data collection could be extended, further capturing information necessary for evaluating new education policies. Policymakers and researchers need to collaborate early in the process and work together to investigate policy effects systematically. Such an approach could overcome the reinvention of the wheel of "bottom-up" policies, as described for the Netherlands. Within such a context, this evaluation spirit would be very well placed, especially since administrative data generation is increasing and *econometric and statistical methods* have developed further (Crato & Paruolo, 2019). Collectively, we see the need for greater research, across a variety of educational contexts, to examine the complex interaction of factors that ameliorate the effects of SES on student outcomes. A greater collaboration between and mutual understanding of stakeholders, policymakers, and researchers for data and research generation could eventually foster a way into more evidence on the complex field of education policies and inequalities. This eventually could reshape future education policy design and, with that, decrease socioeconomic inequalities of education outcomes.

References

Alvaredo, F., Chancel, L., Piketty, T., Saez, E., & Zucman, G. (2017). *World inequality report 2018.* Retrieved from https://wir2018.wid.world/files/download/wir2018-full-report-english.pdf.

Blossfeld, H.-P., Kulic, N., Skopek, J., & Triventi, M. (Eds.). (2017). *Childcare, early education and social inequality: An international perspective.* Cheltenham, UK: Edward Elgar. https://doi.org/10.4337/9781786432094.

Bradbury, B., Corak, M., Waldfogel, J., & Washbrook, L. (2015). *Too many children left behind: The U.S. achievement gap in comparative perspective.* New York, NY: Russell Sage Foundation.

Chmielewski, A. K., & Reardon, S. F. (2016). Patterns of cross-national variation in the association between income and academic achievement. *AERA Open, 2*(3), 1–27. https://doi.org/10.1177/2332858416649593.

Chzhen, Y., Gromada, A., Rees, G., Cuesta, J., & Bruckauf, Z. (2018). *An unfair start: Inequality in children's education in rich countries* (Innocenti Report Card 15). Florence, Italy: UNICEF Office of Research. Retrieved from https://www.unicef-irc.org/publications/995-an-unfair-start-education-inequality-children.html.

Clark, D. (2005). *Politics, markets and schools: Quasi-experimental evidence on the impact of autonomy and competition from a truly revolutionary UK reform.* Unpublished manuscript, Center for Labor Economics, University of California, Berkeley, CA. Retrieved from http://matthieuchemin-research.mcgill.ca/ECON742/paper/clark.pdf.

Contini, D., & Cugnata, F. (2018). *How do institutions affect learning inequalities? Revisiting differences-in-differences models with international assessments.* Department of Economics and Statistics Cognetti de Martiis working paper. Retrieved from https://ideas.repec.org/p/uto/dipeco/201817.html.

Contini, D., & Scagni, A. (2011). Inequality of opportunity in secondary school enrolment in Italy, Germany and the Netherlands. *Quality & Quantity, 45*(2), 441–464. https://doi.org/10.1007/s11135-009-9307-y.

Cordero, J., Cristóbal, V., & Santin, D. (2017). Causal inference on education policies: A survey of empirical studies using PISA, TIMSS and PIRLS. *Journal of Economic Surveys, 32*(3), 878–915. https://doi.org/10.1111/joes.12217.

Crato, N., & Paruolo, P. (Eds.). (2019). *Data-driven policy impact evaluation: How Access to microdata is transforming policy design.* Cham, Switzerland: Springer. https://doi.org/10.1007/978-3-319-78461-8_1.

De Gregorio, J. D., & Lee, J.-W. (2003). Education and income inequality: New evidence from cross-country data. *Review of Income and Wealth, 48*(3), 295–416. https://doi.org/10.1111/1475-4991.00060.

De Witte, K., Smet, M., & Van Assche, R. (2017). *The impact of additional funds for schools with disadvantaged pupils* (SONO research paper 2017.OL3.1/3). Retrieved from http://steunpuntsono.be/wp-content/uploads/2018/10/SONO_2017.OL3_.1_3_vrijgegeven.pdf.

European Union. (2009, May 28). Council conclusions of 12 May 2009 on a strategic framework for European cooperation in education and training ('ET 2020'). *Official Journal of the European Union, 52,* C 119. https://doi.org/10.3000/17252423.c_2009.119.eng.

Han, S. W. (2018). School-based teacher hiring and achievement inequality: A comparative perspective. *International Journal of Educational Development, 61,* 82–91. https://doi.org/10.1016/j.ijedudev.2017.12.004.

12 Cross-National Trends in Addressing …

Hanushek, E. A., Link, S., & Woessmann, L. (2013). Does school autonomy make sense everywhere? Panel estimates from PISA. *Journal of Development Economics, 104,* 212–232. https://doi.org/10.1016/j.jdeveco.2012.08.002.

Hanushek, E. A., & Woessmann, L. (2006). Does educational tracking affect performance and inequality? Differences-in-differences evidence across countries. *The Economic Journal, 116* (510), C63–C76. https://doi.org/10.1111/j.1468-0297.2006.01076.x.

Heckman, J. (2006). Skill formation and the economics of investing in disadvantaged children. *Science, 312*(5782), 1900–1902. https://doi.org/10.1126/science.1128898.

Horn, D. (2009). Age of selection counts: A cross-country analysis of educational institutions. *Educational Research and Evaluation, 15*(4), 343–366. https://doi.org/10.1080/138036109030 87011.

Jackson, M. (Ed.). (2013). *Determined to succeed? Performance versus choice in educational attainment.* Stanford, CA: Stanford University Press.

Jenkins, S. P., Micklewright, J., & Schnepf, S. V. (2008). Social segregation in secondary schools: How does England compare with other countries? *Oxford Review of Education, 34*(1), 21–37. https://doi.org/10.1080/03054980701542039.

Jürges, H., Schneider, K., & Büchel, F. (2010). The effect of central exit examinations on student achievement: Quasi-experimental evidence from TIMSS Germany. *Journal of the European Economic Association, 3*(5), 1134–1155. https://doi.org/10.1162/1542476054729400.

Kerr, S. P., Pekkarinen, T., & Uusitalo, R. (2013). School tracking and development of cognitive skills. *Journal of Labor Economics, 31*(3), 577–602. https://doi.org/10.1086/669493.

Klinger, D. A., DeLuca, C., & Miller, T. (2008). The evolving culture of large-scale assessments in Canadian education. *Canadian Journal of Educational Administration and Policy, 76.* Retrieved from https://journalhosting.ucalgary.ca/index.php/cjeap/article/view/42757.

Meghir, C., & Palme, M. (2005). Education reform, ability and family background. *American Economic Review, 95*(1), 414–424. https://doi.org/10.1257/0002828053828671.

Organisation for Economic Co-operation and Development. (2012, May). *Growing income inequality in OECD countries: What drives it and how can policy tackle it?* (OECD Forum on Tackling Inequality). Retrieved from http://www.oecd.org/els/socialpoliciesanddata/47723414.pdf.

Organisation for Economic Co-operation and Development. (2016a). *PISA 2015 results (vol. 1): Excellence and equity in education.* Paris, France: OECD Publishing. https://doi.org/10.1787/9789264266490-en.

Organisation for Economic Co-operation and Development. (2016b). *Enrolment in childcare and pre-school.* Retrieved from https://www.oecd.org/els/soc/PF3_2_Enrolment_childcare_preschool.pdf.

Rochex, J.-Y. (2012). General conclusion: Priority education policies in Europe, from one "age" and one country to another. In M. Demeuse, D. Frandji, D. Greger, & J-Y. Rochex (Eds.), *Educational policies and inequalities in Europe* (pp. 288–319). London, UK: Palgrave Macmillan.

Rodriguez-Pose, A. (2018). The revenge of the places that don't matter (and what to do about it). *Cambridge Journal of Regions, Economy and Society, 11*(1), 1752–1378. https://doi.org/10.1093/cjres/rsx024.

Schnepf, S. V. (2002). *A sorting hat that fails? The transition from primary and secondary school in Germany* (Innocenti Working Papers No. 92). Retrieved from https://www.unicef-irc.org/publications/341-a-sorting-hat-that-fails-the-transition-from-primary-to-secondary-school-in-germany.html.

Woessmann, L. (2018). Central exit exams improve student outcomes. *IZA World of Labor, 419.* https://doi.org/10.15185/izawol.419.

Correction to: Socioeconomic Inequality and Student Outcomes

Louis Volante, Sylke V. Schnepf, John Jerrim and Don A. Klinger

Correction to:
L. Volante et al. (eds.), *Socioeconomic*
Inequality and Student Outcomes,
Education Policy & Social Inequality 4,
https://doi.org/10.1007/978-981-13-9863-6

The original version of this book was inadvertently published with incorrect author affiliation in the book and also in the chapter "Socioeconomic Inequality and Student Outcomes Across Education Systems". The same has been corrected.

In the book, the affiliation "DG Joint Research Centre, European Commission's Joint Research Centre, Ispra, Varese, Italy" of the author "Sylke V. Schnepf" has been changed to "European Commission's Joint Research Centre, Ispra, Italy."

In the chapter "Socioeconomic Inequality and Student Outcomes Across Education Systems," the affiliation "European Commission's Joint Research Centre, Petten, The Netherlands" of the author "S. V. Schnepf" has been changed to "European Commission's Joint Research Centre, Ispra, Italy."

The updated version of the book can be found at
https://doi.org/10.1007/978-981-13-9863-6
https://doi.org/10.1007/978-981-13-9863-6_1

© Springer Nature Singapore Pte Ltd. 2019
L. Volante et al. (eds.), *Socioeconomic Inequality*
and Student Outcomes, Education Policy & Social Inequality 4,
https://doi.org/10.1007/978-981-13-9863-6_13